Man
For
Humanity

Man For Humanity

On Concordance vs Discord
in Human Behavior

Edited by

JULES H. MASSERMAN, M.D.
Professor of Psychiatry and Neurology
Northwestern University
Chicago, Illinois
President, International Association of Social Psychiatry

and

JOHN J. SCHWAB, M.D.
Professor of Psychiatry and Medicine
University of Florida
Gainesville, Florida
President, American Association for Social Psychiatry

CHARLES C THOMAS • PUBLISHER
Springfield • Illinois • U.S.A.

Published and Distributed Throughout the World by
CHARLES C THOMAS • PUBLISHER
BANNERSTONE HOUSE
301–327 East Lawrence Avenue, Springfield, Illinois, U.S.A.

© *1972*, by CHARLES C THOMAS • PUBLISHER
ISBN 0-398-02354-9
Library of Congress Catalog Card Number: 72-187667

With **THOMAS BOOKS** *careful attention is given to all details of*
manufacturing and design. It is the Publisher's desire to present books
that are satisfactory as to their physical qualities and artistic possibilities
and appropriate for their particular use. **THOMAS BOOKS** *will be true*
to those laws of quality that assure a good name and good will.

Printed in the United States of America
EE-11

Contributors

PAUL L. ADAMS, M.D., *Professor of Pediatrics and Psychiatry, University of Florida, Gainesville, Florida*

JOHN L. CARLETON, M.D., *Santa Barbara Psychiatric Medical Group, Santa Barbara, California*

STANLEY R. DEAN, M.D., *Clinical Professor of Psychiatry, University of Florida, Gainesville, Florida*

JOSEPH W. EATON, PH.D., *Professor of Sociology in Public Health and Social Work Research, University of Pittsburgh, Pittsburgh, Pennsylvania*

ALFRED M. FREEDMAN, M.D., *Professor and Chairman, Department of Psychiatry, New York Medical College, New York, New York*

RICHARD O. FULLER, *Research Center for Group Dynamics, University of Michigan, Ann Arbor, Michigan*

MANFRED HALPERN, PH.D., *Department of Politics and Center of International Studies, Princeton University, Princeton, New Jersey*

VLADIMIR HUDOLIN, M.D., *Professor of Psychiatry, University of Zagreb, and Director, Institut za proucavanje, Zagreb, Yugoslavia*

ARI KIEV, M.D., *Cornell Program in Social Psychiatry, Cornell Medical Center, New York, New York*

SOL KRAMER, PH.D., *Professor of Biology, Department of Psychiatry, and Director, Comparative Behavior Laboratory, University of Florida, Gainesville, Florida*

LEROY P. LEVITT, M.D., *Dean, Chicago Medical School, Chicago, Illinois*

JUAN J. LOPEZ-IBOR, M.D., *President, World Psychiatric Association, Professor of Psychiatry, University of Madrid, Madrid, Spain*

FERGUS H. MANN, A.C.S.W., *Institute of Gerontology, University of Michigan, Ann Arbor, Michigan*

JULES H. MASSERMAN, M.D., *Professor of Psychiatry and Neurology, Northwestern University, Chicago, Illinois*

LOUIS MILLER, M.D., *Chief, National Psychiatrist, Mental Health Services, Ministry of Health, Jerusalem, Israel*

F. THEODORE REID, JR., M.D., *Department of Psychiatry, Northwestern University, Chicago, Illinois*

v

ANNE ROE, PH.D., *Lecturer in Psychology, University of Arizona; Professor Emerita, Graduate School of Education, Harvard University, Boston, Massachusetts*

JOSEPH F. RYCHLAK, PH.D., *Professor of Psychology, Purdue University, Lafayette, Indiana*

ARTHUR M. SACKLER, M.D., *Chairman, International TASN Force on World Health Manpower, World Health Organization; Publisher, Medical Tribune International*

JOHN J. SCHWAB, M.D., *Professor of Psychiatry and Medicine, University of Florida, Gainesville, Florida*

GEORGE GAYLORD SIMPSON, PH.D., *Professor of Geosciences, University of Arizona, Tucson, Arizona*

ELLIOTT P. SKINNER, PH.D., *Franz Boas Professor of Anthropology, Columbia University, New York, New York*

W. CLEMENT STONE, *President, Combined Insurance Company of America; Editor and Publisher, Success Unlimited, Chicago, Illinois*

ROBERT H. STROTZ, PH.D., *President, Northwestern University, Evanston, Illinois*

GEORGE VASSILIOU, M.D., *Director, Athenian Institute of Anthropos, Athens, Greece*

VASSO VASSILIOU, M.D., *Associate Director, Athenian Institute of Anthropos, Athens, Greece*

BRYANT WEDGE, M.D., *Director, Institute for the Study of National Behavior, San Diego, California*

ISIDORE ZIFERSTEIN, M.D., *Fellow for Russian Studies, National Institute of Mental Health, Washington, D.C.*

Introduction

MAN FOR HUMANITY: A PREVIEW OF THE COLLOQUIUM

On May 7, 8, and 9, 1971, a Colloquium on Concordance *vs* Discord in Human Behavior was held by the American Association for Social Psychiatry at Northwestern University, Chicago, Illinois, and Forest Hospital, Des Plaines, Illinois. My introductory remarks were as follows:

Distinguished Guests, Ladies and Gentlemen: As one manifestation of a worldwide reaction among men of goodwill away from hostile confrontations and savage wars toward human empathy, peace and concordance, the International Association for Social Psychiatry was founded in London less than two years ago, and in that short time it has already achieved, through two international congresses and the organization of seven derivative national societies, worldwide scientific prestige and influence. As President of the international association it is my privilege and that of President John Schwab and the other officers of its American division to welcome your participation in our Colloquium on Man *for* Humanity. To add to Mayor Richard J. Daley's and Director Dr. Albert Glass' gracious greetings, I am happy to transmit wishes for the success of our deliberations from Governor Richard Ogilvie and Senators Charles Percy and Adlai Stevenson, III of Illinois, Senator Edmund Muskie of Maine, Chief Justice Warren Burger of the United States Supreme Court, Secretary-General U Thant of the United Nations and other world leaders, all of whom express their regrets that the recurrent crises that keep each of them occupied prevent them from being with us in person.

We have all sought earnestly—and sometimes desperately—to understand the turmoil that seems to be engulfing humanity, and we have read widely, observed closely and thought deeply about the causes of conflict, aggression, violence and war. Throughout, however, we have been sustained by the hope that, since humanity has indeed progressed—however irregularly and asymptotically—from the presumption of a primitive brutality toward more co-operative and encompassing social systems, there must also have emerged eventually predominant adaptational trends toward human collectivism and collaboration—else, simply put, very few of us could have survived. This Colloquium is dedicated to deepening our understanding and fostering the utilization of these consilient tendencies on the broadest possible scale. Applying modern progressive concepts of systems theory, we shall begin with the survival value of protoplasmic syncitia, trace the evolution of multicellular organisms and their later social aggregations, examine the early collectives of *Homo habilis* and then apply whatever fundamental vectors of coherence we can detect to the ultimate hope of the brotherhood of man.

To clarify this evolution, the first plenary sessions will begin with a review by Professor Sol Kramer of the ethologic origins of vital alliances. In this regard, the Darwinian phrase "survival of the fittest" has often been misinterpreted to mean that only the most strong and savage are fit to live; whereas Thomas Huxley, Ashley Montagu and our own George Gaylord Simpson have clearly pointed out that most species have persisted for precisely the opposite reason—namely, conspecific and cross-specific collaboration to the point of individual self-sacrifice. Even among rudimentary plants, lichens can exist only because their component fungi and algae live in symbiosis; so also, in the primitive animate kingdom the common Portuguese Man-of-War (*Physalia pelagica*) may be considered either as a fortuitous contiguity of independent cells, an individualized organism or a cooperative society comprised of various species in a partnership of mutual survival.

Following Dr. Kramer, we shall have the privilege of hearing the world-renowned paleontologist, George Gaylord Simpson, trace the development of human relationships from prehistoric societies to our still ethically dubious present under the intriguing title of "Man Is not a Naked Ape," recalling the aphorism that we have at last found the missing link halfway between the anthropoids and civilized man: it's us. Dr. Paul

Adams, a profound student of human development in the sense that the individual recapitulates the social ontology of our race, will then discuss perhaps the basic paradigm of all human concordance—namely, that the seemingly unselfish devotion of mother to child may be the origin of the latter's enduring faith that perhaps others may also prove to be relatively trustworthy mentors and companions; in effect, our innocent offspring have to be taught racial, class and religious prejudices, else they are in danger of growing up indiscriminatingly and disconcertingly friendly. Indeed, we humans seem to operate according to relatively few ultimate or *Ur*-principles, one of the most important of which is the necessity of social collaboration. First, we strive to satisfy our physical needs and to attain longevity by developing various sciences and skills with which to control our physical and social environments *as we individually conceive them;* second, we quest for interorganismic relationships which sexually or socially serve to perpetuate a cherished segment of our species; and third, we seek to develop implicit philosophies or, in the case of man, wishful metapsychologies and theologies that reassure us as to life's values and purposes. Conversely, when our capacities to pursue these *Ur*-objectives fail and we are faced with unresolved frustrations, conflicts and uncertainties, we develop phobic and other deviant escapist patterns of behavior and may resort to aggressive violence when that also seems necessary to overcome material or animate obstacles to what we consider essential goals.

Dr. Bryant Wedge, Director of the Institute for the Study of National Behavior, will next review techniques of possible intervention when these *Ur*-faiths are transgressed in adverse individual or group transactions, to be followed by Professor Manfred Halperin, a guiding light at the Princeton University Center for International Studies, who will explore man's hope for an effective worldwide code of civilized conduct. Our highly distinguished guest from Spain, Dr. Juan J. Lopez-Ibor, President of the World Psychiatric Association, will then summarize and collate the intellectual proceedings of the morning.

But thought, however searching or profound, retains a pale

Shakesperian cast of futility unless it eventuates in plans for concerted and effective action, which is the central theme for our second plenary session. In that seminar, Dr. Elliott Skinner, an outstanding authority on Africa, will join with prestigious psychiatrists from around the world, including Dr. Joshua Bierer of Britain, Dr. Vladimir Hudolin of Yugoslavia, Dr. Louis Miller of Israel, and Dr. George Vassiliou of Greece to discuss what influences behavioral scientists can bring to bear, not only on the powers that are in their respective countries but also through cultivating universal yearnings for human concordance so that while there is yet time, we can avert a threatening Armageddon.

On the following day, an address by Professor Joseph Eaton will explore the possibility of conciliations in a region that currently most dangerously threatens world peace, the Middle East. However, by far the greater amount of time will be spent in seven seminars apportioned equably among groups especially interested in subtopics highly relevant to human concordance. These workshops will deal respectively with forms of communication, individual and group dynamics, environmental influences, transcultural vectors (including, I trust, the increasingly urgent problems of rehabilitating military personnel dehumanized by present wars) and the re-emergent parochialisms which increasingly threaten economic and racial conflicts and, eventually, an international holocaust. Each workshop will have an academic chairman and secretary, and one or two topical speakers who will present succinct material designed to initiate free discussion; also available will be two well-informed "resource personnel" from among the principle invitees of the Colloquium. The sessions will then phase into a penultimate address by the world philanthropist, W. Clement Stone; a summary by Arthur Sackler and myself; and a terminal open forum for general discussion. Please note that I have said that our sessions will "phase into" rather than "end in," since I hope that this Colloquium will never terminate in the minds and lives of all of us.

Thus, my introduction. I shall leave it to the perceptive reader to appreciate the breadth, cogency, scholarship and literary quality of the ensuing contributions to the Colloquium.

Northwestern University   JULES H. MASSERMAN

CONTENTS

PART III
STUDIES IN TRANSCULTURAL DISCORD
AND CONCORDANCE

PART IV
CLINICAL AND CULTURAL APPLICATIONS

PART V
REVIEWS AND INTEGRATIONS

Man
For
Humanity

PART I

DEVELOPMENT AND COMMUNICATION

Chapter 1

Conflict and Concordance in the Development of Animal Societies

Sol Kramer

A S AN INTRODUCTION to the theme and discussion of this
Colloquium, it might be useful to provide an insight into
some of the biobehavioral mechanisms which have led to the evolution of social behavior. It is therefore my intention (a) to discuss those ethological findings and concepts that are germane to
social behavior, (b) to amplify this with an indication of the
ecodynamics of conflict and cooperation, and finally (c) to indicate the use of ethological concepts in considering human
psychodynamics, social behavior and social psychiatry.

ETHOLOGIC FINDINGS AND CONCEPTS

Charles Darwin demonstrated that the evolutionary viewpoint was as applicable to the study of behavior as to animal
structure. Wheeler [72-74] not only demonstrated that genetically
constant patterns of behavior could be utilized as taxonomic
traits in ants and other social insects but was the first investigator to consistently explore the evolution of animal societies
from an ethologic viewpoint. One of his papers, published in 1903,
was the first to make use of the term "ethology" in its modern
sense. Utilizing both extensive comparative observations of different species, together with experiments, he showed that the
complex and specialized behavior patterns of slave-making ants,
harvesting ants, legionary (army) ants, fungus growing ants
and so forth could be derived from instinctive patterns of activity
generally present among the many species of ants with a relatively primtive social organization. In 1935, Lorenz [42] emphasized the role of instinctive actions in the social behavior of birds.
He not only provided an understanding of the structure of bird

5

societies but laid the foundation for the development of ethology as a discipline.

The findings of ethological studies * have since confirmed the fact that the central nervous system of both invertebrate and vertebrate animals contains genetically determined neuromuscular coordinations termed "fixed motor patterns" and that these patterns of behavior are normally released by key stimuli exhibited by conspecific members of a given species. These key stimuli are termed "releasers," and to a large extent fixed motor patterns and releasers regulate the social behavior of animals. Striking color patterns or markings, scents, calls, songs, other movement patterns or a combination of these may all serve as releasers.

If we follow Tinbergen [69] in considering the study of social behavior as the study of cooperation between individuals, then social behavior may be defined as occurring when two or more individuals interact with each other. As few as two animals may be involved as in courtship and reproduction, thirty or more individuals may be involved in the predator mobbing response of a reproductive "club" of herring gulls, or thousands of individuals may cooperate as in the flight and roosting of a flock of starlings. It is now apparent that fixed motor patterns and the lawful phenomena associated with them have played a central role in the evolution of whatever cooperative, social interactions we find in animals.

In behavioral experiments hitherto conducted in the laboratory, the endeavor was to keep all other conditions constant while a single stimulus was varied. In nature, however, and especially in social situations, the animal is frequently subject to stimuli which might elicit more than one behavioral response. Since fixed motor patterns may be released by the presentation of a key stimulus (provided the animal is in the proper physiological state), the discovery of releasers provided ethologists with unique experimental opportunities. It now becomes possible to combine two or more releasers and study their summation effects, to present an animal with releasers for two different

---

* See the following references: 15, 16, 27, 41, 44, 45a and 67.

```
┌─────────────────────────────────────────────────────────────┐
│              ETHOLOGICAL FINDINGS & CONCEPTS                  │
│                                                               │
│  I. FIXED MOTOR PATTERNS —FMP                                 │
│      • GENETICALLY DETERMINED NEUROMUSCULAR COORDINATIONS     │
│      • TAXONOMIC SPECIFICITY & UTILITY                        │
│  2. RELEASERS (KEY STIMULI)                                   │
│  3. IRM– HYPOTHETICAL INNATE RELEASING MECHANISM IN CNS       │
│  4. LAWFULNESS OF BEHAVIOR                                    │
│      • CONFLICT OF FMP'S ⟶ DISPLACEMENT ACTIVITY             │
│      • REDIRECTED ACTIVITY: FMP DIRECTED AT SUBSTITUTE ANIMAL │
│      • SUPERPOSITION OF FMP'S ⟶ NEW EXPRESSIVE MOVEMENTS     │
│      • INTENTION MOVEMENTS: INCOMPLETE ACTIVATION OF          │
│                            SEQUENCE OF FMP'S                  │
│      • AMBIVALENCE: OBJECT WITH OPPOSING RELEASERS            │
│      • REGRESSION : ACTIVATION OF FMP'S FROM EARLIER LIFE STAGES│
│  5. EVOLUTION OF BEHAVIOR                                     │
│  6. IMPRINTING; BOND FORMATION                                │
│      • CRITICAL PERIODS                                       │
└─────────────────────────────────────────────────────────────┘
```

Figure 1–1. Ethological concepts and findings germane to social behavior.

motor patterns and study what happens when such an internal "conflict" is activated in the central nervous system, or to provide an animal with a single object which contains releasers for two different types of behavior. For example, nesting herring gulls will brood dummy eggs and will carry red-colored objects away from their nests. If we now paint a dummy wooden egg red and place it in the nest of a herring gull, it will first carry away the "red-colored object," then sit down and brood the "egg-shaped object," then again carry away the red object, and so forth. In this way it is possible to study "ambivalent" behavior at the perceptual-motor level.[68]

Ethologists have developed various hypotheses and theories associated with the ways in which such motor patterns function in the central nervous system. Of particular importance to those concerned with human behavior is the fact that there appears to be a certain *lawfulness* associated with these genetically determined neuromuscular coordinations (Fig. 1–1). It thus happens that in a typical conflict situation, neither of the normally released motor patterns occurs, but a third, seemingly irrelevant pattern appears termed a "displacement activity." Such displacement activities very often evolve into signals which other members of the species appear to "understand" and react to accordingly. Thus, the displacement sand-digging of the three-spined stickleback, *Gasterosteus aculeatus,* serves as a threat signal to other sticklebacks at the territorial boundary of a reproductive male, and other males appear to heed this communication by not encroaching on the territory of the male who displays it.

All neuromuscular patterns of activity have corresponding autonomic nervous system patterns associated with them (Fig. 1–2), which normally support the particular behavior an animal may be engaged in at a given moment. Morris [49] has shown that in

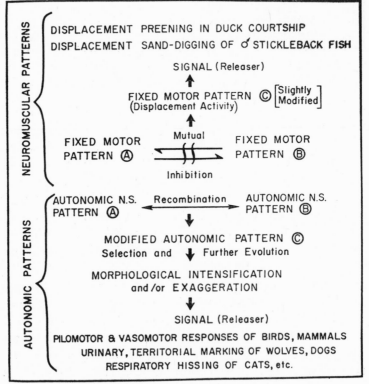

Figure 1–2. Relationship of fixed motor patterns and autonomic nervous system responses in the evolution of signals.

conflict situations we get not only neuromuscular displacement activities but new autonomic patterns, which may result in modified pilomotor, cardiovascular, respiratory or other responses. If these modified autonomic patterns develop some signal function, they often become exaggerated in the course of evolution or combined with structural modifications which make these responses more visible to other animals. Therefore, not only neuromuscular patterns but displacement activities and displacement autonomic patterns of response are subject to intensification or exaggeration through selection and are capable of evolving into communicative signals or releasers of social behavior. The respiratory hissing of snakes, the hissing and spitting of cats, the urinary, territorial marking of dogs and wolves, and the pilomotor and vasomotor signals of birds and mammals fall into this category (Fig. 1–3).*

Furthermore, there appears to be a continuous spectrum of behavior from the simple inherited reflexes of animals to the more complex sequences of motor patterns which comprise a functional behavior response. Whenever the stimulus for a complete response is of low intensity or is combined with a lowered physiologic state of the animal, various incomplete sequences may occur. Consequently an animal may display any transition from slight indications of a specific behavior pattern, referred to as *intention movements,* to complete sequences of an action chain. A bird may bend its legs, stretch its neck or flutter its wings (all of which represent movements initiating the normal pattern of flight), thereby indicating an intent, or incomplete impulse, to fly. It should be noted that while the all-or-

---

* Masserman [46] has demonstrated that experimental neuroses induced in cats result in the same stereotypes of anxiety, phobias, hypersensitivity, regression and psychosomatic dysfunctions observed in human patients. Many of these dysfunctions, such as rapid heart rate, full pulse, catchy breathing, raised blood pressure, sweating, trembling, erection of hair, gastrointestinal disorders, persistent salivation, etcetera, are mediated by the autonomic nervous system. The same basic relationship between the neuromuscular system and the autonomic nervous system is involved in animal and human psychosomatic dysfunctions and in the evolution of animal signals as a result of conflict of fixed motor patterns. Consequently I have sometimes referred to the *psychosomatic signals* of animals. For many a clinician these psychosomatic manifestations in man are also interpreted as a signal of conflict and a cry for help.

none law of physiology holds true for the *motor unit* (a nerve fiber together with all the muscle fibres it supplies), it does not hold for the *sequences of motor patterns*. In given nerves, only a small number of nerve fibers may be "recruited" which then only partially activate a given sequence—and it is this principle which apparently provides the basis for intention movements.

Still another type of lawful phenomenon observed in animals

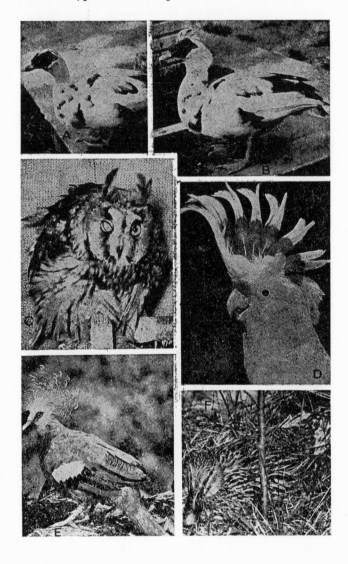

is the *superposition* of two separate motor patterns into a new behavioral combination or expression. For example, an aggressive goose will extend its neck while a fearful one bends it. When the superposition of these two responses results in an extended, partially bent neck, it indicates a mood of fearful aggression. Dogs likewise have been shown to superpose the two responses of fear and aggression which give rise to subtle nuances of fearful and aggressive responses, which lead to the development of new expressions.

Regressive Behavior

As part of the bonding ceremony of herring gulls, the female begs for food from the male with the same posture and begging movements that herring gull chicks use with their parents. The male, in fact, often responds to this behavior by regurgitating food and feeding her, just as he would respond to a food-begging chick. Masserman [46] indicated that adult dogs and cats would resume their previously recorded puppyish or kittenish characteristics after experimentally being made neurotic. Both examples are referred to as *regressive behavior*.

There are numerous recorded instances wherein fixed motor patterns associated with an earlier stage of development are reactivated, not only in other animals but also in man. A child who has been walking bipedally for months sometimes reverts to crawling locomotion in the presence of an infant sibling or when his mother fusses admiringly over a neighbor's younger

---

Figure 1–3. Feather postures (pilomotor response) in the evolution of bird signals. (*A*) Male hybrid Muscovy duck. (*B*) Same animal, crest and neck feathers erected. (*C*) Long-eared owl. *Asio otus*, in conflict between attack and escape. Note two groups of erected crest feathers ("the ears") and ruffled body feathers. (*D*) Leadbeater's Cockatoo, *Kakatoe leadbeateri*, lives in large social flocks. The crest feathers are not only elongated but display an orange and yellow pattern when erected. (*E*) The highly modified, permanently erected crest feathers have become a new structure in the Victoria Crowned Pigeon, *Goura victoria*. (*F*) A mallard hen on her nest, conflicted between continuing to brood her eggs and escaping, spreads her white tail feathers, just before flying off a few seconds later. (Photographs D and E with permission of the San Diego Zoological Society; remaining photographs by the author.)

child. In LSD psychotherapy thirty-, forty- and fifty-year-old patients exhibit sucking reactions of such intensity that the therapist feels obliged to provide an object or even a hand for the patient to suck on.[38]

We have come to think of regressive behavior so exclusively in a psychological context that we overlook the significance of the neuromuscular foundations of such behavior. At the very least we must consider that the neural mechanisms responsible for such behavior are still present in the central nervous system and subject to reactivation. Furthermore, we often think of regression as an undesirable mode of behavior. Kortlandt [32a] points out that just before juvenile cormorants in Holland are about to migrate south in the fall, they reactivate the parental relationship and return to begging for food for a day or two, then fly off towards an unknown destination in Africa. When presented with an unknown or fearful object or situation, infant rhesus monkeys and children alike return to clinging to their surrogate or real mothers before exploring the new object. Even on the adult human level the capacity for intimacy is correlated with the ability of sexual partners to revert temporarily to infantile modes of expression and sexuality. Fried [20] suggests that some psychotherapists may be so preoccupied with ego strengthening that they fail to see or support the apparent regulatory function of passing phases of ego regression.

Redirected Activity

In a dominance hierarchy of chickens, a higher ranking individual may drive a lower ranking bird from a feeding area. In such a feeding situation the lower ranking bird may be motivated to peck back, but the fear of the higher ranking bird may inhibit its doing so. In a very definite sense, this is a conflict between fear and aggressive behavior. If a still lower ranking bird should be present or pass by, the displaced chicken will direct its aggression towards the low ranking passerby, sometimes even while fleeing from the first bird. This is termed "redirected activity" and is most probably equivalent to the concept of object displacement in psychoanalysis.

In the fighting behavior of the Burmese jungle fowl, *Gallus gallus spadiceus,* displacement feeding or even pecking at the ground may occur, but as the fighting mounts in intensity so does the intensity of pecking. If often becomes an "aggressive pecking" and in this instance it is difficult to determine whether "displacement feeding" or redirected pecking from a rival onto an object, or onto the ground itself, is taking place—in the fashion that an angry person bangs his fist on the table instead of striking whomever has aroused his anger. Likewise during an actual fight between two jungle fowl, both attack and escape may be activated, and in addition to the occurrence of irrelevant activities, the motivation for fighting itself may become ambivalent. Consequently, although Kruijt [36] recognizes the usefulness of the concept of displacement activity, he is reluctant to use the term and prefers to simply describe and analyze which motor patterns are being aroused in a particular instance and which irrelevant behaviors are occurring.

Transitional Activities

Likewise, Lind [39] has pointed out that during behavior studies of various species of birds, individuals frequently change over from one action to another when it is least expected, and when no conflict or thwarted situation can be occurring; instead, there appears to be a gradual transition between two activities through a motor pattern common to both behaviors. For example, when a sheldrake, *Tadorna tadorna,* preens its feathers it dips its bill into the water at intervals, lifts and shakes its head, then continues to preen. It happens that when it dips its head down to the water the duck stops and takes a drink before continuing to preen. In one instance of fifteen bill dippings, eleven are followed by "head-shaking—preening," but four are followed by "drinking—head-shaking—preening." Lind considers that the bill dipping motor pattern is a preliminary to drinking as well as to preening and that even in a preening situation, the performance of bill dipping acts as a transition to drinking.

Again, during high intensity bathing a sheldrake on the surface of the water dips its forebody into the water with its neck drawn back, with its wings and hind quarters tilting into the air. This movement is akin to the preliminary motor pattern of bottom-feeding. Lind has noticed several instances during bathing where immediately after dipping its forebody down during bathing, the duck actually begins to bottom-feed for two to three seconds, then resumes bathing. The forebody in the water and hindquarters in the air is a transitional behavior common to both bathing and bottom-feeding behavior.

All of these lawful phenomena such as displacement activities, ambivalent responses, intention movements, superposed movement patterns, regressive behavior and so forth have been shown to be responsible for the evolution of the many signaling or communication systems which play such a vital role in the evolution of social behavior. Before proceeding further along these lines, however, it would be useful to clarify the various ways in which biologists, ethologists and others use the term "conflict."

BIOLOGICAL MEANINGS OF CONFLICT

Several diverse types of biological responses or interactions are sometimes designated by the term "conflict." These may be classified as (a) intraindividual conflict, (b) conspecific conflict and (c) interspecific conflict. In diverse animal species, all three categories of conflict have resulted in the evolution of mechanisms which contribute to or enhance social behavior.

Intraindividual Conflict

By intraindividual conflict I mean to designate a conflict of responses within a single animal, such as approach or avoidance in courtship rituals, flight or aggression in fighting for a territory, etcetera. It is this internal conflict of antagonistic responses which gives rise to the displacement activities * mentioned

---

* It should be noted that when ethologists use the term "displacement," they refer to a conflict of motor patterns and the consequent activation of a *displacement motor pattern*. When psychoanalysts and psychiatrists refer to "displacement," they generally refer to a displacement of *objects*. Thus Fenichel, in discussing Freud's analysis of Little Hans refers to the fact that fear and hatred of the father were displaced to a horse. Ethologists refer to the change of a behavior pattern from one object to another as *redirected activity*. Dollard and Miller (1950) have also used the term "displacement" in a psychological context similar to but not equivalent to ethological usage.

previously. Internal conflict and displacement activity of this type was initially described by Kortlandt in a study of the European cormorant, *Phalacrocorax carbo sinensis*. Since that time many ethologists have called attention to the regular and predictable occurrence of displacement activities in a variety of animals.

Although Tinbergen [68] suggested that displacement activities may provide outlets for surplus impulses which might disturb or otherwise damage the central nervous system—that is, that they have a homeostatic function—we still know practically nothing about their underlying neurophysiological mechanisms which would account for their predictable characteristics. Nevertheless some studies have been undertaken to assess accurately their lawful regularity of occurrence or predictability. For example, Van Iersel and Bol [29a] carried out a study of displacement preening in two species of terns (*Sterna sandwichensis* and *S hirundo*). Preening, which is known to occur as a displacement activity in many species of birds, occurs as a normal motor pattern immediately after bathing. It also occurs in terns after copulation, after an alarm signal is given, during nest relief ceremonies, during brooding or in connection with aggressive displays. The authors carried out careful quantitative analyses of preening behavior in relation to all of the forementioned behavior. Their findings indicate that different fixed motor patterns mutually inhibit each other in specific ways as follows:

1. Brooding of eggs inhibits escape, nest-building, aggression and preening.

2. At high intensities, brooding of eggs and escape are mutually inhibitory.

3. If at the same time, therefore, escape and incubation are sufficiently but not too unequally activated, a conflict will result.

4. Such conflict may give rise to either preening or more frequently head-shaking as a displacement activity.

Combined observations and measurements made of preening after strong alarm calls and during alarm experiments indicate a definite correlation between both *frequency* and *intensity* of displacement preening and the strength of the escape drive. A definite correlation was also shown to exist between intensity of preening and the strength of the incubation drive.

The study of displacement activities occurring in a variety of animals indicates that they originate from other fixed motor patterns. In conflict situations, however, these motor patterns are released out of their original function and context. The fact that two types of displacement activities, preening or head-shaking, occur in the conflict situations of terns studied by Van Iersel and Bol raises a further question. What determines which fixed motor patterns of those available to an animal will be utilized as a displacement activity in a conflict?

In an endeavor to answer this question, Van Iersel and Bol made a study of the nest-relief ceremonies of the sandwich tern. Both the male and female tern incubate their eggs. While one parent incubates, the other leaves the nesting area, usually for several hours. Upon the mate's return, the brooding bird leaves the nest, and the returning mate settles on the eggs. Sometimes this exchange is made quickly and smoothly on signal of the returning mate, but very often the exchange goes more slowly. When the brooding bird does not get off the nest at once, preening and nest-building occur as a displacement activity in both the brooding and the relieving bird. What determines whether displacement preening or displacement nest-building will occur?

Since one bird is on the nest and the mate is ready to take its place, it can be assumed that the drive or impulses for brooding behavior are present in both birds. On the other hand the presence of some other bird in the nesting territory arouses either aggressive or escape behavior. If aggression is aroused, there is a conflict between incubation and aggression, and displacement preening occurs. If escape is aroused, there is a conflict between incubation and escape and displacement nest-building occurs (Fig. 1–4). Since both birds have a drive to incubate, the choice between displacement preening or displacement nest-building depends on whether escape or aggression is the more strongly aroused conflicting pattern. Furthermore, the intensity of displacement preening was shown to be correlated

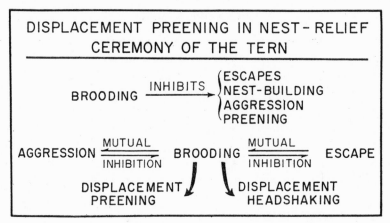

Figure 1-4. Factors effecting the "choice" of displacement activity in the tern.

with the strength of both incubation and escape. In other words, the intensity of the expression of a displacement activity is correlated with the intensity of the conflict.

Thus a conflict situation may be defined as one in which two opposite systems of covert motor activity are simultaneously activated but mutually inhibit each other. There also appear to be other types of situations, however, when displacement activities occur as in the courtship of the stickleback fish. When the female suddenly stops following a courting male, the latter may start fanning with its gill fins (displacement fanning), or if one of two fighting domestic cocks suddenly flees or is quickly removed, the remaining one may begin displacement food-pecking. All these behavioral relationships are derived from visible, gross behavior, but it would seem that both the conflict of responses and the resulting displacement activities must involve lawful and as yet little understood central nervous system mechanisms.

In the human realm we normally subsume this type of internal conflict under the heading of emotional tension resulting from incompatible inner needs or drives. It should be noted that emotional responses also involve underlying fixed motor patterns; in a succeeding section their role in human behavior and character formation will be noted.

Conspecific Conflict

In utilizing the term "discordance" in the theme of this collo-quium, we undoubtedly have in mind conspecific conflict—two or more individuals being at variance, quarrelsome or in dis-agreement. In actual fact intraindividual conflict and conspe-cific conflict are often dynamically interrelated, for it is most frequent that when two individuals of the same species oppose, court or cooperate with each other that internal patterns of responses are activated which are in conflict with each other. These internal conflicts then give rise to displacement activi-ties, and the displacement activities very often give rise to threat or appeasement gestures which then contribute to the social behavior or the social hierarchical system of which they are a part. Ethological studies have provided us with some insight regarding the evolution of these communicating systems.

The most common conflicts of conspecific animals are known from the fighting that occurs during seasonal activities that have to do with territorial behavior and mating. The displace-ment sand-digging of the stickleback fish occurs during the territorial fighting which often develops between reproductive males. The tendency towards aggression is increased with prox-imity of a territorial male to its own nesting area, and the tendency to escape an aggressive male is increased with the increased distance of an encroaching male from its own terri-tory. Thus it comes about that at some distance from the nests of two adjoining males a territorial boundary is established, where, theoretically, the tendency to behave aggressively and the tendency to escape balance each other. It is here that displace-ment sand-digging occurs. Displacement sand-digging has appar-ently become sufficiently ritualized so that it now acts as a threat signal to a neighboring male stickleback. Thus displacement sand-digging (which differs in slight respects from normal, func-tional sand-digging associated with building a nest) has itself become a releaser which inhibits further encroachment on the territory of the male that displays it. In other words, the dis-placement activity resulting from the intraindividual conflict between aggression and escape has evolved into a signal or releaser which mediates the territorial conflict of two adjoining males. The resulting "concordance" has emerged from the conflict.

The males of the mouthbrooding cichlid fish, *Tilapia mossambica* construct spawning pits in our laboratory in unusually close proximity—that is, within 10 to 14 inches of each other. It is not unusual to have three or four pit-digging, reproductive males maintaining their several spawning pits in an average 23-gallon tank. When these males first begin to dig spawning

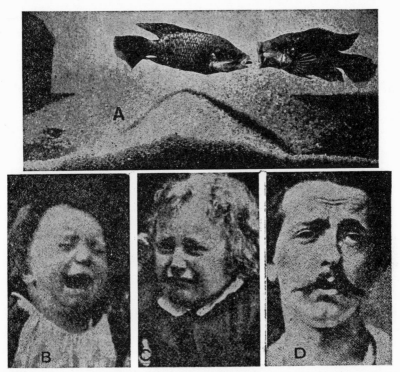

Figure 1-5. *Conspecific conflict:* (*A*) Ritualized threat between male *Tilapia mossambica* with spawning pit territories at extreme right and left. (Photograph by the author.)
Intraindividual conflict: (*B*) A child crying. (*C*) Moderate (partially inhibited crying) in an older child. Note the raised eyebrows. (*D*) An actor simulates grief. Note the furrowed frontal muscle contractions which raise the eyebrows and prevent the eye closing, crying pattern. (All illustrations from Charles Darwin: *The Expression of the Emotions in Man/and Animals.*)

pits they sometimes engage in actual fights; they circle each other and nip at each other's sides. But very quickly these fights give way to ritualized threat behavior in which two adjoining males swim back and forth at each other, first one advancing an inch or two, the other retreating an inch or two, then the second fish advances and the first retreats (Fig. 1–5, *A*). If the intensity of their threat behavior brings them closer than they wish, they flare their mouths open at each other, then both retreat to spitting gravel and continuing the construction of their spawning pits without approaching each other. Very often in these cases the territorial line is not an imaginary boundary but an actual mound of gravel constructed by the two fish as they spit gravel towards each other's spawning pits. These ritualized threats enable these adjoining males to maintain their spawning pits next to each other day after day, week after week, with little or no actual fighting taking place between them. If the ecological environment is changed, however, either as the result of covering up their spawning pits or rearranging the pots and slate in the tank, momentary fights may again take place but they again quickly merge into ritualized patterns of threat behavior. In *T sparrmani* threat behavior also occurs between pairs of fish forced to defend territories in the confines of a 20-gallon aquarium, but these threats are hardly ritualized and frequently give way to actual attacks.

These ritualized patterns of behavior have evolved again and again in the animal kingdom, and their adaptive value lies in the fact that they enable animals to fight for a territory without actually killing the rival. Thus Eibl-Eibesfeldt [15] has shown that male marine iguanid lizards, *Amblyrhynchus cristatus*, of the Galápagos Islands establish and defend mating territories on small areas of rocky terrain. In this case, also, ritualized displays and fights take place which are not damaging to the rivals. The possessor of a territory first attempts to intimidate an encroaching male by specific display patterns (themselves probably displacement activities), but if this fails, the two males butt their heads against each other and engage in head-pushing. The struggle ends with the weaker animal adopting a submissive posture, crouching low on its belly and being permitted to retreat. Biting rarely occurs, and clawing each other with their sharp talons apparently never occurs in these ritualized fights between males. The conflict is resolved by a ritualized show of strength in which neither of the contestants kill or even maim each other.

Interspecific Conflict

At the Max Planck Institute for Behavioral Physiology in Germany, it was common to see a gaggle of geese resting, preening or otherwise engaged on land at the edge of the lake. But in this case the seventy to seventy-five geese which made up the group consisted of several different species—greylags, Canadians, snow-geese, whitefronts, pink-footed geese, etcetera. Suddenly a neck and head would shoot straight up, and within less than a second or two at the most, all the necks would be similarly erected with the geese ready to move off. Inspection would invariably reveal that a strange dog or other animal had approached the area—sometimes still at a distance. The vertical "stiff neck" is an alarm signal frequently displayed on sight of a predator, which all the other species of geese respond to in similar fashion as soon as one alarm is given.

The presence of a predator is frequently responded to by one member of a herd of animals with some particular stance of attention. Very often such a response or a portion of it may evolve into a signal, through intensification or exaggeration. An alarmed whitetail deer, *Odocoileus virginianus,* raises its head at attention, brings its ears forward, raises its tail and fluffs the white hairs on the underside of its tail and on its spread anal flanks. The pronghorn antelope behaves similarly. At attention, the great ears of the mule deer, *O hemionus,* twist forward, spreading 25 percent larger than the whitetail's. At calving time, a herd of forty or fifty hinds of red deer may separate into families, with the mother hind alert to any source of alarm. Should danger threaten, she gives a warning bark, which signals the other herd members to fix their eyes on the source of the disturbance and then move off. Each hind is thus a potential sentinel for the entire herd, but apart from this adaptive value,

Figure 1–6. Interspecific conflict signals. (*A*) Adult female Thomson's gazelle looking around, relaxed. (*B*) Adult male showing long-necked, alert posture. (After Fritz Walther.) (*C*) Pronghorn antelope, *Antilocarpa americana*, sighting danger—showing spread, elongated white flank hairs. (After E. T. Seton, with permission of the publishers, Charles T. Branford Company, Newton, Mass.)

signals which result from responses to other (predator) species also promote group coordination and social cohesion.

The social coordinating function of alarm signals is most clearly seen in African herds of grazing animals. Walther[71] has pointed out that in herds of Thompson's gazelle, *Gazella thomsoni*, in East Africa, individual animals stop grazing and look around every few minutes—although in some cases an individual animal may graze for as long as fifteen minutes. Since "tommies" often occur in large herds, there is great probability that at least one animal has its head up all the time. As soon as one member of the herd is alerted to a suspicious movement or unknown form, it erects its neck, puts its ears forward, lowers its croup and tenses its muscles. Other gazelles are alerted by the alert posture of a single animal or more so by an additional snort of alarm. As a result of these responses to alarm postures or sounds, a potential predator has little opportunity to take a member of the herd by surprise. Alert behavior may also lead to all members of the herd converging on a suspicious object for a closer look or smell. Tommies twitch their flanks immediately before running off, but this movement is not always a danger signal. It is generally the last link (before running) in a chain of action normally seen in intraspecific behavior in relation to another dominant animal.

When a bachelor gazelle enters the territory of another male, the territory owner walks closer with presented horns to drive the intruder away. In this situation the complete behavior sequence takes place. The bachelor (a) lowers his head and turns it alternately to right and left, then (b) begins to stamp with all four legs, (c) pushes his nose against his inguinal region, (d) scratches his head or neck hastily with a hind leg, (e) *shakes the flank* and (f) then runs off in a gallop. When performed in this context, flank movements never provoke flight reactions in other gazelles. All these movements appear singly or in the same sequence when an animal is covered by insects; they thus appear to be body care movements. When one animal is confronting another, there is conflict between running or standing absolutely still (another fixed motor pattern), and it is in this context that the complete sequence of movements appears. Walther points out that shaking the flanks is the last link in the sequence before flight, and it is exclusively in the flight from predators that the first movements drop out, and the abbreviated terminal sequence occurs and may serve as an alarm.

In this context it is most interesting to see that the interspecific alarm apparently evolved from a conflict situation normally occurring between two animals within the same species. Thus, aspects of intraindividual conflict, conspecific conflict and interspecies conflict all became involved in the predator alarm signal of Thomson's gazelle.

EVOLUTION OF AN INVERTEBRATE SOCIETY

Extremely complex systems of insect social organization have evolved several times, as in the termites (order Isoptera) and the ants, wasps and bees (order Hymenoptera). As our human heritage is derived from the vertebrate evolutionary line it might seem pointless to consider an invertebrate society, especially in a colloquium on social psychiatry, were it not for the fact that biologically lawful behavior and principles appear to be operating similarly in the evolution of invertebrate and vertebrate social systems alike. The principles to which I wish to draw attention for the purposes of this colloquium are (a) behavioral continuity, (b) the transformation of behavioral functions, (c) the relationship between anatomical and behavioral evolution and (d) the biosocial control of the production of phenotypes (castes).

The Hymenoptera may be taken as an example of insect societies, since an excellent study emphasizing their behavioral evolution has recently been completed by Malyshev,[45] a Russian investigator. Central to such societies, as developed independently among the wasps and hornets on the one hand and the bees on the other, is the close relationship between female parent or female workers and the larval offspring. Such a complex relationship cannot develop haphazardly; it must develop out of previous motor patterns, for how does such behavior develop from the relatively primitive sawflies (Tenthredinoids) which, other than depositing eggs in the tissues of plants with the aid of their saw-like ovipositors, show no relationship with their larval offspring? Malyshev first traces a line of evolution from species in which the larvae crawl out of the plant tissue to feed (exophytic) to those in which *the larvae began to remain in the plant tissue to feed* (endophytic). In response to the now *parasitic larva,* and probably to accessory gland substances from the ovipositor of the female, the tissues of the plant proliferate to form a special enclosure or "gall" around the larva. The larvae in turn soon lost their appendages for locomotion and became *relatively sedentary larvae.* Some females now began to lay their eggs in the already formed galls parasitized by other Hymenoptera species; they become *secondary parasites.* In the process the secondary parasitic larva began to feed not on the plant tissue, but on the tissue of the primary insect larva (which experiments confirm they will do). The larvae have now transformed from being plant feeders to being *animal feeders.*

The female parents evolved motor patterns from laying an egg inside the gall, to laying it directly onto the host egg inside the gall, then onto the host larva inside the gall, then parasitized free-living insect larvae outside the gall. Since the victims were active, it is likely that the ovipositor which penetrated the gall and conveyed a cell-proliferating substance now penetrated the host larva and produced a substance, or toxin, which *penetrated and paralyzed the victim.* This permitted the female parent to manipulate and hold the quiet victim, while she securely fastened the egg to the body of the host larva. *Meanwhile the ovipositor had become functionally and anatomically transformed into a stinger.*

Some female parasites parasitized species of larvae which burrowed in the soil and after depositing an egg on the host pushed the victim deeper into its burrow and closed up the burrow. Malyshev conjectures that this had the selective advantage of preventing other parasite species from laying an egg on an already parasitized host. Some species of wasps began to bury their victims, which was *the beginning of nest construction,* an extremely important innovation for the later evolution of social organization.

Some species, as in *ammophila* now built their nests first, then provisioned it with a large caterpillar, laid an egg on or near the victim, then closed the nest. Others provisioned their nests with larger numbers of smaller caterpillars, then many tiny larvae, aphids, etcetera. These behaviors provided the background for the shift from *mass provisioning* to *progressive provisioning,* in which the parent supplies the cell with food from day to day as the larvae develop and as is needed. The smaller prey meant that food could be easily flown to the nest instead of laboriously dragged, and the female could now construct a second cell, deposit an egg and start to rear a second, then a third larva. *This was the beginning of the simultaneous rearing of several larvae by one parent.*

Some wasps, such as the hornet *Vespa,* began to supply their larvae with *masticated food,* while the larvae in turn secreted drops of saliva, or other exudates, which the parent fed upon— the beginning of a mutual food exchange or *trophallaxis.* At this point we have arrived at the evolution of the social wasps, but an extremely important behavioral characteristic separates the bees from the wasps. Wasps feed their larvae on animal food, while bees feed their larvae on the nectar and pollen of flowers. In German they are in fact called "Blumenwespen" or flower wasps. Nevertheless for all the carnivorous habits of wasp larvae, adult wasps always continued to be plant feeders. Although bees are not considered to have originated from the vespoid wasps but from the burrowing sphecoid wasps (Fig. 1–7), there are some species of vespoid wasps that are beginning to mix their own plant food with the saliva and masticated food fed to their larvae. This suggests how the intimate feeding relationship between adults and larvae of the highly social species of bees came about. Without the change from mass provisioning to progressive provisioning which resulted in masticated food (with saliva), mouth-to-mouth feeding and the combination of nectar and pollen with

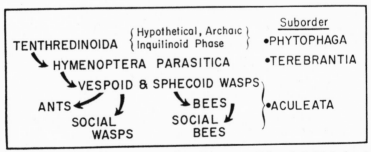

Figure 1–7. Evolution of social Hymenoptera. (After S. I. Malyshev.)

animal food, it is unlikely that the transformation to nectar, pollen and bee milk feeding (a salivary gland secretion) could have come about.

All of the behavioral relationships described above, except the hypothetical inquiniloid sawfly phase, are known from living species of Hymenoptera. When we speak of behavioral continuity then, we mean that new behaviors are not brought about haphazardly but are intimately related to the previous fixed motor patterns which a group of organisms have evolved.

Behavioral continuity and the transformation of behavioral functions are intimately related, as is the relationship between anatomical and behavioral evolution. A structure akin to the saw-like ovipositor of the sawflies which was used merely for inserting eggs into plant tissue was modified to insert eggs and produce plant galls, then further elongated and specialized for the insertion of eggs into the thickened tissues of another host's gall by a parasitic gall wasp. This ultimately resulted in the evolution of a stinging organ capable of locating and paralyzing the locomotion-controlling ganglionic mass of their prey. Likewise the continuing importance of nectar gathering ultimately led to the evolution of the elongated, combined sucking (for nectar gathering) and mandibilate mouth parts (for nest construction) characteristic of bees. The specialized epidermal cells, the oenocytes, which normally produce a waterproof waxy substance for the cuticle of insects were concentrated and transformed into wax glands for the production of a specialized material, beeswax, for the construction of the comb—not unlike the way the sweat glands of primitive mammals became concentrated and localized to produce a special secretion—milk of mammary glands. In the bees, however, it was the pharyngeal salivary glands which became specialized and enlarged for the production of "bee milk" or royal jelly. Many more examples of the all-important transformation of functions both behavioral and physiologic (is behavior not physiologic?) could be given which affected the evolution of social behavior and organization in these insects. Two of the most important examples have to do with the biosocial control of the castes and sex of colony members and the utilization of successive age stages of worker bees for further behavioral specialization.

The bee colony itself determines the production of reproductive queen bees and nonreproducing female worker bees. The eggs of these two castes are genotypically the same. If the larvae which hatch from them are fed exclusively on "bee milk" they become adult female queens, if fed on bee milk initially, then pollen and nectar, they become adult female worker bees. They are *nutritional phenotypes.* These two castes actually represent a split of female functions—the queen lays eggs exclusively, the female workers tend to the young and the hive. In addition, by controlling the construction of the size of the cells, the worker bees determine whether the queen will lay fertilized eggs which develop into females or nonfertilized eggs which develop into males. Whether the female workers feed larvae, build comb, forage, etcetera, depends on various stages of activity of the pharyngeal glands and the wax glands or whether both sets of glands are involuted, which is correlated with the age of the worker (Fig. 1–8). But the behavioral needs of the colony can influence the physiologic activity of these glands, just as the physiologic state of the glands is capable of influencing the behavior of the workers.[53]

It should be noted that among many species of wasps there is no morphological difference between the queen and her workers. One female is behaviorally antagonistic to the other females and suppresses their egg-laying activity. These females then carry out other female care functions and become "worker wasps." In the honeybee, the queen secretes a chemical substance which is mixed with the general food supply and suppresses the development of the ovaries of the worker bees. One might well consider that this reproductive "conflict" between the queen and worker bees plays a central role in the behavioral developments characteristic of the honeybee society. Once these behavioral relationships were established as among various other groups of bees, the unique communication system of honeybees dances described by von Frisch [21] and Lindauer [40] could then be evolved.

SOME EVOLUTIONARY ASPECTS OF
SOCIAL INSECTS (Hymenoptera)

1. FREE-LIVING EXOPHYTIC LARVA (SAWFLIES)
   → SEDENTARY, ENDOPHYTIC LARVA (GALL WASPS)
   → PARASITIC, CARNIVOROUS LARVA
   - EGG PARASITISM → LARVA PARASITISM
   - HOSTS LEADING AN OPEN LIFE
   - TRANSFORMATION OF OVIPOSITOR INTO STINGER

2. VESPOID ADAPTATIONS
   - DIRECT CONTACT & HANDLING OF ADULT PREY
   - CONCEALMENT OF PREY; NEST CONSTRUCTION
   - MASS PROVISIONING → PROGRESSIVE PROVISIONING
   - MASTICATION OF FOOD; MOUTH-TO-MOUTH FEEDING
   - TRANSFORMATION FROM ANIMAL FOOD TO NECTAR
                                    (& POLLEN)

3. APOID (BEE) ADAPTATIONS
   - MOTOR PATTERNS FOR CARE OF OFFSPRING
     Mass Provisioning → Progressive Provisioning
   - PARENT IN CONTACT WITH PROGENY
     Several Consecutive Broods
     Extended Life Span of Parent
   - SPECIALIZED COMMUNICATIVE SYSTEMS

4. BIOSOCIAL CONTROL OF CASTE PRODUCTION
   - NUTRITIVE PHENOTYPES
   - SPLIT IN MATERNAL FUNCTIONS
     Reproduction || Larva-Colony Care & Foraging
     (Queen) || (Female Workers)

5. ADAPTATION OF BEHAVIORAL PROPENSITIES
   OF SUCCESSIVE AGE GROUPS
   - FEEDING LARVAE ⎫   • BUILDING COMB ⎫
   - CLEANING CELLS ⎬ 1-10   • STORING FOOD ⎬ 10-20
   - RECONNAISSANCE ⎭ days   • GUARDING HIVE ⎭ days
   - FORAGING FOR POLLEN & NECTAR⎬20 days → DEATH

Figure 1–8. Some behavioral transformations in the evolution of social wasps and bees.

VERTEBRATE SOCIAL ORGANIZATION

Diverse social structures have evolved independently among various vertebrate groups of animals. Just as in the Hymenop-

tera, however, behavioral continuity and behavioral transformations have played a central role in these developments.
Likewise lawful behavioral responses, superposition of motor
patterns and displacement activities, and their subsequent selection and ritualization, play an important role in mediating
vertebrate social interaction. Of course, the more animals interact together, the more opportunities for conflicts occur.

In some social organizations conflicts play an open and active
role in the social structure; in others it is masked so that the
social group appears to be working in complete cooperation and
concordance. To understand the evolution of vertebrate social
systems we would have to rely on the same comparative methodology that has been so effective in enabling us to understand
the evolution of vertebrate anatomy. But in tracing the evolution of vertebrate structure we can lean heavily on fossil
materials, as well as on our knowledge of living species. While
gross behavioral information is often inferred from fossils, we
have almost no fossil records of fixed motor patterns and less
evidence regarding the evolution of social behavior. Therefore
we must rely heavily on comparative descriptive studies of the
behavior of living species and on a great deal of inferential reasoning. Very few thoroughgoing comparative studies of the social
behavior of vertebrates have been made such as Tinbergen and
his students are carrying out for gulls, although diverse investigators are now undertaken for primates. Nevertheless, the
descriptive and experimental studies of social behavior made
during the past two decades have yielded considerable information.

As seen from only some of the examples depicted in Figure
1–9, vertebrate social structures may vary from open or closed
anonymous groups to those in which individual recognition plays
an important role, from temporary social structures to persistent
social organizations. In open anonymous groups, such as schools
of fish or flocks of birds, any species member may join the group
or leave it. Schools of fish appear to have some adaptive value in
regard to predator avoidance and feeding. Likewise, flocks of
birds appear to have some value with regard to feeding, preda-

```
┌─────────────────────────────────────────────┐
│    SOCIAL GROUPS & ORGANIZATIONS              │
│  1.OPEN ANONYMOUS GROUPS                      │
│      SCHOOLS OF FISH                          │
│      FLOCKS OF BIRDS                          │
│  2.CLOSED ANONYMOUS GROUPS                    │
│      TERRITORIAL MICE, RATS                   │
│  3.COLONIES OF REPRODUCTIVE BIRDS             │
│      HERRING GULLS, TERNS                     │
│      CORMORANTS, GANNETS, PELICANS            │
│  4.PACKS OF HUNTING MAMMALS                   │
│      WOLVES - FAMILY STRUCTURE, PLUS          │
│                 SUCCESSIVE GENERATIONS        │
│                 OF YOUNG; RANK ORDER          │
│      HUNTING DOGS - NO RANK ORDER             │
│  5.HERDS OF MAMMALS                           │
│      DEER, ANTELOPE, SHEEP, GOATS, etc.       │
│      HORSES, ZEBRA                            │
│      FUR SEALS, SEA LIONS, etc.               │
│  6.PRIMATES                                   │
│      MATERNAL- INFANT AND FAMILY              │
│      STRUCTURE TO HIGHLY                      │
│      COMPLEX. SOCIAL ORGANIZATIONS            │
└─────────────────────────────────────────────┘
```

Figure 1–9. Some examples of vertebrate social groups.

tor alarm and migration. Ducks and geese not only migrate together but feed together. Passerine birds not only feed together and migrate together but roost together in trees at night. The rounded appearance of a bird with fluffed feathers to provide an insulating pocket of warm air is a signal that another bird may approach closer than the usual social distance. This often results in birds "clumping" together and sharing their body heat at night. However, this is only true of those species that have "contact signals" such as species of finches; in similar situations swallows and starlings avoid body contact.

By contrast, only group members are tolerated in *closed anonymous groups,* such as exist among mice and rats. Group members do not recognize one another individually but determine group membership on the basis of a collective odor due to urinary markings.[15] Strangers from outside the group are attacked vigorously, but within the group conflicts are slight and there is no rank order. Dominant individuals only rarely develop. On the other hand when a group of rats are kept in a limited space but supplied with adequate food, both dominant males and submissive homosexual males that do not compete for females develop in the colony. According to Calhoun,[5] in such *"limited space"* situations, there is a disintegration not only of normal rat group behavior but also of nesting behavior and the care of the young.

Colonies of reproductive birds form temporary seasonal social structures. For example, during autumn and winter herring gulls feed, sleep and migrate in flocks. In spring, the flock visits the breeding grounds where it breaks up into several "clubs" which consist of paired birds and unpaired individuals that court one another in this area. There may be ten or twelve or more pairs of birds in the club area that start nest-building and defend a small nesting area within the club area. Unpaired aggressive males may also defend a courting area until they mate, then build nests together. There may be four, five or six clubs areas within a reproductive colony, and the club areas are often separated by 50, 75 or 100 yards. Gulls rarely settle or build nests in the in-between areas but settle down in the club areas; they are obviously attracted to the presence of other gulls. Once within the club, however, they actively defend their nesting or courting area against each other. Physical features of the terrain undoubtedly play some role, but the spacing of the nests appears to be the result of the forces of social attraction and aggressive behavior between pairs.

To defend their nesting area, three types of threat behavior have evolved: (a) a mild upright posture with stretched neck advancing toward a stranger or intruder; (b) grass-pulling, which is a stronger threat; and (c) choking—when male and female face a neighboring pair together, often pecking on the ground and uttering a rhythmic, hoarse sort of cooing call. Other gulls respond to these threats by retreating. Sometimes actual fights break out between gulls if the threats are not heeded. In the midst of this constant conflict between pairs, the individual members of the pair cooperate with each other in brooding the eggs (which are never left alone—one member incubates while the other is off feeding), the hatching chicks are sheltered and protected from other adults, and both parents respond to the begging pecks of herring gull chicks by regurgitating food and feeding them. When invaded by a predator, a dog or even a man, the adults utter an alarm call, all members of the club fly up into the air and proceed to "dive bomb" the intruder. They swoop down, one after the other, sometimes scrape their legs over the head of the intruder and drop regurgitated food or feces. Even though I know that such attacks are not actually damaging, I have always found them extremely distasteful. Though temporary, a breeding colony of gulls has a definite social organization which combines both conflict and cooperative patterns of behavior.

Open conflict plays a significant role in the temporary social organizations that form during the reproductive season of many diverse groups of animals. The ritualized head pushing fights which marine iguana males (Reptilia) of the Galápagos Islands carry on have already been mentioned. During the reproductive season the adjacent territories of the males may each contain several females. These reproductive groups form a very loose social structure in which cooperative behavior is almost nonexistent, except during actual courtship.

Similar seasonal social structures develop among fur seals and sea lions. The seals have few or minimal social ties during most of the year, but when they gather on the Pribilof Islands during the summer reproductive period which lasts some four months, a social structure emerges. The older males arrive first and each takes possession of a specific territory, but not without considerable fighting between them. When the females arrive some four weeks later, they appear to choose to enter the territories of specific bulls. There is some evidence that the females (and their female offspring) return in general to the same territory year after year. Spectacular threats, rushes and serious fighting continue duing this period when the females give birth to off-spring resulting from the mating of the previous year. While each female cares for its solitary pup, the bulls protect their entire harem of females and pups. The pups very shortly begin to as-sociate with each other in groups called "pods," but each female continues to suckle her own pup. After several weeks the pups start to enter the water, after which they very quickly become adept swimmers.

It is only after the pups are born that the cows come into heat again, and sexual activity reaches its own peak. Virgin females seek the company of harem females, and the larger harems break down into smaller female groups at this time. Young bachelor seals also occupy the islands during this reproductive period but remain together in their own areas around the breeding terri-tories. They attempt to capture and mate with females but are no match for the larger bulls. In such circumstances, it is not surprising that considerable size dimorphism occurs between the older bulls, the younger bachelors and females. A territorial bull may weigh eight times or more as much as a seventy-pound female. It is not until the height of the estrous period is over, and the emaciated bulls stop defending their territories and re-turn to the water that there is a general mixing of bulls, bachelors, cows and pups. With the reproductive and sexual periods over, the social structure disintegrates, and the seals separate and head south again for the winter.

Although bull seals constantly herd their females together, their social structure is again different from herds of grazing animals. According to Darling,[14] who studied the red deer of Scotland, these animals utilize both a highland summer terri-tory and a lowland winter territory, but in the presence of storms, insect attacks or strangers, they will move along well-trodden paths from one territory to another. The most stable group of the herd consists of females and their young, which are guarded until they are three years of age. After their third year, males join the less-organized herd of stags, while the females re-main together. The female herd is led by a dominant hind, who herself has a young deer with her, is extremely vigilant and investigates and warns the herd of all potential dangers. Several older females may cooperate with the chief hind, not only in warning of danger but in determining the movements of the herd in feeding and in the seasonal migrations. During the rutting season, however, the male groups break up, invade the female territories, round up hinds and keep them in harems during brief mating periods. Aggressive displays and fights occur during this period, and the stag who is in charge of the harem mates with the females as they come into heat. But after a week or so the exhausted stag is driven off by another who takes his place. The females cooperate with the male in sexual activity only and not in defense of their harem territory.

It appears that the constant attentiveness of the females to their mother over a three-year period and their subsequent time spent in the female herd is responsible for the stability of the female herd and the dominance hierarchy. By contrast, the male herd is looser, no dominance hierarchy develops and there is less cooperative behavior. Aggression between males, however, is confined to the rutting period. In contrast to seals, red deer are centered around a stable, year-round, matriarchal type of organization interacting temporarily with a looser group of males. Species of sheep also display a similar type of matriarchal social organization.

The wolf pack displays a type of social structure which is largely derived from the family unit—although in some instances two or more separate packs may join temporarily to form a larger pack. Normally the pack consists of a parental male and female and several successive broods of offspring that cooperate in chasing, attacking and killing their prey. When the parental female is having a litter, she does not hunt but is fed by the male or other pack members—a further indication of cooperative behavior. On the other hand the dominant parental male appears to suppress all sexual activity of the other males in the pack, and this is apparently accomplished with a minimum of conflict or fighting. Dominance relationships are established while the pack animals are developing in each new litter and the resulting hierarchy of relationships appears to have great stability. Strong social relationships and dependencies develop between pack members, but ultimately some of the older males will leave, find mates and establish packs of their own. The original parental pair maintain a permanent relationship, very often for life. Dominance, friendly submission, subordination, suppression of behavior and highly adaptive cooperative behaviors are thus effectively blended together in the wolf pack type of society.[95] On the other hand, African Cape hunting dogs, *Lycaon pictus,* also cooperate in hunting down, attacking and killing prey considerably larger than themselves, but no rank order occurs in their social structure.

These few examples of social organization should suffice to demonstrate that not only is there great diversity in the types of social structures that have evolved, but that conflict and cooperative behavior go hand in hand. We may put the matter even stronger by stating that in many instances it can be demonstrated that the signals or communication which promote social behavior and cooperation have been derived directly from lawful responses growing out of the conflict situation. The cooperative response very often contains both the conflict and its resolution.

The stickleback fish which has established a nesting territory that is aggressively defended against other males must resolve the strong aggressive impulses which are at their height during this time. The zigzag courtship dance with which the male greets an approaching female is a resolution, in part, to this aggressiveness. Since she does not have the red belly characteristic of males, but a white one with enlarged eggs, the male appears to begin to attack her, then inhibits this attack and moves toward the nest he has prepared. These combined motor patterns result in the zigzag courtship dance to which the female responds by following the male towards the nest. Proof that aggressiveness is involved is indicated by the fact that under various circumstances males actually bite females during a zigzag dance and these attacks are identical with those delivered on males. It is the forward movement towards the female which may result in biting the female, whereas the sideward leap away from her may suddenly change into a leading to the nest. If a female shows up when the male is not quite finished with nest-building and he is showing little or no nest-leading activity, he will be inclined to bite and attack the female and even drive her off. On the other hand, the stronger the sexual drive, the less biting is shown by the male during courtship. Thus the motor patterns of attack and nest-leading make up one zigzag movement, and from this Seven-ster [58] inferred that courtship is a mixture of sexual and aggressive activities.

Likewise, in the egg relief ceremonies of cichlid fish, it is not uncommon to see one of the parents making exaggerated S-shaped movements and even biting the mate, as occurs in *Tilapia zilli*. In *T sparrmani, Aequedens pulcher* and other cichlids, the female sometimes becomes so aggressive after spawning that she drives her own mate away from the egg site, as well as other fish. Also, in *T sparrmani* when aggressive behavior is increased by the presence of two or more parental pairs in the same tank, males sometimes turn against and attack their own female mates (Kramer, unpublished observation).

Many ritualized behavior patterns which mediate social or cooperative behavior thus represent a "balance" between potentially antagonistic elements. When either internal or external factors are changed, the balance changes, and the aggressive portion of the conflict may break out anew. This applies not only to ritualized behaviors but to others as well. Two pairs of pigeons had each built nests on the floor of a pigeon loft, instead of in the nesting boxes provided. The second pair had to cross quite close to the nest of the first pair, and there was considerable overt aggression between these two pairs initially. After a few days, however, both pairs became habituated to the situation and accepted the presence of the other pair without overt conflict. At this point I decided to move the first of the floor nests into the nesting box and succeeded in doing so by placing the nest on successive slabs of wood 1½ inches thick every few hours, then moving it an inch or two at a time towards the nesting box. In this way I succeeded in moving the nest about

1½ feet up to and into the nesting box in the course of a day. The next day, however, it was apparent that the conflict between these two pairs whose nests had been separated by 5 feet, and were now separated by 3½ feet, had broken out anew. Each time the second pair passed by they were again attacked, but after about one and one half days the pairs again became habituated to the situation and overt conflict had disappeared.

It should be emphasized, of course, that not only fixed (inherited) motor patterns but learned behaviors enter into many aspects of the development of social behavior. Fixed motor patterns do not, however, appear to become more plastic and transform into learned behaviors, as Lorenz [43] pointed out, either phylogenetically or ontogenetically. Fixed motor patterns and the capacity for learned behavior appear to be two separate types of adaptation and evolution. There is no justification for opposing phylogenetically determined fixed motor patterns and ontogenetic learning mechanisms, since fixed motor patterns may mature or emerge during ontogeny. Fixed motor patterns may drop out of the behavioral repertoire just as they have evolved and be replaced by learned behaviors, or learned behaviors may be inserted between or interlaced with innate behavior patterns. The fact that an animal species may have evolved a high capacity for learned activities, as in man, is no indication, as we shall see subsequently, that fixed motor patterns play no role in that animal's social behavior or organization.

ASPECTS OF CONFLICT, TRANSFORMATION AND COOPERATION IN PRIMATES

We normally think of primates as social animals, but even here a tremendous diversity of social groupings has been reported among different species. Bourliere [2] has pointed out that even within a given family or subfamily the structure of primate societies is far from being uniform. Moreover, the same types of social organization may be found in very different groups. For example, monogamous family groups exist among both the lemurs (Indridae) and the anthropoids (Hylobatinae). Even within a group such as the Lemuroidea, some species show no more social groupings than do some insectivores or ro-

Time of Census	Total of Individuals	Adult Males	Females with Infants	Other Adult Females	Juveniles	Infants	Reference
January, 1932 .	26	3	4	7	8	4	Carpenter, 1934
May, 1932 . .	27	4	1	10	11	1	" "
January, 1933 .	29	4	5	5	10	5	" "
May, 1933 . .	30	5	3	9	10	3	" "
March, 1951 .	17	1	3	6	4	3	Collias and Southwick, 1952
November, 1955	14	1	3	1	6	3	Altmann, 1959

Figure 1–10. Variation in group composition among the howling monkeys, *Alouatta palliata* of the laboratory group of Barro Colorado Island. (After F. Bourliere.)

dents (the aye-aye, *Daubentonia madagascariensis* is solitary and nocturnal). Others live in lasting family groups and still others form large bisexual groups. *Lemur macaco* generally lives in small groups of from four to fifteen animals in territories which they defend against other groups of their species. At night, however, these separate groups join together to form large nocturnal groups that disperse again at sunrise.

There also appears to be considerable variability in the size and structure of social groups wihin a single species, whenever a group has been studied over a period of years or in different ecological communities. Figure 1–10 indicates the variation in group composition among the howling monkey (*Alouatta palliata*) laboratory group on Barro Colorado Island during six separate years from 1932 to 1955. The factors that determine group size and integration are still far from being understood.

On the basis of careful counts of fifty-one groups in 1932 and 1933, Carpenter indicated a group size range from four to thirty-five individuals. The average grouping tendency in howlers was as follows: three males plus eight females plus three dependent infants plus four juveniles and an unknown number of solitary, transitional, nongroup-living males. On the average there were more than twice as many adult females in a group as adult males (but note the variation in the laboratory colony of howlers from five males and twelve females in 1933 to one male and nine females in 1951), and Carpenter wondered what factors determined what he termed the "socioeconomic sex ratio" for a given species. Genetic factors, the intragroup pattern of competition and cooperation, male and female sex needs and capacities, the developmental rate of infants and juveniles, ecological conditions and differential mortality rates must all enter into producing the socioeconomic sex ratio and group size. Southwick, Beg and Siddiqi, in studying the adaptations of rhesus monkeys in various habitats in Northern India from 1959 to 1960, noted that temple and forest living social groups were distinctly larger in overall numbers than village, canal bank and other habitat groups (Fig. 1–11). Ecological conditions not only influenced group size but behavioral interactions as well.

Among howler monkeys, males play a major role in controlling group movements, regulating intragroup status and in defending and maintaining the integrity of the group against other organized groups in the area. The ritualized howling battles and threats, which take place when two separate groups run into each other, appear to play a significant role in promoting social

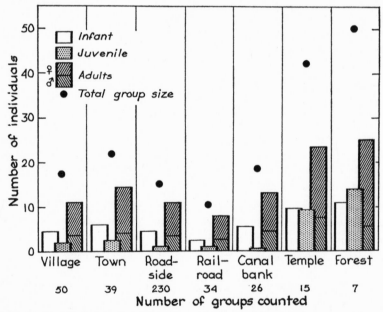

Figure 1–11. Variation in group size and composition of rhesus monkeys in different habitats in North India. (After C. H. Southwick, M. A. Beg and M. R. Siddiqi, 1965, with permission of Holt, Rinehart & Winston, Inc., Publishers.)

cohesion. Just as the alarm signals promote social cohesion with-in herd animals and reproductive colonies of birds, so inter-group agonistic behavior not only serves to defend the group territory but also to integrate primate social structure. On the other hand, dominant males come and go within any given group, and it appears to be the female subgroups which determine what-ever measure of year-after-year group stability exists. They may even influence male "decisions." According to Carpenter, it ap-pears highly improbable that distinct cohesive groups ever merge and fuse permanently unless two such groups are very unbalanced in their composition.

Ground inhabiting nonhuman primates are often more ag-gressive and appear to have a more highly structured social system than do arboreal species, but this is not always the case, as the arboreal howling monkeys of Barro Colorado Island attest. While aggressiveness, territoriality, dominance and group struc-ture appear to be closely related to ecological considerations, factors other than whether a species is ground inhabiting or arboreal must also enter into the social organization, as they do in determining the socioeconomic sex ratio. The arboreal Nilgiri langur (*Presbytis johnii*) has a less-structured, social grouping behavior, according to Poirier,[78] but the mothers also have a less intimate relationship with their infants and wean them earlier than other primate species.

Where social groupings have been established among primate species, we frequently find strong dominance relationships and dominance hierarchies as well. Dominance hierarchies serve to minimize actual aggressive encounters between members of a social group, but it is conceivable that such dominance relation-ships could operate against the social cohesion of the group. Let us examine several examples of how primates appear to resolve these seeming antagonistic forces within their social structures.

Parental licking or grooming of young occurs in many species of mammals and primates. In addition, nonparental allogroom-ing behavior occurs in many but not all species of higher pri-mates.[62] It would appear, further, that those species with a strong dominance hierarchy, such as occurs in macaques and baboons, show more allogrooming behavior than in those species with a less well-defined hierarchial organization. In some species, as in the baboon *Papio ursinus,* the less dominant individuals most frequently groom the more dominant individuals, so that dominant males are the most frequently groomed individuals (by both other males and females). If a troop leader or dominant primate approaches an animal of lower rank, the latter would normally give way, move off or othewise seek to avoid contact. But it is just in this context that many allogrooming bouts are initiated by invitation of the dominant animal. The animal soliciting grooming very often places himself, notwithstanding his dominance, in a submissive and potentially dangerous position, facing away from the subordinate individual. By placing himself, in a submissive position and inviting grooming, the dominant animal appears to have transformed a conflict situation into one that promotes rather than discourages interaction with lesser ranking individuals. While primate grooming behavior is primarily of importance as regards its cleaning be-behavior function, allogrooming appears to have developed a secondary function which promotes social interaction and social cohesion.

Allogrooming also serves as appeasement behavior when female rhesus monkeys wish to approach a mother and her infant [54] or a female rhesus may allogroom a male in an effort to overcome his aggressive tendencies.[7] Likewise Wickler [76] has presented an argument for the fact that presentation of the anogenital region by males, which normally serves as a sexual invitation, has been secondarily modified as a kind of appeasement behavior to counterbalance intragroup antagonistic tendencies. Not only females but also young, lesser ranking males use this behavior as a submissive pattern of behavior in relation to more dominant individuals. According to Chance,[9] attacks in rhesus monkeys may be foiled when the object of attack suddenly presents, diverts the aggressor from attacking and stimulates him to mount instead. Dominance mounting of males as well as females has been observed in a number of baboon species, macaque species, Cercopithecus and other genera. Likewise, in the squirrel monkey, *Saimiri sciureus,* genital display, in the form of penile erection, is a ritual, derived from sexual behavior but serving social and not reproductive purposes.[51] It is in fact a signal of dominance relationships, frequently exhibited by the alpha-animal, less often seen in lower ranking group members. Wickler refers to these forms of sexual behavior (also present in other mammals, as well as primates) as "sociosexual signals" since they have secondarily been transformed from their original reproductive function to serving social functions.

Thus, there are many instances, not only among insects, fish, birds and mammals but in the complex behavioral interactions of primates, in which motor patterns serving one function are transformed, modified or elaborated to serving additional functions. This is particularly true for the muscles and motor patterns of the face whose primary function was to manipulate and masticate food and to direct the perceptual organs of smell, hearing and vision. These muscles have secondarily been modified to provide not only mammals but especially primates with both complex facial displays and subtle forms of facial expression which serve social communication and behavior.[29] Without in any way minimizing the equally valuable and illuminating descriptive studies of primates undertaken by anthropologists and others, it is this zoological and evolutionary approach focused on the motor components of behavior which characterizes the thinking of ethologists. It appears just as valid a methodology for analyzing the complex behaviors of primate social systems, as for less complicated behaviors of lower vertebrates.

As already mentioned, it had generally been thought that male dominance relationships largely determined the social behavior and organization of many primate species. Where attention has been paid to female social relations, dominance relationships have also been found to exist.[31,57] In many species of primates, dominance relationships are not readily visible, and this appeared to be the case after seven months of field studies on the vervet monkeys (*Cercopithecus aethiops*) in Zambia by Lancaster.[37] When daily experimental feeding of a social group of fifty-five vervets was begun in the eighth month, however, male and female hierarchies emerged from the clear-cut succession of individuals that approach the feeding area. Without this experimental manipulation the female hierarchy would not have become clear since lower ranking individuals had previously exhibited a high rate of avoidance behavior.

Young adult female vervets and juveniles not only take their rank from their mothers but can count on the support of relatives if they should find themselves faced with a dominance encounter. In addition, younger members of such female subgroups often form coalitions with each other against adults. In one instance a three-month-old vervet and a one-year-old female (probably the mother's younger sister) formed a successful coalition against an unrelated adult female. Very often these coalitions are successful not only against older, stronger animals but against animals higher in the dominance hierarchy. Thus if a dominant adult male tried to maintain exclusive control of a desirable feeding area, a coalition of younger but related animals would form against him, drive him off, even chase and threaten him. Of 145 coalitions observed during an eight-month period, ninety-one were aimed at the dominance hierarchy. Although these coalitions are very often successful, even against top-ranking males, no actual attacks occur and they never seemed to affect the rank of the dominant animal. According to Lancaster the female vervet subgroups and the opportunities they afford for coalitions not only appear to ameliorate the effects of male dominance and even to protect them from threats or bites of dominant animals but to curb the absolute power of top-ranking individuals. Coalition conflict thus appears to promote social cohesion rather than diminish it.

ETHOLOGY, ECODYNAMICS AND EVOLUTION

All animals have their own particular habitats, such as a wooded area, a desert, a shoreline, and within these habitats, each animal may be restricted to an ecological niche. When an animal, either alone or as part of a group, defends a subdivision of such an ecological niche against other species members we generally refer to this subdivision as a territory. Territories may be temporary or permanent and are often marked, or staked out, by glandular or urinary markings, songs, calls, threats or other signals that are recognized and responded to by other members of the species. Such species not only have behavior patterns for locating and signaling appropriate territories but aggressive behavior for defending them as well.

Calhoun demonstrated that by confining territorial rats which normally do not form dominance relationships to a limited space, both dominant and submissive animals are developed. If domestic hens are provided ample space and their food is regularly scattered, very little aggressive pecking behavior is seen. Their classic pecking order was demonstrated by confining them to a limited space and placing their food in a central area. Eventually the other hens will not even approach the food area, so long as the dominant alpha animal is feeding. If the alpha animal is removed, the next lower ranking hen takes her place. Dominance relationships may be established by behavioral signs other than actual aggressive conflicts, but if an aggressive conflict does break out, very often a single fight is all that is necessary to settle the rank of the individuals involved. Dominance hierarchies not only serve to minimize conflicts but often operate to structure a closed social group. In the Burmese jungle fowl, according to Kruijt,[36] the social rank order starts to develop during the first stage of aggressive behavior from three weeks of age onward but becomes fully established during the second stage from fifty to eighty days of age. Strange birds that are introduced into such an established rank hierarchy are initially attacked by all members of the social group.

As indicated previously, in Calhoun's "behavioral sinks" there occurs not only a disintegration of normal rat group behavior but also of nesting behavior and the care of the young.[6] In North India, not only do the different habitats appear to influence the numbers of individuals in the social groups of rhesus monkeys but their behavior as well. The temple monkeys utilized a more restricted home range and showed increased aggressive behavior, when compared with the groups in other habitats.[61] Under the crowded conditions of zoos, chimpanzees, baboons and rhesus

monkeys are known to show more vicious attacks towards cagemates, often resulting in their death, than in the field where the
dominance hierarchy, cooperative behaviors, threats and ample
opportunity for escape and return help to maintain the integrity of the social group.[56]

Space is but one of the many physical factors in the environment capable of modifying the social behavior of animals. The
presence, mood and numbers of other animals and the behavioral
context in which they find themselves have also been shown to
modify behavior lawfully. How then can we reconcile the ethological concept of fixed motor patterns and the many behavioral
modifications that every observer records whenever a given
species is investigated closely?

Such behavioral modifications as occur both phylogenetically
and ontogenetically are the resultant of the lawful interaction of
internal factors, both hormonal and behavioral, the presence of
other species members and their behaviors, and physical aspects
of the environment. I have coined the term "ecodynamics" to
refer to this interaction of the fixed motor patterns within
an organism with its environment. Ecodynamics play a role in
the evolution of new behaviors and in the behavioral modifications that are seen to occur within the life cycles of given individual animals.

In an earlier section of this chapter, it was pointed out that
the behaviors emerging from a conflict, or mutual inhibition of
two motor patterns, give rise to lawful behaviors in the form of
displacement activities. These displacement activities, if they
have adaptive value, may be intensified or combined with structural modification, or ritualized as the result of natural selection,
and thus evolve into new behaviors. But the fact that displacement sand-digging has evolved as a territorial threat in sticklebacks can hardly be viewed as an accident or chance event.
Tinbergen [68] has pointed out that many fish tend to bend forward and downward in a balanced hostile situation and that in
the three-spined stickleback this behavior pattern of sand-digging
is part of the nest-building activity of a territorial stickleback, and
the presence of sand at the territorial line where the conflict

between attack and escape occurs undoubtedly played a role in determining which of the many motor patterns was initially selected by the central nervous system for displacement activity. Furthermore, sand-digging is the first in the sequence of nest-building activities to be activated and explains why this motor pattern and not others in the nest-building sequence, came to be utilized in boundary displacement.

The above example suggests how the ecodynamics of the situation—the conflict between attack and escape at the boundary line, the tendency of a territorial fish to engage in nest-building, the forward-downward posture, the presence of sand at the boundary, etcetera—all combined to lead to the evolution of displacement sand-digging as a threat signal. Once selected and ritualized, however, male sticklebacks make this threat movement whether or not sand is present at the boundary line.

Similar ecodynamic considerations may determine much of the so-called modifiability, or plasticity, of behavior observed in individuals of a species in a particular ecological and social context. The intent of this statement is simply to call attention to this biologically important and often overlooked category of behavior, not to imply that genetic variability of behavior does not also occur. On the contrary, without genetic variability selection could not occur. In our laboratory, we have studied the egg-fanning behavior of the peacock cichlid, *T sparrmani*. Both parents fan the eggs—that is, move their pectoral fins rapidly to circulate water and oxygen over the eggs while remaining in place over them. During a given 15-minute period we can time the number of seconds each parent spends fanning and find the female generally spending slightly more time than the male in doing so. But from time to time gross variations in the distribution of fanning occurs. Sometimes the female does all or almost all of the fanning, more rarely the male does.

If we observe these variations we often find that one of the parents approaches the eggs to fan but is driven off by the other. In the particular case below it was noted that the female sometimes permitted the male to fan, sometimes drove him off, which suggested the following experiment. We timed the fanning be-

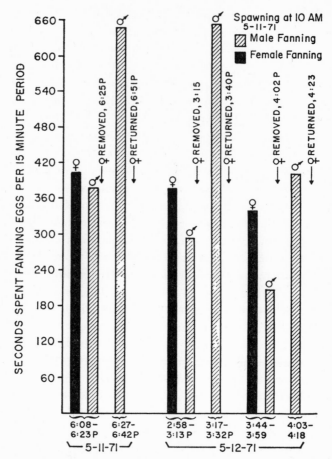

Figure 1-12. Male fanning of eggs in *Tilapia sparrmani,* with and without the presence of the female.

havior of both parents, then immediately afterward removed the female and timed the fanning behavior of the male alone. In each case the time spent by the male in fanning increased from 72 to 125 percent more than in the presence of the female (Fig. 1–12). The shared fanning behavior of male and female appears to represent an ecodynamic balance between the fanning drive of both parents, the strength of the bond between them, the level of aggression aroused, etcetera. The motor patterns of fanning and aggressive behavior are fixed, but the dynamic way in which these factors interact is capable of producing considerable modification of behavior. Similarly, Southwick *et al.* concluded that the differences in behavior of rhesus monkeys in various habitats in India were primarily quantitative rather than qualititative differences in basic behavior patterns and that "all rhesus observed, regardless of habitat, seemed to possess a basically similar behavior repertoire." In many similar cases it can be shown that the so-called behavioral plasticity is brought about by ecodynamic and quantitative modification of fixed motor patterns.

We have gone to some lengths to show that the social behavior of animals is based on the presence of fixed motor patterns and that these motor patterns are subject to certain lawful responses. These lawful responses—displacement activities, intention movements, regressive behavior, etcetera—are particularly likely to emerge in the conflicts that occur both between animals and within animals, and they in turn, through selection and further evolution, give rise to more complex rituals, ceremonies, signals and other communication interactions which not only mediate social behavior but underlie the various forms of social organization, which have repeatedly evolved in nature. Moreover, conflict and cooperation are being continuously balanced and integrated in animal societies. We must now consider in what way, if any, these findings and principles underlie human social systems and whether an understanding of these concepts can contribute to social psychiatry.

ETHOLOGY AND SOCIAL PSYCHIATRY

Social psychiatry as a discipline is considered to have begun as a dialogue between clinical psychiatry and the new profession of social work just before World War I. Since then it has been alternately taken over and discarded by psychiatrists and sociologists. Therefore, social psychiatry has been variously regarded (a) as a subbranch or research specialty wholly within psychiatry, enabling psychiatrists to discover and deal with the ways in which social problems affect individual patients; (b) as a division of sociology; (c) as an interdisciplinary area between psychiatry and sociology and (d) as concerned not with the treatment of individuals at all but with social units such as the neighborhood, the community or society at large. Some look upon social psychiatry as an action-oriented discipline, others regard it as an endeavor to better understand how people adapt to their social structure and what forces tend to damage or enhance their adaptive capacities. Whatever their orientation, disciples generally agree with Kiev that social psychiatry is fundamentally concerned with the varied interrelationships between the sociocultural environment and the individual.

Bell and Spiegel [1] suggest, however, that just as the mind-body dichotomy had to be given up as unfruitful, so the individual-society distinction requires reexamination. They are somewhat chagrined that in the current atmosphere of haste attempts to conceptualize the field, to elaborate theories and to devise new methods of research have largely fallen by the wayside. Since Reusch [55] is of the opinion that sociological and psychological abstractions should be left to sociologists, psychologists and psychoanalysts, it is, I believe, legitimate that an ethologist might provide an ethological model that may have some value for social psychiatry today.

While the concepts and tools of anthropology, sociology, social psychology, social work and epidemiology have been brought to bear on the problems of social psychiatry, the concepts of biology have hitherto been limited largely to neurophysiology and neuroendocrinology. Some considerable attention is now being paid, however, to biobehavioral concepts as developed by ethologists, which emphasize an evolutionary approach to the area. Neither sociology nor social psychology (nor general systems theory, transactional theory, existentialism, etcetera) has attempted to incorporate an evolutionary framework into its conceptualizations. Even in anthropology physical anthropologists more or less confine their thinking to the evolution of structure, while cultural and social anthropologists largely ignore any consideration of evolution.*

Few would argue with the statement of Thiessen [66] that "behavior is the outcome of genotype developing within a milieu of environmental and social influences." Its acceptance, however,

still leaves room for different conceptualizations regarding the
nature of these influences. Through what mechanisms are these
influences brought to bear on the individual? Anthropologists,
psychologists and sociologists have primarily regarded the environmental influence in terms of learning theory—that is, that
the culture, or representatives of it, simply teach the infant members of their societies how to behave. Cultural anthropologists frequently make a "strawman" of freudian instinct theory. If men
possessed rigid instincts, they argue, how could any culture possibly modify human behavior? Some theorists recognize phylogenetically given behaviors but separate them from the learning
process during early ontogeny. Little consideration is given to
yet another possibility—namely, that the social environment,
by facilitating,[77] repressing or overexciting phylogenetically
given patterns of behavior during ontogeny, programs and structures these behavior patterns in each individual. Fixed motor
patterns are integrated by the environment into unique com-
binations, which bring about altered physiological responses,
which alterations modify the very processes of growth and development of each infant and child. Through a modification of early
behavior, the culture structures or "grows" these response patterns into the organism. If the only influence which a culture
provided was to teach the individual ways of behaving, then it
would be relatively simple for individuals to unlearn maladapted
patterns of behavior and substitute more satisfying ones. This
is precisely what patients with acute behavioral problems find
so difficult, sometimes impossible, to do, to the vexation of their
psychotherapists.

It is this realm of behavior, termed the "unconscious," which
the psychiatrist attempts to grapple with on an individual level,

---

* There are exceptions to these statements. The anthropologist Hallowell [25,26] also
drew attention to this tendency among anthropologists and has himself provided
some of the best anthropological writing on the significance of behavioral evolution
for an understanding of society. His emphasis on the formation of personality structure, though not written from a fixed motor pattern ethological viewpoint, shares
several features with the present author's concepts. Likewise Gerth and Mills [24]
have emphasized the role of character structure in sociology, and Fletcher [22] has
discussed the implications of ethology for sociological theory. Masserman's *The
Biodynamic Roots of Human Behavior* [47] is a similar effort in psychiatry.

a realm which often defeats both his efforts and the conscious intentions of his patients. Freud emphasized this point in his theory of "unconscious resistance" which is regularly and lawfully aroused in each patient during the course of therapy. What mechanism accounts for resistance? For all his emphasis on the phenomenon, Freud never provided any insight into the biological processes underlying this resistance, nor did he explain the mechanism of repression. Without an adequate understanding of the biological mechanisms that enter into repression, the nature of the individual and the individual-society relationship will always remain blurred. It is precisely in this domain of the interrelationships of the sociocultural environment and the individual, that ethological concepts can make a contribution to social psychiatry.

ETHOLOGY AND HUMAN CHARACTER STRUCTURE

The relation of ethological concepts to human character formation, which the following material summarizes, has been outlined by the writer in several publications.[33-35] The psychoanalytic concept of "character" and the psychological definition of the term "personality" share much in common. Both terms refer to the totality (and organization) of an individual's behavioral and emotional tendencies and attitudes. I prefer the European term "character structure" since it emphasizes the fact that these characteristic patterns are not simply learned but possess some organizational structure of their own, a consideration which has a particular implication for social psychiatry.

I have frequently taken biologists to task for not interesting themselves in psychodynamic theory, but it is equally true that most psychiatrists are little interested in biology. "The trouble is," wrote Alex Comfort in a provocative essay, "that we seem to lack a common-room, or any other daily contact, which could bring working biologists and working psychoanalysts into proximity, or even collision. The marriage of psychoanalysis and biology is long overdue and likely to be fertile, and each has a great deal to teach the other." We have so often repeated the dogmas about man's uniqueness (so is every other species unique)

dvisability, perhaps impossibility, of jumping from
-ω human behavior (why then the huge research investment in animal behavior?) that we have cut ourselves off from
serious examination of this essential area. What is required for
such examination is simply a valid connecting link between
these two fields, and the fixed motor patterns of ethologists,
together with what we have already learned from psychodynamic theory, gives every indication of providing such a link.

Man's capacity for learning and the capacity of a culture to
transmit to each new generation its accumulated knowledge
and wisdom has undoubtedly played an important role in the
evolution of man and human social organizations. Even more
essential to every society is the fundamentally biological relationship which every individual must repeat successfully and
without which no social system can maintain its integrity. That
essential bit of biology is embodied in the mother-infant relationship. We have not only the studies of Spitz [64,65] and Engel [17]
on anaclitic depression but the parallel studies of Spencer-Booth
and Hinde [63] on depression in rhesus monkeys and those of
Kaufman and Rosenblum [30] on depression in pigtail macaques
to indicate that depression is not merely a psychological reaction,
nor even a uniquely human one, but a fundamentally biologic
primate response which occurs when the mother-infant relationship is interfered with through separation in early infancy.
Nevertheless, the subject of "maternal deprivation" is treated
as if it refers only to psychological deprivation. All the evidence
now points to the fact that what we have termed "maternal
deprivation" actually refers to phylogenetically determined sen-
sory inputs and behavioral outputs essential to the normal
development of both primate and human infants. It is further
apparent that such deprivation can and does lead to various forms
of growth modification and failure. [50] The infant's phylogenetically adaptive behaviors have been inextricably woven into the
physiology of his growth processes. Psychic development and
somatic growth can no longer be regarded as distinct or separate entities.

Bowlby [3,4] early called attention to the value of reformulating
psychoanalytic theory in biological and ethological terms and to

the significance of the infantile motor patterns of sucking, clinging, smiling, following and crying for attachment behavior and bond formation with the mother. These and many other fixed motor patterns play an additional hitherto unsuspected role in human development. They are responsible for the neuro-muscular modifications of each child, which ultimately gives rise to human character structure. Without such phenotypic modification, human society as we know it in its many cultural manifestations would not be possible.

Hooker's [28] study of the prenatal origins of human behavior amply confirms the fact that the human fetus, like the embryos of other vertebrates, goes through an orderly succession of neuro-muscular sequences. This results in the infant's capacity to utilize an array of fixed motor patterns which ensure attachment to its mother and subsequent phases of maturation. These include respiratory movements, rooting, sucking, various spinal and postural reflexes, grasping, the neuromuscular coordinations of swimming, creeping, crawling, quadruped and biped walking and the motor patterns of crying, smiling and other emotional re-sponses. In addition, an array of hitherto unsuspected vertebrate motor patterns, such as gasping respiration, pelvic and other right-ing reflexes, etcetera, which if activated by the environment could result in individual response tendencies.

Hans Selye tells the story of a man who, after getting drunk on whisky and soda, rum and soda, and gin and soda, concluded that he must avoid soda water if he wanted to remain sober. The words "whisky," "rum" and "gin" would rarely result in masking their common alcoholic content. Nevertheless a se-mantic difficulty still exists when we speak about respiration, rooting and sucking reflexes, postural reflexes locomotion, ma-nipulation, emotions, behavior, attitudes and so forth. Instead of recognizing that all these responses are mediated by or involve the neuromuscular system, many of us still consider these terms to represent distinct or unrelated entities. Since there are ap-proximately two hundred and twenty some odd pairs of muscles in man, not only do many different categories of response share muscles in common, but their state of tonus or tension at any given time influences all these responses. Furthermore, if Jacobson [29b] is right in his physiologic demonstration of complete neuromuscular relaxation and the reports of his subjects that they are devoid of thought processes during this state, then even thinking may be correlated with the activity and state of the neuromuscular system.

Each infant comes into the world with certain fixed motor patterns (barring perinatal insults) that adapt it for an intimate relationship with its mother. By her activity, the mother facilitates, or releases, various patterns of behavior in the infant, or fails to provide some of them with an opportunity for expression, or actively suppresses some behaviors. From the point of view of what is contained in its central nervous system, the infant is *phylogenetically programmed* at birth. As a result of utilizing these specific behavioral interactions with the mother, then other family members, the infant's basic neuromuscular responses are secondarily *ontogenetically programmed*. To translate this ethological concept into psychoanalytic terminology, the infant's instinctual *id* functions can only be carried out by means of its fixed motor patterns, while the fate or experience of those motor patterns in the outside world (the individual way in which they are combined or integrated) make up its *ego structure*. That special portion of the ego experience and attitudes which results from the desire to maintain and prolong the close bond with the mother and to avoid confrontation with the powerful father, even to the point of reaction formation against its own id impulses, gives rise to *superego* formation, the chief function of which is the inhibition or limitation of satisfactions—that is, the repression of behavior.

Several features of these early mother-infant interactions deserve to be emphasized. First, all these early behavior patterns are taking place simultaneously with the rapid growth processes occurring during infancy and childhood. It has been amply documented that physiologic modification during active growth modifies the nature of that growth. Behavioral modification, which always involves autonomic, endocrine and other physiologic changes, is equally capable of modifying growth processes,

with the result that these early behaviors become anchored in
the total somatic changes which are occurring at this time.
There is no separate development of somatic and psychic structure, but a simultaneous integration which the term "character
structure" is meant to embody.*

Secondly, character structure is the resultant of *all* the behavior
patterns that have become integrated in a characteristic way
during early development. Although the oral, anal and genital
functions of psychoanalytic developmental theory play a pre-
ponderant role in this integration, they are not the only motor
functions that contribute to its development. The early respiratory pattern of the newborn infant is extremely vulnerable to
perinatal insult and subsequent environmental modifications.
Erikson [18] recognized this in referring to an initial *oral-respira-
tory-sensory stage* of human development. Just as Freud linked
the psychological traits of orderliness, frugality and obstinacy to
anal character structures, so Erikson links such traits as basic
trust, shame, doubt, initiative, guilt, a sense of incompetence,
confusion, etcetera, with the outcome of specific behavioral
(motor) stages of early development. The motor patterns are
an integral part of *psychobiological* development.

Thirdly, the way in which any given mother patterns her
infant's fixed motor patterns is only indirectly related to the
culture or subculture to which she belongs. This ontogenetic
patterning is more directly and specifically the result of her own
capacity for relatedness, her own character structure.

These concepts are roughly indicated in Figure 1–13. The motor
patterns of the infant are programmed by the infant's immediate environmental experiences, which will normally be provided
by the mother. Combined as they are with autonomic, endocrine
and growth functions, these basic response patterns are gradually structured in the individual, not simply learned. Karen
Horney recognized this relationship when she spoke of neuroses

---

* Some of the mechanisms involved in altering growth during the mother-infant
relationship are discussed in a previous publication of the writer.[35]

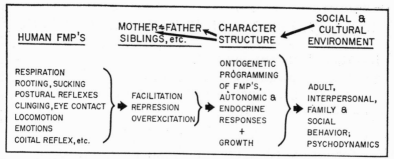

Figure 1–13. Some interrelationships of human fixed motor patterns, the mother, family, the social and cultural environment and character structure.

as being altered forms of growing. In this sense all human beings are *neuromuscular phenotypes.**

Once formed, adult character structure represents not only the individual pattern of emotional responses and the mediator of interpersonal and family behavior but the mechanism through which the social environment influences social behavior (Fig. 1–14). It is largely through the character structure of the parents that the social environment or culture exerts an indirect influence on the developing infant and child, as far as the patterning of its basic responses are concerned. The character structure of the father, the relationship of the father and other members of the extended family to the mother, and other factors are all capable of influencing what behaviors the mother will respond to, facilitate or suppress in the infant. Likewise the socioeconomic, political and technological environment, as it directly influences family structure and dynamics, is also capable of influencing man's biopsychosocial development and structure. We have now entered the field of human psychodynamics, but it should be apparent that these behavioral relationships which surround the infant and child differ little at this biological level from those

---

* To be accurate we should refer to modifications of the perceptual-motor systems, since historically speaking these two systems are always intimately coordinated in the course of both evolution and individual development. Modifications of behavior are equally capable of modifying perceptual discrimination as shown by White and Held,[75] Smith and Smith [60] and others.

```
┌─────────────────────────────────────────────────────────┐
│                                                           │
│     BIOLOGIC ASPECTS OF HUMAN SOCIAL SYSTEMS              │
│                                                           │
│   1.MATERNAL-INFANT BONDING                               │
│   2.EXTENDED INFANTILISM & DEPENDENCY                     │
│   3.ONTOGENETIC PROGRAMMING OF PHYLOGENETICALLY           │
│     FIXED MOTOR PATTERNS                                  │
│                                                           │
│                  GROWTH↓PROCESSES                         │
│   4.PRODUCTION OF NEUROMUSCULAR PHENOTYPES                │
│                        ↓                                  │
│   5.HUMAN CHARACTER STRUCTURE                             │
│      • INDIVIDUAL PATTERN OF EMOTIONAL RESPONSES          │
│      • BASIS OF INTERPERSONAL & FAMILY BEHAVIOR           │
│      • MECHANISM THRU WHICH SOCIAL ENVIRONMENT            │
│          INFLUENCES SOCIAL BEHAVIOR                       │
│      • PSYCHOSOMATIC BACKGROUND FOR RESPONSES TO STRESS,  │
│          INVASION OF PATHOGENS,OTHER NOXIOUS AGENTS, DRUGS│
│                                                           │
└─────────────────────────────────────────────────────────┘
```

Figure 1–14. The continuing biologic aspects of all human social systems.

ecodynamic determinants of behavior which ethologists deal with when analyzing the evolution of social behavior and organization in animals.

As a structural concept, character formation involves a consideration of the biological roots of repression. As already mentioned, Freud himself apparently failed to explore, with his usual depth and tenacity, the nature of the forces responsible for repression, but Fenichel drew attention to the fact that "the physical effects of the state of being dammed up emotionally are readily reflected in the neuromuscular system." It was Charles Darwin, however, who provided an insight into repressive mechanisms when he endeavored to understand how the continuous impulse to cry, coupled with a desire to inhibit this expression, led to the expression of grief.

Crying as an expression involves both the impulse to cry out, which many young animals do when separated from their mothers, coupled with the reflex closing of the eyes (Fig. 1–5, *B*) that accompanies any violent expiration whether by screaming, coughing or sneezing. The fixed motor pattern of crying, therefore, involves a large group of muscles which include the zygomatic muscles, the labial levator muscles, the mouth angle depressors, the quadratus (for screaming) and the orbicular muscles of the eyes, the nose pyramidal and the eyebrow corrugator muscles (for closing the eyes). To stop crying, a child endeavors to keep his eyes open, and to do so he must prevent the contraction of the orbicular, pyramidal and corrugator muscles, and this he does by counteracting their contraction with a contraction of the central fasciae of the frontal muscles of the forehead (Fig. 1-5, C, D). In doing so he raises the eyebrows at an oblique angle, characteristic of a grief-stricken person. If a child endeavors to look at an object against the background of a sunny sky his eyes close reflexly, but in his endeavor to keep them open so as to focus on the object, he also contracts the central portion of the frontal muscles. In this situation he also employs a similar interaction of two sets of motor patterns.

In ethological terms the expression of grief is a superposition of two motor patterns, the crying motor pattern together with the frontal muscle inhibiting pattern. If this reaction occurs in a young child over a period of time, both the physiology and structure of the face are altered when he reaches adulthood. To my knowledge, the motor pattern of every impulse the child is called upon to repress requires that another motor pattern be utilized to inhibit it.* The "forces" of repression, the inhibited impulses, the "defense mechanisms" and so forth are all brought about and maintained by motor patterns, which together with the motor patterns of the original impulses become superposed or locked together in the body of the individual.

Thus, just as animal rituals, ceremonies, etcetera, contain the original conflicts which gave rise to them and may be demonstrated again and again by altering the intensity of one or the

---

* Maya Angelou provides one of the most discerning descriptions of this process. "How could an eight-year-old contain that much fear? He swallows and holds it behind his tonsils, he tightens his feet and closes the fear between his toes, he contracts his buttock and pushes it up behind the prostate gland." (In *I Know Why the Caged Bird Sings*. New York, Random House.)

other of the two conflicting motor patterns or by a change in the ecological conditions, so human character structure, which makes social structure possible and determines its development, also embodies conflict and may be released in myriad ways by changes of the social (ecological) environment. These conflicts can be released in the play therapy techniques of Melanie Klein, in which the motor components are readily observable. They are also present in the abreactions of adult psychotherapy, wherein the transference as well as verbalization effects a gradual relaxation of the neuromuscular system and a provocation of both secondary and original, primitive impulses. In psychotherapy wherein lysergic acid diethylamide has been used as an adjunct, numerous therapists have reported both the variety and intensity of early motor patterns, including infantile sucking, aggressive biting responses, clinging, ambivalent behavior and even motor manifestations associated with the birth experience.

In character analytic vegetotherapy, as developed by Reich,[52] a direct endeavor is made to loosen the characteristic body attitudes and to set free previously inhibited affects, which are seen as a vital part of the defense mechanisms. The resistances of the patient are seen as *character resistances,* accompanied by corresponding muscular attitudes or a *muscular armor,* which represents an essential part of what is psychologically referred to as inhibition.

Reich not only delineated the dynamic relationship between inhibition, repression and the musculature, but he specifically described the motor pattern of crying and its inhibition in almost ethologic terms. Thus when an individual attempts to suppress the impulse to cry, he not only tenses the muscles in the lower lip, but he must also inhibit all those muscles of the mouth, the jaw and the throat which would become active in the process of crying. Consequently, it is seldom that individual muscles become tense or spastic; rather *muscle groups* forming a functional unit from a vegetative point of view do so.

At this point it is difficult to avoid the feeling that I am calling attention to material which is common knowledge to every psychiatrist. All psychiatrists and psychoanalysts intuitively evaluate the nonverbal aspects of patient communication throughout, their analyses. Long before the current interest in "body language" not only therapists but kinesiologists and orthopedic surgeons could agree that "psychological elements" contribute to every individual's posture and movements.

It is insufficient, however, simply to recognize the psychological elements of posture and nonverbal communication. The biologically lawful basis for their validity requires incorporation into a general concept of human development. In this contribution I have emphasized the ethological concept of fixed motor patterns and the lawful ways by which they give rise to mechanisms for mediating social behavior and organization throughout the animal kingdom. All the evidence suggests that such biobehavioral functions as are found in animal ecodynamics are an equally intrinsic part of the evolution of human social behavior and organization.

Contrary to the views of so many cultural and social anthropologists today, the culture does more than simply pass on its accumulated traditions and knowledge. Largely through the repression of behavior, it effects a deep-rooted biological and structural modification of each individual. Far from the oft-repeated statements of behavioral scientists that instinctual mechanisms are of minor importance in human society, this hypothesis suggests that the various motor patterns with which each infant is born are central to human character formation. "It is paradoxical," wrote Hallowell in an address to the American Anthropological Association in 1949, "that whereas opponents of human evolution in the nineteenth century were those who naturally stressed evidence that implied discontinuity between man and his primate precursors, anthropologists of the twentieth century, while giving lip service to organic evolution have, by the special emphasis laid upon culture as the prime human differential, once again implied an unbridged gap between ourselves and our animal forbears—no culture frees the infant from the fundamental conflict arising from the biologically rooted impulses on the one hand and the demands of parents or parent surrogates on the other, nor the need for some internal reso-

lution of such conflicts." Furthermore, by confining themselves
to the structural background of human evolution (as in physical
anthropology) and the structural products of human activity
(as in archeology), anthropologists have until recently neglected
the biological basis of the evolution of human behavior.

Normally each culture biologically and empirically produces
the character structures required for its environment and social
structure. In this sense the character structures are adapted to
environmental needs. In overlooking the biological roots of
social structure, especially in an age of rapid change, the "social
unconscious" produces character structures which defeat the
avowed goals of society, just as the unconscious motivations of
the individual defeat his conscious goals. One of Western Society's avowed goals, for example, is stable marriage and family
life; yet it appears to be producing more and more character
structures incapable of the intimacy which family life requires.

If the internal resolution of human conflict is not merely a
learned phenomenon but a biologically structured one,* as I
have suggested, then it would appear that social psychiatry would
be required to give some consideration to developing knowledge
and conceptualizations that will enable society to "grow" the
character structures capable of living in concordance in the
face of continuing ever-present conflict and change. According to
Sade,[57] the sum of the dynamics of the individual life cycles
comprises social structure to be found in a group of primates.
This suggests that the amount of concordance or discordance in the social structures of the primate man will always
be directly related to the biologically rooted character structure
of its members and the social (ecological) changes that occur.

Investigators in diverse fields have called attention to the

* The hypothesis of this chapter is that the motor patterns are structured. Kalmus,[80] in treating a similar theme dealing with the origins of society, writes, "though it is possible to describe certain types of the behavior of social animals—and of course man—as arising from a conflict between such hypothetical antagonistic entities as the id or the ego, it is very doubtful whether these exist in any organized way." If the ego represents the experiential resultant of the activity of the motor patterns *combined with the processes of growth,* it too must possess some degree of structure at some biological level in the organism.

significance of biological, ethological and evolutionary concepts for human behavior—Simpson and Roe,[59] Hallowell [25] and Chapple [10] in anthropology; Ambrose,[79] Bowlby,[4a] Masserman [47] and Reich [52] in psychotherapy and psychoanalytic theory; Peiper [50a] in pediatric neurology; and Fletcher [22] in sociology. Nevertheless the biosocial structuring of fixed motor patterns in human character formation has not yet been adequately realized. It would appear that this concept could provide a significant direction of thought and theory regarding the biosocial roots of concordance and discordance in human society.

SUMMARY

As animals have entered into more extensive relationships with each other, conflicting responses have been aroused, and through lawful behavior reflecting biologic solutions within the central nervous system, a variety of new responses have been elicited. Since these new responses are the result of existing fixed motor patterns and the various stimuli of other animals or physical factors in the environment, I have termed this process "ecodynamics."

Whenever these responses have proved to be of adaptive value, their continued and often exaggerated use has been incorporated into the genetic makeup of these evolving animals through natural selection, just as other adaptive attributes have been so incoporated.

This has resulted in those fixed motor patterns, releasers, courtship dances, dominance relationships, territorial and other ritualized behaviors which mediate social behavior and have led to the structuring of animal organizations—that is, the courtship dances, ceremonies and rituals contain both the elements of the conflicts and their biologic solutions.

These same fixed motor patterns continue to operate in the human species where they give rise to an ontogenetic patterning of responses, or the production of neuromuscular phenotypes, resulting in the formation of human character structures. Human character structure (with its embodiment of needs and conflict) is the mediating factor in all human social systems.

REFERENCES

1. Bell, N. W., and Spiegel, J. P.: Social psychiatry: Vagaries of a term. In *Social Psychiatry* (Vol. 1), edited by A. Kiev. New York, Science House, 1969.
2. Bourliere, F.: Patterns of social grouping among wild primates, In *Social Life of Early Man*, edited by S. L. Washburn. Chicago, Aldine, 1961.
3. Bowlby, J.: An ethological approach to research in child development. *Br J Med Psychol, 30:*230–240, 1957.
4. Bowlby, J.: The nature of the child's tie to his mother. *Int J Psychoanal, 39:*350–373, 195.
4a. Bowlby, J.: *Attachment.* Attachment and Loss Series, Vol. 1. New York, Basic Books, 1969.
5. Calhoun, J. B.: Population density and social pathology. *Sci Am, 206(2):*139–148, 1962.
6. Calhoun, J. B.: A behavior sink. In *Roots of Behavior,* edited by E. L. Bliss. New York, Harper & Brothers, 1962.
7. Carpenter, C. R.: Sexual behavior of free-ranging rhesus monkeys *(Macaca mulatta)*. *J Comp Physiol Psychol, 33:*113–142, 1942.
8. Carpenter, C. R.: Societies of monkeys and apes. In *Primate Social Behavior,* edited by C. H. Southwick. Princeton, Van Nostrand, 1963.
9. Chance, M. R. A.: Social structure of a colony of *Macaca mulatta. Anim Behav, 4:*1–13, 1956.
10. Chapple, E. D.: *Culture and Biological Man.* New York, Holt, Rinehart & Winston, 1970.
11. Comfort, A.: *Darwin and the Naked Lady.* New York, George Braziller, 1962.
12. Darwin, C.: *The Origin of Species* (6th ed.). New York, D. Appleton, 1885 (1859).
13. Darwin, C.: *The Expression of the Emotions in Man and Animals.* Chicago, University of Chicago Press, 1965 (1872).
14. Darling, F. F.: *A Herd of Red Deer.* London, Oxford University Press, 1937.
15. Eibl-Eibesfeldt, I.: *Ethology, the Biology of Behavior.* New York, Holt, Rinehart & Winston, 1970.
16. Eibl-Eibesfeld, I., and Kramer, S.: Ethology, the comparative study of animal behavior. *Q Rev Biol, 33:*181–211, 1958.
17. Engel, G. L.: *Psychological Development in Health and Disease.* Philadelphia, W. B. Saunders Company, 1962.
18. Erickson, E. H.: *Childhood and Society.* New York, W. W. Norton & Co., 1950.
19. Etkin, W.: Cooperation and competition in social behavior. In *Social Behavior and Organization Among Vertebrates,* edited by W. Etkin. Chicago, University of Chicago Press, 1963.

20. Fried, E.: *On Love and Sexuality*. New York, Grove Press, 1961.
21. Frisch, K. v.: *Bees, Their Vision, Chemical Senses and Language*. Ithaca, Cornell University Press, 1950.
22. Fletcher, R.: *Instinct in Man*. New York, International University Press, 1957.
23. Gellhorn, E., and Loofbourrow, G. N.: *Emotions and Emotional Disorders*. New York, Harper & Row, 1963.
24. Gerth, H., and Mills, C. W.: *Character and Social Structure*. New York, Harcourt, Brace & World, 1953.
25. Hallowell, A. I.: Personality structure and the evolution of man, *Am Anthrop, 52:*159–173, 1950.
26. Hallowell, A. I.: Culture, personality and society. In *Anthropology Today*, edited by A. L. Kroeger, Chicago, University of Chicago Press, 1953.
27. Hinde, R. A.: *Animal Behavior*. New York, McGraw-Hill, 1966.
28. Hooker, D.: The *Prenatal Origin of Behavior*. Lawrence, University of Kansas Press, 1952.
29. Huber, E.: *Evolution of Facial Musculature and Facial Expression*. Baltimore, Johns Hopkins Press, 1931.
29a. Iersel, J. J. A. v., and Bol, A. C. A.: Preening of two tern species. A study on displacement activities. *Behaviour, 13:*1–88, 1958.
29b. Jacobson, E.: *Progressive Relaxation* (2nd ed). Chicago, University of Chicago Press, 1938.
30. Kaufman, I. C., and Rosenblum, L. A.: The reaction to separation in infant monkeys: Anaclitic depression and conservation-withdrawal, *Psychosom Med, 29:*648–675, 1967.
31. Kawamura, S.: Matriarchal social ranks in the Minoo-B troops: A study of the rank system of Japanese monkeys. *Primates, 1:*149–156, 1958.
32. Kiev, A. (Ed.): *Social Psychiatry* (Vol. 1). Introduction. New York, Science House, 1969.
32a. Kortlandt, A.: Aspects and prospects of the concept of instinct. *Arch Neerland Zool, 11:*155, 1955.
33. Kramer, S.: Ethology and human character formation. *Int Psychiatry Clin, 2:*303–350, 1965.
34. Kramer, S.: Fixed motor patterns in ethologic and psychoanalytic theory. In *Science & Psychoanalysis*. Vol. 12: *Animal & Human*, edited by J. H. Masserman. New York, Grune & Stratton, 1968.
35. Kramer, S.: Behavioral science and human biology in medicine, *New Physician, 18 (11,12):*891–901, 965–978, 1969.
36. Kruijt, J. P.: Ontogeny of social behavior in Burmese red jungle fowl. *Behaviour* Suppl. No. 12, 1964.
37. Lancaster, J. B.: Female brooding: Social relations between free-ranging adult female vervet monkeys, Monographed paper, American Anthropology Association Meeting, San Diego, California, November, 1970.
38. Leuner, H.: Psychotherapy with hallucinogens. In *Hallucinogenic Drugs and Their Psychotherapeutic Use*, edited by R. Crockett et al. London, H. K. Lewis & Company, Ltd., 1963.

39. Lind, H.: The activation of an instinct caused by a "transitional action." *Behavior, 14*:123–135, 1959.
40. Lindauer, M.: *Communication Among Social Bees.* Cambridge, Harvard University Press, 1961.
41. Lorenz, K.: The comparative method in studying innate behavior patterns. In *Physiological Mechanisms in Animal Behavior.* Fourth Symposium of the Society of Experimental Biology, Cambridge University Press, 1950.
42. Lorenz, K.: Der Kumpan in der Umwelt des Vogels. *J Ornithol, 83*:137–213, 289–413, 1935. (English translation: Companionship in bird life. In *Instinctive Behavior,* edited by C. H. Schiller. London, Methuen & Company, 1957.)
43. Lorenz, K.: *Evolution and Modification of Behavior.* Chicago, University of Chicago Press, 1965.
44. Lorenz, K.: *Studies in Animal and Human Behavior* (Vol. 1). Cambridge, Harvard University Press, 1970.
45. Malyshev, S. I.: *Genesis of the Hymenoptera.* English translation of 1966 Russian edition. London, Methuen & Company, 1968.
45a. Marler, P. R., and Hamilton, W. J.: *Mechanisms of Animal Behavior.* New York, John Wiley & Sons, 1966.
46. Masserman, J. H.: *Behavior and Neurosis.* New York, Hafner Publishing Company, 1964 (1943).
47. Masserman, J. H.: *Biodynamic Roots of Human Behavior.* Springfield, Charles C Thomas, 1968.
48. Mills, J. S.: *A System of Logic.* New York, Harper & Bros., 1846 (1843).
49. Morris, D.: The feather postures of birds and the problem of the origin of social signals. *Behaviour, 9*:75–111, 1956.
50. Patton, R. G., and Gardner, I. L.: *Growth Failure in Maternal Deprivation.* Springfield, Charles C Thomas, 1963.
50a. Peiper, A.: *Cerebral Function in Infancy and Childhood.* New York, Consultants Bureau, 1963.
51. Ploog, D. W., Blitz, J., and Ploog, F.: Studies on social and sexual behavior of the squirrel monkey *(Saimiri sciureus).* *Folia Primatol (Basel)*, *1*:29–66, 1963.
52. Reich, W.: *Character Analysis.* New York, Orgone Institute Press, 1949.
53. Ribbands, R.: *The Behavior and Social Life of Honeybees.* Bee Research Association, Ltd, London, 1953.
54. Rowell, T. E., Hinde, R. A., and Spencer-Booth, Y: "Aunt"-infant interaction in captive rhesus monkeys. *Anim Behav, 12*:219–226, 1964.
55. Ruesch, J.: Social psychiatry: an overview. In *Social Psychiatry* (Vol. I), edited by A. Kiev. New York, Science House, 1969.
56. Russell, C., and Russel, W. M. S.: Primate male behavior and its human analogues, *Impact Sci on Soc, 21*:63–74, 1971.
57. Sade, D. S.: Determinants of dominance in a group of free ranging rhesus. In *Social Communication Among Primates,* edited by S. A. Altmann. Chicago, University of Chicago Press, 1967.
58. Sevenster, P.: A casual analysis of a displacement activity (Fanning in *Gasterosteus aculeatus* L.) *Behaviour,* Suppl. No. 9, 1961.

59. Simpson, G. G., and Roe, A. (Eds.): *Behavior and Evolution.* New Haven, Yale University Press, 1958.
60. Smith, K. V., and Smith, W. M.: *Perception and Motion.* Philadelphia, W. B. Saunders Co., 1962.
61. Southwick, C. H., Beg, M. A., and Siddiqi, M. R.: Rhesus monkeys in Northern India. In *Primate Behavior,* edited by I. DeVore. New York, Holt, Rinehart & Winston, 1965.
62. Sparks, J.: Allogrooming in primates: A review. In *Primate Ethology,* edited by D. Morris. London, Weidenfeld & Nicholson, 1967.
63. Spencer-Booth, Y., and Hinde, R. A.: The effects of separating rhesus monkey infants from their mothers for six days, *J Child Psychol Psychiatry, 7:*179–197, 1967.
64. Spitz, R. A.: Hospitalism: An inquiry into the psychiatric conditions in early childhood. *Psychoanal Study Child, 1:*53–74, 1945.
65. Spitz, R. A.: Anaclitic depression. *Psychoanal Study Child, 2:*313–342, 1946.
66. Thiessen, D. D.: Stickleback zigzags to monomorphic marking, *Contemp Psychol, 10:*246–248, 1965.
67. Tinbergen, N.: *The Study of Instinct.* Oxford, Clarendon Press, 1951.
68. Tinbergen, N.: Derived activities; their causation, biological significance, origin and emancipation during evolution. *Q Rev Biol, 27:*1–32, 1952.
69. Tinbergen, N.: *Social Behavior in Animals.* New York, John Wiley & Sons, 1953.
70. Tinbergen, N.: The evolution of signaling devices. In *Social Behavior and Organization Among Vertebrates,* edited by W. Etkin. Chicago, University of Chicago Press, 1963, pp. 206–230.
71. Walther, F. R.: Flight behavior and avoidance of predators in Thomson's gazelle *(Gazella thomsoni Guenther 1884)*. *Behaviour, 34:*184–221, 1969.
72. Wheeler, W. M.: Ethological observations on an American ant *(Leptothorax emersoni Wheeler)*. *Arch Psychol Neurol, 2:*1–31, 1903.
73. Wheeler, W. M.: An ethological study of certain maladjustments in the relation of ants to plants. *Bull Am Nat Hist, 22:*403–418, 1907.
74. Wheeler, W. M.: *Ants—Their Structure, Development and Behavior.* New York, Columbia University Press, 1910.
75. White, B. L., and Held, R.: Plasticity of sensorimotor development in the human infant. In *The Causes of Behavior,* edited by J. F. Rosenbluth and W. A. Smith. Boston, Allyn & Bacon, 1966.
76. Wickler, W.: Socio-sexual signals and their intraspecific imitation among primates. In *Primate Ethology,* edited by D. Morris. London, Weidenfeld & Nicolson, 1967.
77. Winnicott, D. W.: *The Maturational Processes and the Facilitating Environment.* New York, International University Press, 1965.
78. Poirier, F. E.: The Nilgiri langur *(P johnii)* troop: Its composition, structure, function and change. *Folia Primat, 10:*20–47, 1969.
79. Ambrose, J. A.: The study of human social organization: A review of current concepts and approaches. *Symp Zool Soc (Lond), 14:*301–314, 1965.

80. Kalmus, H.: The social organization of animal communities: Origins and general features. *Symp Zool Soc (Lond)*, *14*:1–12, 1965.
81. Leyhausen, P.: The communal organization of solitary mammals. *Symp Zool Soc (Lond)*, *14*:249–263, 1965.

Chapter 2

Man Is Not a Naked Ape

ANNE ROE AND GEORGE GAYLORD SIMPSON

THE ANCESTRY OF MAN has been distinct from that of the living apes for at least 15,000,000 years, which can be conservatively reckoned to mean more than 750,000 generations. A figure of well over a million generations is quite probable. In the course of that time, these animals evolved from what must reasonably be called "apes" in the vernacular into men as we see them— as we *are* them—today. The lineages that remained apes were not static either, but they changed much less. We still share with living apes many anatomical and a few behavioral traits probably inherited from the common ancestry. The changes are nevertheless profound, even in anatomy but especially in behavior. The recent apes and indeed all of man's surviving fairly close relatives live in groups and have social structures, variable in kind and in complexity. We may conclude that this—group living—is one of the oldest evolutionary influences on our behavior. To it have been added many features unique in intensity or in kind, so that the extrapolation from our relatives or from reasonably inferred ancestry is not obvious or simple.

It must be evident that the evolutionary background is not only relevant but also essential to an understanding of man, including his social behavior with both its concordant and its discordant factors. As neither of the authors is an anthropologist, sociologist or psychiatrist, we assumed that our role in this symposium was to supply background for the main thesis. Thus, the background we shall attempt to supply here will concern evolutionary biology and psychology.

The importance of these subjects was quite evident to Darwin, whose intense interest in human behavior and social relationships arose even before he became an evolutionist. Unfortunately, for

69

some time after Darwin, evolutionary concepts in sociology were dominated by what was wrongly called Social Darwinism and was concerned largely with the equally misleading slogans of "the struggle for existence" and "the survival of the fittest." Only in quite recent years has there been a marked increase in more defensibly scientific studies of evolutionary aspects of behavior and societies. We like to think that among the stimuli for those studies were the two conferences and subsequent symposial volume on *Behavior and Evolution*,[29] organized and edited by us, with broad backing from a wide spectrum of disciplines previously less inclined to pursue joint investigations in this field.

As examples we may mention that studies of phylogeny and morphological evolution have become less purely anatomical and more functional or behavioral [24,30]; there has been the great expansion of behavioral genetics in an evolutionary framework [5,18,36] and a similar increase in evolutionary studies on neuroanatomy and neurophysiology [2] (also a symposium is now being organized by R. B. Masterton as a future example). Several other fields could be cited but not all can be followed up here. One more must be emphasized, however: the tremendous increase in studies of primate behavior always implicitly and usually explicitly in evolutionary terms. (The subject was not separately treated in the 1958 volume, although it was repeatedly mentioned and both Nissen and Carpenter, pioneers in this field, were present at the conferences and wrote chapters in the symposium; more recent studies of high quality are so numerous that to specify an example might seem invidious; Scott, 1967, and McClearn, 1970, are reviews including this subject and other aspects of evolutionary psychology.)

PHYLOGENY

Long before the recent florescence of evolutionary behavioral studies, there was intense interest in deciphering the material ancestry of man and the anatomical changes involved in it. This continues unabated. The direct evidence, consisting of skeletal and dental remains of fossil forms in or related to the human ancestry, increases almost from day to day. Nevertheless it is still quite incomplete, so that views as to human phylogeny still depend to considerable extent on inference, sometimes highly speculative and hence entailing ardent disagreement among students of the subject. Nevertheless knowledge attained now presents a general picture of adequate probability for our purposes without undue concern for detail.

Claims for occurrence of a primate in the late Cretaceous period, perhaps 70 million years ago, are questionable, but undoubted primates are known in considerable abundance and variety in the middle Paleocene epoch, some 60 to 65 million years before present ("b.p.," the standard abbreviation for this measurement). All are prosimians or pre-monkeys. Fossils from the late Oligocene epoch of Egypt strongly suggest that at that time, more or less 30 million years b.p., both true Old World monkeys, cercopithecoids, and apes, hominoids, existed, although in such primitive and similar forms that their origin from prosimians and differentiation from each other may not have been much earlier, geologically speaking. Through much of the Miocene epoch, roughly 25 to 15 million years b.p., there was a widespread and common but still not really very well-known complex of varied primitive apes in Africa, Europe and southern Asia, usually called dryopithecines after the first-named genus, *Dryopithecus*. (That fossil ape was named by Lartet in 1856, even before Darwin's *Origin of Species,* although Darwin did not have occasion to discuss it explicitly until the *Descent of Man,* 1871.) Although the question is still moot, there is now an apparent consensus that the dryopithecines as a group included ancestors both of the higher recent apes (excluding gibbons) and of man.

For a long time there was an apparent gap in the record from late Miocene epoch to early Pleistocene epoch or quite approximately from 15 to 2 million years ago. Now a good case has been made out for presence of a human ancestor, distinct from that of any recent ape, by the late Miocene epoch about 15 million years b.p. There is thus a probability that the crucial divergence of apes (pongids) and men (hominids) had occurred before that date. Incidentally, the direct paleontological evidence is conclusively opposed to dates inferred indirectly and on dubious, apparently erroneous, assumptions by some molecular biologists.[31]

The creatures known as australopithecines, now universally accepted as partly primitive and partly divergent hominids, all near and some probably in our direct ancestry, have long been known from the early to early-middle Pleistocene epoch, say 1½ to ½ million years b.p. Recently several fossils of the late Pliocene members of that group, from more or less 5 to 2½ million years b.p., have been discovered; however, the facts of this discovery have not been adequately published yet. Although australopithecines have been positively identified only in Africa, it is unlikely that they were confined to that continent and the limited known distribution may be an artifact of preservation and discovery.

Perhaps already in the earliest and surely by the beginning of the middle Pleistocene the more gracile of the australopithecines were grading into *Homo*. Some time before 500 thousand b.p. they had reached definable status as *Homo erectus* (the group of fossils formerly variously called *Pithecanthropus, Sinanthropus, Atlanthropus*, etcetera) which in turn by about 250 thousand b.p. was grading into modern man, *Homo sapiens*.

(Most of the relevant recent fossil finds are mentioned in Simons,[32,33] and the most closely pertinent previously known fossil hominids are discussed in Coon.[7] These are polemic and to some extent biased works, like practically all publications about human origins, but they provide introductions to the basic literature. All but the latest African discoveries of ancient hominids are catalogued, without bias, in Oakley and Campbell.)[23]

EVIDENCE ON ANCESTRAL BEHAVIOR

The direct observation of ancestral behavior is obviously impossible. To keep inferences from indirect evidence within reasonable limits of confidence requires more self-restraint than has commonly been shown. In plainer language, much that has been said on this subject is no better than guesswork and should not be taken as serious results of research. As one example among many, one can find quite definite statements that the australopithecines did or did not have language (in the human sense). In fact from all evidence now available it is absolutely impossible to determine whether they did or not.

In dealing with the fossil evidence, a distinction must be made among several categories of behavior, categories that do not occur at once to most students of *Homo sapiens* as a present, going concern. Perhaps most basic is the distinction between what has been called first-order and second-order behavior.[34,35] First-order behavior includes such things as posture, locomotion or various separate and related motions of parts of the body. Second-order behavior involves more extended activities or patterns into which first-order behavior is compounded. Examples are the relatively simple, largely innate and stereotyped courtship activities of some birds and the sometimes more complex, largely learned and modifiable courtship activities of humans.

A great deal can be learned about first-order behavior but practically nothing about second-order behavior from fossil remains. There are numerous relevant studies on early hominids, most interestingly so far on early Pleistocene australopithecines by Napier.[3,9,22,39] Such studies have shown with sufficient confidence that those particular hominids walked upright and had grasping hands similar to those of *Homo,* but that both hand and leg functions were probably not yet fully at the *Homo* level.

Similar efforts have been made to draw ethological and behavioral inferences from the teeth of the australopithecines but in our opinion those studies do not merit much confidence. Two of the most popular concepts are that reduction of the anterior teeth, especially the canines, accompanied their substitution by artificial weapons and that the large cheek teeth of the more robust australopithecines indicate a herbivorous diet and the smaller cheek teeth of gracile australopithecines a more carnivorous diet. But there is considerable evidence that the anterior teeth of *Homo* are still efficient weapons (see Every, 1970), and from the indifferently omnivorous cheek tooth pattern of *Australopithecus, Homo* and many other primates, rodents, etcetera, it is quite impossible as far as now demonstrable to determine whether their possessors are more vegetarian or carnivorous.

From fossil remains alone, very little can be inferred as to the second-order behavior of our ancestors and still less about their sociology, which can be considered third-order behavior. Fortunately we are not wholly confined to the fossils, and other evidence does permit some, although still limited, inferences of a higher order. For one thing, there are artifacts associated with early hominid remains even as far back as the late Pliocene epoch. Modern apes occasionally show behavior that involves tool-using of a very simple sort and even by stretching a point can be said to modify objects for use as tools. However, none of them produce anything comparable to the known made equipment of the early australopithecines, and they seem to be mentally quite incompetent to do so. It is also extremely unlikely that their direct ancestors ever achieved this sort of behavior.

The most important point here is that the australopithecines had brains that were within the relative size range of Recent apes and yet demonstrably had at least one form of second-order behavior, tool-making of an extensive and fairly complex sort, of which the Recent apes are mentally incapable. We therefore conclude that by the late Pliocene epoch, at the latest, our ancestors' brains were not yet quantitatively but definitely qualitatively different from the brains of apes.

It is obvious that Recent humans and apes have very different behavior and also different brains. The brain of *Homo sapiens* is decidedly larger, both absolutely and relatively, than that of any ape. The important point that has been added is that a qualitative difference preceded that difference in brain size. Man is not a large-brained ape. He is a *different*-brained animal. The "large-brained ape" concept is a fallacy related to or indeed inherent in what Julian Huxley has called the "nothing but" fallacy and we may call the "naked ape" fallacy.

The increasingly numerous studies of nonhuman primate behavior are interesting in themselves, but they are also supported as throwing light on human psychology and sociology. The comparative method of approach to historical (evolutionary) problems is legitimate and often fruitful, but it is full of pitfalls, nowhere more than here. On the whole Recent apes retain more characteristics of the ape-human common ancestry than humans do; Recent monkeys retain more from the monkey-ape common ancestry and Recent prosimians more from the prosimian-monkey common ancestry. With regard to anatomy and first-order behavior, those points are sufficiently substantiated by fossil evidence. However, it does not follow that second-order and third-order behavior observed in Recent apes, monkeys or prosimians therefore occurred in our own ancestry at progressively more distant times in the past. Still less does it follow that we still retain such behavioral traits, even in cryptic form, after our radical divergence from all those other lineages of primates. That is more likely than not to fall into the naked ape fallacy, as all too familiarly demonstrated by the author of the naked ape catchword itself,[21] by some other popularizers [1] and even occasionally by a really able and otherwise sound scientific student of animal behavior.[19]

When Darwin wrote *The Descent of Man* (1871), he took pains to point out resemblances of mankind to apes and lower primates not only anatomically but also psychologically. He specified that in some nonhumans and in inchoate form, at least, there occur such things as pleasure, pain, happiness, misery, love, pride, jealousy, shame, magnanimity, rage, excitement, dread, imitation, attention, memory, imagination, reason and the use (but not manufacture) of tools. But it was necessary in Darwin's day and it was his whole aim in that work to show that human characteristics are not altogether unique and that their derivation by evolution from "lower animals," in fact from primeval apes, is plausible. It is remarkable that so many students of behavior are still following the same line, although they have no need at all to prove what Darwin did adequately prove just a century ago.

Interest in ferreting out and explaining resemblances between man and other animals is indeed perennial, but we submit that it is now more important, even more interesting, and still more difficult to specify and explain the characteristics in which man differs from his closest relatives, the things that do make us human. In short, we need to know in more detail and greater depth why in fact we are *not* naked apes.

The problems involved here are far from solved. Some can be delimited, although not completely specified, by general knowledge of evolutionary processes. The beginning of hominid divergence from the apes (pongids) must have been by the separation of a population that became a new species; this normally occurs when a marginal group becomes isolated and ceases to interbreed regularly or at all with its former fellows. Marked divergence of the new specific lineage, such as did eventually occur in our ancestors, is not likely to follow unless the lineage is somehow impelled to evolve a new kind of adaptation. Such an impulse is most likely to occur when the ancestral ecological niche is no longer open to the diverging population, either because it is filled by adequate competitors or because in a changed environment that niche is absent. There must then be some other niche that the population can enter, for otherwise it will just become extinct, which is by far the most common outcome of such a situation. If such a new niche does exist and variants in the population are viable in it, natural selection will lead to increased adaptation divergent from the ancestry. If, as certainly happened in our own ancestry, the niche changes, especially if the population itself continuously affects the ecology, adaptation by natural selection may continue over many generations and lead to profound changes at every level of anatomy, function and behavior.

Just where and how the first species that initiated a lineage toward man, divergent from later apes, arose is not known and perhaps is not knowable. If the ancestral population in its early stages had remained ecologically similar to its fellow apes, it is reasonably certain that it would either have merged with those apes before full genetic isolation arose or have become extinct. Thus it is probable that the separate lineage that was to lead to man did early become ecologically distinct and start into a new adaptive niche. As to just what the initial distinction was, the consensus has it as hunting-gathering in organized bands in plains or savannas rather than forests and probably with a change in food habits.[3] We agree that those conjectures are reasonable, but some are trivial and the evidence for others is exiguous.

The earliest hominids were necessarily hunter-gatherers because that is true of all their fairly close relatives and of Recent men living under primitive conditions. Bipedality seems more likely to be adaptive in savannas than in forests, but the very earliest hominids were probably not yet fully bipedal and they may have entered savannas because they became bipedal rather than becoming bipedal because they lived in savannas. Another line of evidence, that of associated faunas, is anomalous because early hominids are found associated with both forest and savanna animals and in any case it is doubtful whether they habitually lived with the animals associated with their fragments in death. As we have indicated, change from herbivorous to more carnivorous food habits is not evident from their teeth, and also there is evidence that some apes and monkeys are more carnivorous than was previously supposed. It is practically certain that the earliest hominids did live in bands with some organization, but there is no direct evidence as to the detailed nature of that organization. Such details are found to differ quite markedly in related nonhuman primates; compare, for examples, the different group relationships observed among various bands of chimpanzees by Kortlandt,[16] Goodall [12] and Reynolds and Reynolds [26] or among different baboons by Zuckerman,[41] Washburn and DeVore [40] and Kummer.[17]

Although many fascinating observations have since been made, we do not really have more solid conclusions about the evolution of social behavior in our remote ancestry than those reached by Thompson in the 1958 book previously mentioned. He said that "In summary, it may be stated that the evolution of social behavior is a broad and complex problem" and gave as his principal conclusion the "disappointing . . . broad generalization" that "with increasing ability to abstract, a potential for complex group behavior is gradually built up, culminating in man."

Nevertheless the essential nature of the adaptations that started our ancestry on its separate way and that have led to us is quite clear: these adaptations are within the broad scope of culture in the anthropological sense. There have been many attempts to define culture, some of them downright confusing, and the literature of the subject is enormous. We shall not attempt to review it but can happily refer to two discussions by

Hallowell [14,15] which seem to us to make much of the other literature superfluous.

It will be recalled that man-made tools constitute the only
considerable direct evidence of the behavior of early hominids.
These artifacts are by any definition a part of human culture.
and their early appearance in the fossil record supports and
emphasizes the view that culture is precisely the crucial hominid
adaptation. The further point should be made that culture is
a *biological* adaptation. The capacity for culture is genetic and
was certainly fostered by natural selection. That is the key to
the unique nature of the human species and to its evolutionary
origin.

Objections have been made to that conclusion, for example
it has been seriously maintained that a brain a little better
than that of a gorilla would have sufficed for man. That is
perhaps a somewhat subtle but still a glaring example of the
naked ape fallacy. The implication is that natural selection would
only have produced a slightly superior ape. That is not at all the
case. When the hominid lineage separated from that of the apes,
it went in a different direction, not toward a better ape but
toward a new kind of animal. Once started in that new direction,
its thrust was not to improve on the basic apish ancestry but to
evolve better men—that is, animals with capacity for culture in
its many manifestations increasing through the generations.

It has been repeatedly emphasized that language is the most
unique and one of the most important of the manifestations of
culture. All normal men have language, and human society could
not have taken the forms it has if the capacity for language had
long been lacking in our ancestry. It did not arise in the ancestry
of any other animals now living. That statement has been
queried, and there has recently been some partly polemic discussion of it, but it is maintained by a strong consensus of linguists
and others concerned (see, for example, the recent brief review, with citations, by Fillenbaum).[10]

Just as culture is a biological adaptation requiring genetic
changes, so language, one of the major manifestations of culture, once established, is the major vehicle for the transmission

and alteration of cultures. The fact that the capacity for language requires a brain which is structurally different from that of any ape is beyond dispute. The very beginnings of these differences were probably present in the earliest hominids, and natural selection took it from there. Although we can tell almost nothing of the internal organization of the brain from fossil "brain" (endocranial) casts, we do know that the increase in brain size which accompanied the evolution of *Homo* followed the use of tools. Quite apart from size, a slight change in associative pathways or in numbers of associative neurons would have a spiraling feedback effect on the whole process. It is an easy speculation that behavioral changes in individuals with favorable variation in brain structure might well relate to dominance positions and hence to reproductive advantage.

Obviously, the ability to speak, however rudimentary the forms or however small the variety of the vocalizations, would have enormous selective value. The essential structural differences between men and other living primates with regard to the capacity for language are apparently not in the development of peripheral structures—that is, the muscular and other properties of the vocal organs, but in the structure of the brain, in both cortical and subcortical areas. Comparison of the brains of modern apes and of man demonstrate present differences and may suggest how they arose.

The greatest relative growth of the human brain compared to that of the subhuman primates is in the inferior parietal region. Geschwind [11] points out that this region, placed between the association cortexes of the three nonlimbic modalities, vision, audition and somesthesis, provides the basis for the formation of nonlimbic associations and hence the anatomical basis for language—or at least for object-naming. Furthermore some cortical areas in the brain of man have no parallel in the brains of apes. Penfield and Roberts [25] state that

> There are four cortical areas in which a gentle electrical current causes a patient, who is lying fully conscious on the operating table, to utter a long-drawn vowel sound which he is quite helpless to stop until he runs out of breath. Then, after he has taken a breath, he continues helplessly as before. Other animals lack this inborn vocalization

transmitting mechanism in the motor cortex. . . . Curious as it may seem, this is the most striking difference between cortical motor responses of man and other mammals, and it seems likely that it bears some relationship to man's ability to talk. Another striking peculiarity of the human motor cortex, which may also bear some relationship to speaking and writing, is the relatively large area devoted to mouth . . . and the relatively large area of hand as well.

Again we may ask, what started all this? What brought language into the picture? It is hard to see any *necessity* for the development of symbolic language in the manner of life of the australopithecines, for example.

Surely they must have been capable of the sort of expressive vocalizations characteristic of the great apes today, and some have speculated that speech developed from increasing differentiations of these vocalizations. However, it is hard to see what selective advantage such refinements might have. Perhaps some modification of alarm cries, for example to denote the nature of the danger could be helpful, but the essential element is simply that danger is present and the direction from which the alarm came would clearly locate the source of the danger. In both man and animals, emotional expression is adequately served by gesture, nonverbal vocalizations and facial expression. We must look elsewhere for the source of language.

Thinking is not dependent upon speech. It may be, but is not necessarily, facilitated by language. A great deal of thinking in other than verbal terms is not unusual and in fact is particularly relied upon by persons engaged in such activities as experimental physics for whom translation into verbal or even nonverbal symbolic terms can be a considerable chore. (This may be a difficult point for psychiatrists and psychologists to accept, since they are generally a thoroughly verbal-thinking lot!) Vygotsky [38] has insisted that thought and speech have different roots, developing independently of each other, but that in man these two lines of development eventually meet and that thereupon "thought becomes verbal and speech rational." Such a fusion does not develop in other primates. Vygotsky also suggested that "speech was born of the need for intercourse during work." The idea that the earliest form of speech was

object-naming [11] ties in neatly with this, as well as with the undoubted importance of the (concurrent?) development of tool-
making.

It is tempting to speculate about the daily life of pre-man,
as one of us has done previously.[27]

> Let us suppose that this pre-human group lived for a considerable
> period in a situation which provided them with a degree of continuing
> security from enemies, that there was adequate vegetable and perhaps
> marine food in the rear vicinity and that this diet was supplemented
> by hunting. Whether only some of the adult males went on hunting
> expeditions, or all of them is not of great importance (except that
> if all went we must assume even greater security since none were then
> present to protect the females and young). That small groups of young
> males may split off from the group for short periods is not uncharac-
> teristic of other primates, and an easy extension of such behavior would
> permit them to go on hunting forays. If the group continued to live
> in the same spot, such forays would inevitably become increased in
> length of time, since they would have to go farther and farther afield.
> They would be limited in the amount that could be transported at any
> one time. When they returned to the group, it is clear that to be able
> to communicate their observations to others of the group would be of
> the greatest advantage. Bees can do as much, and for the same reason.
> Sharing of the experience of those who went different places and those
> who stayed at home would have many advantages other than just the
> acquisition of food—greater group cohesiveness, greater skills, etc.

Certainly it would not have been a difficult step from using
vocables to denominate tools or materials, or the location of materials from which they could be made, to using other vocables
to denominate different individuals, including the self. In the
degree of his awareness of self and others and of the world
around him we find one of the greatest differentiations between
man and his relatives. Hallowell [15] speaks of the "distinctive psychological focus of consciousness in *Homo sapiens*—the capacity for self-objectification which is so intimately linked with
the normative orientation of all human societies" but points out
that the evolutionary aspects of this development have hardly
been touched upon. He remarks that

> . . . representation and articulation of a sense of self-awareness is
> contingent upon the capacity for the symbolic projection of experience
> in socially meaningful terms, i.e., in a mode that is intelligible inter-

individually. . . . Outward behavior can be perceived and imitated through social learning in non-hominid primates. Emotional experiences can become contagious. But what is privately sensed, imaged, conceptualized, or thought cannot be imitated or responded to without an overt sign extrinsic to the experience itself. . . . There is no evidence to suggest that either the chimpanzee or any other non-hominid has developed a traditional means whereby it is possible for an individual to represent himself and other objects and events to himself as well as to others. . . . Speech, through the use of personal pronouns, personal names, and kinship terms made it possible for an individual to symbolize and thus objectify himself in systems of social action. Self-related activities, both in the past and in the future, could be brought into the present and reflected upon. What emerged was a personality structure in which ego processes and functions had become salient at a high level of integration—self-awareness.

It is probable that the development of self-awareness was the precursor for several other human characteristics. Acquisitivity, for example, the conception of personal property, can be seen as a natural extension and one which has had many effects. It may be the major determinant for the fact that man is the most manifestly aggressive primate. It may also be at the basis for many patterns of sexual interaction and is probably a more important source for sexual jealousy than is the sexual drive itself.

The ego functions must also have been a major factor in the increase in man of exploratory drives and perhaps also in the development of such other drives as those for beauty, for understanding and for self-actualization, which are characteristic of him now, although in enormously varying degrees.

The degree to which any man in any society and to which most men in all societies have developed self-awareness has been an important variable in our history from the earliest human societies to the present. While a good argument can be made for the proposition that it is only through further and intensive development of this capacity in all men everywhere that the species has any chance for survival, it is not without its dangers. Many, many of the turbulent developments of the last decade, from the struggles of the new nations to student riots are most readily explicable in terms of the enormous increase in awareness of how other people live as compared to how ego lives. This concern with the individual and with interpersonal interactions is demonstrated as a broad change in the shift in occupational patterns in our society, where in recent years there has been a major increase in the percentages of persons in personal service activities of one sort and another. Such a shift is also shown in interest patterns over the last forty years, to some increase in interest in interpersonal activities of various sorts, a shift toward extroversion.[4] Gottesman [13] has suggested a genetic component in the introversion-extroversion dimension; and it is not inconceivable that extroverts marry more often or have more children.

Associated with this has been another great shift in social structures at least from earliest historical days to the present. This shift concerns the relative size of the ingroup to the total group. By this we mean the percentage of the population who have some reasonable degree of control over their own lives, in terms of living place, occupation and all the rest. Even as late as medieval times, vast numbers of humans had very little control over their lives.

The immensity of this change is implicit as one reads through the four volumes of Churchill [6] on the *History of the English Speaking Peoples*. More and more individuals, especially in the industrialized societies (even the communist ones) have been able to make their own decisions about more and more aspects of their lives. The extent to which these possibilities have been felt and acted upon in another matter.[28]

Nevertheless, these possibilities have increased for many. Why then do we find a major complaint of many (and not only the young) people in our own society that they are lost in the mass, that their own needs and wishes are ignored by the Establishment? Indeed, how can we explain that to an uncomfortable extent, these things are true? Perhaps the answers can be thought of in terms of a "critical mass." Perhaps there is a point beyond which participant democracy is simply impossible and no tinkering with communications or systems or anything else can remedy the situation. If so, the only possible solution is clear enough, but where is the will to institute it and how can it be done?

No one that we know of has asked the question, How small a

human population and how distributed geographically and otherwise can retain all the cultural (including technological) benefits of modern man and still provide for each member a rich life with a sense of worth and purpose? All men are of one species—if any survive, the species does—and from that viewpoint it makes no difference what may be the color of their skins, their political or religious institutions, their fads and fancies. What does matter, though, is that the gene pool should contain as many variants as possible, for advance depends upon the possibilities for recombinations.

Culture is the most characteristic human adaptation. It strongly affects but does not supplant other aspects of evolution. Both cultural and more strictly biological evolution are continuing in our species. We can offer no prediction of a remote outcome.

REFERENCES

1. Ardrey, R.: *The Territorial Imperative*. New York, Atheneum, 1966.
2. Bullock, T. M.: Evolution of neurophysiological mechanisms. In *Behavior and Evolution,* edited by A. Roe and G. G. Simpson. New Haven, Yale University Press, 1958, pp. 165–177.
3. Campbell, B.: *Human Evolution*. Chicago, Aldine, 1966.
4. Campbell, D. P.: Changing Patterns of Interests Within the American Society. (Mimeographed) Center for Interest Measurement, University of Minnesota, Minneapolis, 1967.
5. Caspari, E.: Genetic basis of behavior. In *Behavior and Evolution,* edited by A. Roe and G. G. Simpson. New Haven, Yale University Press, 1958, pp. 103–127.
6. Churchill, W. S.: *History of the English Speaking Peoples* (Vols. 1–4). New York, Dodd, Mead and Company, 1956–1958.
7. Coon, C. S.: *The Origin of Races*. New York, Alfred A. Knopf, 1962.
8. Darwin, C.: *The Descent of Man and Selection in Relation to Sex.* London, Murray, 1871.
9. Day, M. H., and Wood, B. A.: Functional affinities of the Olduvai hominid 8 talus. *Man, 5:*429–455, 1968.
10. Fillenbaum, S.: Psycholinguistics. *Ann Rev Psychol, 22:*251–308, 1971.
11. Geschwind, N.: The development of the brain and the evolution of language. In *Report of the 15th Annual R.T.M. on Linguistic and Language Studies.* (Monograph Series on Language and Linguistics No. 17), edited by C. I. J. M. Stuart. 1964.

12. Goodall, J.: Chimpanzees of the Gombe Stream Reserve. In *Primate Behavior*, edited by I. De Vore. New York, Holt, Rinehart & Winston, 1965.
13. Gottesman, I. I.: *Heritability of Personality: A Demonstration.* Psychological Monographs, 1964, vol. 77, No. 9 (Whole No. 572).
14. Hallowell, A. I.: The structural and functional dimensions of a human existence. *Q Rev Biol, 31:*88–101, 1956.
15. Hallowell, A. I.: Self, society, and culture in phylogenetic perspective. In *The Evolution of Man, edited by S. Tax.* Chicago, University of Chicago Press, 1960, pp. 309–371.
16. Kortlandt, A.: Chimpanzees in the wild. *Sci Am, 206(5):*128–138, 1962.
17. Kummer, H.: *Social Organization of Hamadryas Baboons: A Field Study.* Chicago, University of Chicago Press, 1968.
18. Lindzey, G., Loehlin, J., Manosevitz, M., and Thiessen, D.: Behavioral genetics. *Ann Rev. Psychol, 22:*39–94, 1971.
19. Lorenz, K.: *On Aggression.* New York, Harcourt, Brace & World, 1966.
20. McClearn, G. E.: Behavioral genetics. *Ann Rev Genetics, 4:*437–468, 1970. Also with minor changes and references omitted in *Behav Sci, 16:* 64–81, 1971.
21. Morris, D.: *The Naked Ape.* New York, McGraw-Hill, 1967.
22. Napier, J.: *The Roots of Mankind.* Washington, D.C., Smithsonian Institute, 1970.
23. Oakley, K. P., and Campbell, B. G.: *Catalogue of Fossil Hominids.* Part 1: *Africa.* London, British Museum (Natural History), 1967.
24. Olson, E. C.: Vertebrate paleozoology. New York, Wiley-Interscience, 1971.
25. Penfield, W., and Roberts, L.: *Speech and Brain Mechanisms.* Princeton, Princeton University Press, 1959.
26. Reynolds, V., and Reynolds, F.: Chimpanzees in the Budongo Forest. In *Primate Behavior, edited by I. DeVore.* New York, Holt, Rhinehart & Winston, 1965, pp. 368–424.
27. Roe, A.: Psychological definitions of man. In *Classification and Human Evolution,* edited by S. L. Washburn. Chicago, Aldine, 1963, pp. 320–331.
28. Roe, A., and Baruch, R.: Factors Influencing Occupational Decisions: A Pilot Study. Harvard Studies in Career Development, No. 32., Cambridge, 1964.
29. Roe, A., and Simpson, G. G. (Eds.): *Behavior and Evolution.* New Haven, Yale University Press, 1958.
30. Romer, A. S.: Phylogeny and behavior with special reference to vertebrate evolution. In *Behavior and Evolution,* edited by A. Roe and G. G. Simpson. New Haven, Yale University Press, 1958, pp. 48–75.
31. Sarich, V. M. and Wilson, A. C.: Immunological time scale for hominid evolution. *Science, 158:*1200–1202, 1968.

32. Simons, E. L.: Recent advances in paleanthropology. *Yearbook of Physical Anthropology*, 1969, pp. 14–23.
33. Simons, E. L.: The origin and radiation of the primates. *Ann NY Acad Sci, 167*:319–331, 1969.
34. Simpson, G. G.: The study of evolution: methods and present status of theory. In *Behavior and Evolution*, edited by A. Roe and G. G. Simpson. New Haven, Yale University Press, 1958, pp. 7–26.
35. Simpson, G. G.: Behavior and evolution. In *Behavior and Evolution*, edited by A. Roe and G. G. Simpson. New Haven, Yale University Press, 1958, pp. 507–535.
36. Spukler, J. N. (Ed.): *Genetic Diversity and Human Behavior*. Chicago, Aldine, 1967.
37. Thompson, W. R.: Social behavior. In *Behavior and Evolution*, edited by A. Roe and G. G. Simpson. New Haven, Yale University Press, 1958, pp. 291–310.
38. Vygotsky, L. S.: *Thought and Language*, edited and translated by Eugenia Hanfmann and Gertrude Vakar. Published jointly by MIT Press, Cambridge, and John Wiley & Sons, New York and London, 1962.
39. Washburn, S. L.: *The Study of Human Evolution*. Eugene, Oregon State System of Higher Education, 1968.
40. Washburn, S. L., and DeVore, I.: Social behavior of baboons and early man. *Viking Fund Pub Anthrop, 31*:91–105, 1961.
41. Zuckerman, S.: *The Social Life of Monkeys and Apes*. London, Rutledge and Kegan Paul, 1932.

Chapter 3

Sociopsychiatric Contributions

Juan J. Lopez-Ibor

I POSE THE FOLLOWING PROBLEM: With what authority can a psychiatrist speak on a theme so filled with difficulties as "Man and Humanity"? One of my teachers, during the period of my psychiatric training, said that the topic of the so-called psychopathic personalities really overflows the psychiatric field and that the only thing the psychiatrist can do is bring forth the knowledge he has of what is authentically pathological for the interpretation of what is normal. As if this obstacle were not enough, one has to add the fact that there has been no epoch in the history of human thought in which so much has been spoken about man, yet with so relatively little known about him. Montaigne said, "I have not seen monster nor miracle in the world more manifest than I, myself . . . the more I look for myself and know myself, the more I am astounded by my deformity, the less I understand myself."

Erasmus was the great humanist of the Renaissance who tried to know man *from man himself.* According to Erasmus, man is one with his life, with all that life brings with it of sadness and joy, of deception and hope. Man—who is subjected to the blows of destiny, to all forms of illness and finally to death—is a weak being and makes mistakes. In Erasmus' "In Praise of Madness" (Encomium Moriae), we find one of the best interpretations of the confines of what is human: The supreme happiness and well-being to which men aspire, including believers, is nothing but a type of madness. "Observe," he says, "that Plato glimpsed something of this when he wrote that the delirium of lovers was the happiest of all." In effect, he who loves ardently does not live within himself but within the object of his love. When the spirit tries to separate itself from the body, when the organs

87

are not used properly, delirium is produced. What other meaning could be had in such everyday expressions as "to be beside oneself," "be yourself" and "he is himself again"?

The first question which we should ask in relation to this problem is to know if man is a being whose "biological evolution" is complete or if he is still a changing being with a future. There exists a certain *plasticity* of the human body and there are changes in its morphology in relation not only to illnesses but also to the environment. Young people today, especially in the Western World, have larger physiques, so that the Don Quixote type predominates over the Sancho Panza type—that is, leptosomatics predominate over pyknic types. This has been statistically proved by comparing the heights of soldiers in recent military service with those of the first World War—changes apparently not due to either nutritional habits or physical activities but possibly related to the wealth of *psychic stimuli* which cause hyperfunctional growth. In historical contrast, Emperor Septimio Severo had to lower by 10 centimeters the height required of individuals admitted to the Roman legions.

The evolution of the biological "superman" was anticipated by Nietzsche and Goethe. Neurologically, E. Dalke was one of the first to propose that the physique of man would depend, in great part, on the enlargement of the frontal cortex, with an enrichment of his faculties and understanding. Bergson and Teilhard de Chardin held analogous ideas, and Spatz spoke of a continuation of what V. Economo called "the process of cerebration." In contrast, I incline towards Scheler's theory that man conforms to a general biological law that what can be accomplished decreases at higher evolutionary levels.

But that man morphologically may be a finished form does not mean that he is that functionally. The human child is born unfinished and defenseless but with greater plasticity and potential than any other organism, especially in communication. A one-year-old monkey is capable of producing the same number of different sounds as a seven-month-old baby, but when the latter is eight months old, he already begins to imitate words and develop language. The human hand is also less specialized than the upper extremities of the monkey and thereby more adaptable. That same *capacity of expression* of the hand and of movements of the body affirms that man's relation to the world is different from that of the animals closest to him.

No one doubts that we are in a moment of transition. The Second World War seems to have been the boundary that separated two epochs. But historic boundaries are never that concrete. Even after the First World War one could foretell the entrance into a new historic age, characterized by a struggle, inhibitions and repressions. Opposite Apollonian man, Dionysian man seems to be born anew. The cult of the body, the erotization of life, the search for new forms that seem more primitive and alike in their way of life are all manifestations of that change. Our superdeveloped technology threatens to destroy the milieu in which we live. The efficacy of democracy seems to decrease. The artificialities of the toil and the culture stand out. Man has been liberated from many physical constraints, but it is also true that he is now subject to the threat of tedium and the loss of his own personality. In some respects, the Western ideal of the hero has been transformed into the more oriental concept confronting the pains of human existence by means of the art of patience. An Indian myth relates that the young god Krishna, after having battled in vain with the serpent of the world who had a stranglehold on him, upon hearing his divine father's call remembered that this was not his nature and so released himself by yielding each part of his body to the pressure of the bonds. In contrast, Western man, beginning with the Titans, has sought to determine his own destiny through being Lord of the world.

Even in the relation between the sexes one observes how these Dionysian tendencies are accompanied by a new elevation of the value and power of women. The man of the technical world has searched for the knowledge of the world through super-rational or computerized models, but dissatisfaction grows. The rapidity of such in the changes corresponds to the *process of historic acceleration* in which we live and from the fear that these too swift changes cause chaos in contemporary societies.

When Jaspers published a book about the possible effects of the atom bomb after the Second World War, he ended it with a conclusion that was practically an ode to despair. There was no way, according to him and von Weizsacker, to avoid the forthcoming catastrophe. These meditations basically are very much like those of Immanuel Kant about the impossibility of perpetual peace; the tendency towards the *universalization of power* acts inexorably (perhaps moved by means of occult anxiety) on the human communities that we call states.

This tendency is counteracted by the necessity of a more paradisiacal life. As Ernest Lee Tuveson says, the idea of progress is no more than a metamorphosis of the idea of redemption. Nevertheless, history shows that each new dimension of experience creates a new sensibility. Technological progress has not yet created the new sensibility nor the new ethics which are needed, and all the experiments that are made are merely peripheral and only adequate for small groups of transitory existence. Progress, moreover, is never unitary or unidirectional but complex and cyclic. History does not have *by itself a meaning, rather it acquires significance through the new attitudes of man.* As the poet T. S. Eliot said

> We cannot think of a time that is oceanless
> Or of a future that is not liable
> Like the past, to have no destination.

Chapter 4

Communication in Human Concordance:
Possibilities and Impossibilities

JOSEPH F. RYCHLAK

MEANING IS IMPORTANT to the human animal. As humans we are "processers" of meanings which we often create and then transmit or communicate to others. Not all psychologists accept the view that man does anything so unique as create meanings. They view him as a kind of blind "mediator" of events outside his meaningful realm of understanding. Yet I believe that meaning is essential to man's existence. When we speak of communication we must therefore be speaking somehow of meaning-dispersion and proper understanding, and when we speak of concordance we must also be speaking of an "understanding that allows for harmony" in interpersonal relations.

However, concordance in terms of meanings has its *limits*, because of the *bipolar nature of meaning*. That is, although there are many extraneous reasons for why men may disagree as to which "meaning" being expressed is the one they advocate—such factors as personal, class or national motivations, the problems of making our ideas clear, language differences and so forth—there is an even more basic reason for "some" discordance in human behavior, and it has to do with the dialectical nature of human reason and meaningful understanding. Though he did not appreciate the precedent, Sigmund Freud found this very discordance within the meaning-creations of a *single* person, so that psychoanalytical man is rent with conflicting wishes and has constantly to seek compromise solutions to this internal dialectic.

When I speak of the "dialectic" or dialectical conceptions or dialectical reasoning I no doubt wave a term which has myriad definitions and is therefore not entirely communicative. I find in my classes that students have great difficulty catching the spirit of what it means to think of things in life in dialectical fashion. In my mind, the term "dialectic" carries the signification and connotation of opposition, reversal, taking either side of an arbitrary point in argument, twisting a premise into its obverse and so forth. When I say that meanings are bipolar, I refer to the fact that language takes on dialectical features, so that "high" literally means "low" and "left" means "right" in one sense of the case. To know one meaning is to know the other. If I point to a chair and say "That is a chair," this rudimentary operational definition is not dialectical of course, except only in the sense that any assertion like this can be challenged with its opposite: "That is *not* a chair," meaning the existence asserted can be challenged. The dialectic here is "existence versus nonexistence" but insofar as many nouns and many prepositions are concerned we have a nondialectical usage. These terms are frozen and fixed, serving signpost functions or ancillary roles in the expression of ideas.

The dialectical usage, on the other hand, is intrinsically related to action and especially evaluative terms, and where we see the dialectic in ascendance, there we see a style of thought which is invariably fluid, dynamic and, above all, *conflict*-laden. The early Grecian intellect is a case in point. Anaximander, for example, in what is probably the *first* philosophical argument on record suggested that the basic elements of life were in opposition to one another—air is cold, water moist and fire is hot. Heraclitus' view of change was predicated on the assumption that opposites in life were in a constant state of strife. Empedocles spoke of his well-known "four elements" of earth, air, fire and water as constantly stirred by the *opposites* of "love and strife." These uses of a dialectical tactic are on the side of heuristic aids. They use a dialectical "model" of opposition and thus oppose events with each other. But there was also a use of the dialectic in discourse which was first singled out by the Greeks as an almost divine method of arriving at truth.

I refer here to the dialectic of Socrates. Socrates learned his skills in dialectical discourse from the early philosopher-lawyers known as "Sophists," men who made use of this capacity for reasoning through opposites to twist the case of their opponents in legal debate and carry off the day for their side when the judicial decision was rendered. Socrates raised the dialectic to a new level and took the manipulative aspects of this form of discourse out of central focus—calling it "sophistry" (in a pejorative sense) to use oppositional discourse to sway another to your *predetermined* point of view. The spirit of the dialectic for Socrates and Plato was "free." They believed knowledge to be "one," with "many" aspects of the common body of knowledge interrelated through opposition. The world was not "made up" of many unrelated "bits" of matter. Since "up" defines "down" and "straight" defines "crooked," why not find "truth" by beginning with "error"? Why not find "beauty" by admitting from the outset that it is easier to define "ugliness?" By starting at one pole and applying our naturally *dialectical reasoning capacity,* we can in time arrive at the other pole—*for all things are ultimately related.* Meanings are bipolar and even multipolar.

So it was that Socrates would pose a question for a student and then, by reasoning from the opposite of what the student said, encourage a flow of thought which eventually led to what he took to be new truths. If the student chose A, Socrates defended not-A; if the student chose not-A, Socrates defended A. It was all the same, for Socrates did not believe that he had any knowledge or, as we say today, "information" to "communicate" to the student. Socrates never wrote a book *precisely* because he did not believe that knowledge was programmed in this fashion. He was not skillfully and deviously manipulating his students to come to say what he intended that they say in the "dialogues." This is how we interpret him today because Plato wrote down these exchanges as if they were prearranged "programs" for student-manipulation. Socrates would have called this sophistry! From his viewpoint, all men had potential knowledge at their disposal, and through the exercise of the dialectic in discourse they could both come to know their mutually attainable truth by beginning with ignorance.

It was Aristotle who eventually revolted against this discursive approach to knowledge. He was, in a sense, the first tough-minded theoretician and seems to have rankled at what today we would call the "armchair" features of the Socratic dialogue where two men talked and talked, and though a lot went on, it all seemed so far removed from the real world of "facts."

Aristotle made his case in terms of man's *reasoning* ability, by which he meant that given certain premises, other things flow from the ordering of these premises. Aristotle seems to have been the father of the classical syllogism. We all know this classical sequence: "All men are mortal. This is a man. Hence, this man is mortal." The initial assumption ("All men are mortal.") is termed the *major premise*, the secondary denotation ("This is a man.") is called the *minor premise*, and the deduction ("Hence, this man is mortal.") made thereby is called the *conclusion*. Flowing from premises to conclusions constitutes reasoning, *and*, said Aristotle, there are at least two major types of reasoning to be seen in man. Here is a quote from the *Topics*,[1] in which Aristotle states:

> Now reasoning is an argument in which, certain things being laid down, something other than these necessarily comes about through them. (a) It is a "demonstration," when the premises from which the reasoning starts are true and primary, or are such that our knowledge of them has originally come through premises which are primary and true: (b) reasoning on the other hand, is "dialectical," if it reasons from opinions that are generally accepted.

Now, I want to emphasize two things here: (a) First, keep in mind that the distinction between dialectical and demonstrative reasoning deals *only* with the way in which we arrive at our premises—and especially our major premises—in thinking through some matter. *All* men can and do reason both ways, but when we move to a dialectical strategy, says Aristotle, we are often ready to rely on opinions rather than facts. This brings us to our second point (b), having to do with what Aristotle meant by "primary and true." He meant that the major premise of a demonstrative style of reasoning was in no way arbitrary or fraught with error. What this boils down to is a form of tautology. That is, earlier when I mentioned pointing to a chair and expressing the proposition, "That is a chair," the tautology was in the statement "Chair is chair." This is what an operational definition always amounts to: The antecedent and consequent factors of the proposition are identical. Another type of "primary and true" tautological statement is of the sort: "All bachelors are unmarried." There is a tautological relationship within this proposition which can be analyzed out and made plain without having to look about in the environment.

But the point for our purposes is that when we reason demonstratively we do *not* accept the general proposition that a meaning can be bipolar. A bachelor is not both married *and* unmarried. Aristotle was to call this the "law of contradiction," which is defined in a general sense as "A is not not-A." Whereas the dialectician finds in such contradictions an invitation to learning, the demonstrative reasoner finds only confusion, inconsistency and, above all, *error*. The demonstrative reasoner wishes to minimize and indeed remove all such dialectical impossibilities, viewing opposites as *different*. The dialectician is drawn to the insights of paradox and irony. In a real sense "error" for the demonstrative reasoner is simply the lack of clarity; if things were clear then all would be "true." What is not "primary and true" is therefore meaningless. The dialectician likes to rummage about in the garbage pail of error, where he finds the greatest truths. Error is for the dialectician an active principle—just as cogent to proper understanding as is truth.

In the evolution of modern science over the ages since Aristotle, the demonstrative image of man was to gain ascendance as a model for man.[2] I do not mean that there were no advocates of the dialectic, for there surely were. Hegel is one philosopher usually cited. But in the main, thanks to science's great emphasis on being *accurate,* the methods of science all rest on demonstrative assumptions. Mathematics is demonstrative reasoning *par excellence,* and it can be shown how dialectic was eclipsed with the rise of mathematical science. The British Empiricists, beginning with Bacon and running through Hobbes and especially Locke, were extremely influential in going several points up on Aristotle as "tough-minded" philosophers. Whereas Aristotle at least had man reasoning both demonstratively and dialectically, Hobbes and Locke essentially equated human reason with mathematics.

Today, we see the Lockean image of man reflected in behavior-
ism and cybernetics theory, where man is said to mediate inputs
into outputs, as if these were always primary and true bits of
substance combining in pseudomathematical fashion into higher
order ideas. Even "feedback" conceptions rely on "primary and
true" assumptions. The machine-man challenges neither his
original program nor the information "fed back" following some
mediational adjustment.

Machines reason *only* demonstratively. The Ten Commandments, which come down on one side of an issue, fed into a
machine would teach it ten moral ways of behaving, and so it
would behave. But the Ten Commandments fed into a *man*
teach ten possible ways of sinning *as well as* ten possible moral
behaviors. What happens to the man is a question of his coming
down on *one* or the *other* side of the meanings being conveyed.
It is this bipolarity of meaning which thrusts man into the "ex-
istential predicament" of having to choose, and in choosing he
seeks a kind of self-assurance known as "reasons." What are the
reasons for behaving this way over that way? The main focus
here is that man also "wonders" about the "unexpressed meanings" in the communications of another. "Why is that a sin? Why
is that *always* a sin? Why am I being admonished like this in the
first place?"

The human being that we know ourselves to be cannot "turn
off" such self-reflections. Messages are clear only to the tautol-
ogizing intellect of a demonstrative machine. When we think of
the multiplying factor of the emotions in such situations, how
fantastically complex must this question of communication be!
I think it is significant to note that artistic expression is most
often put into words through a "tension of opposites" phrasing.
Freud once remarked to Fliess that man was indeed a "bundle
of contradictions" as the poet had claimed he was. Whether we
think of Hamlet's tortured self-exclamation—"To be or not to
be"—or Iago's teacherous self-observation—"I am not what I
am"—the respective conflict in moral decision and deceitfulness
of apparent reality is best captured as a dialectical matter. Religious conflict, ethical decisions and indeed emotive behaviors of

all varieties, including humor, can be seen to have a dialectical side in which opposition generates a tension and incongruity mounts to a needed release.

There is a side to man, a side we *must* acknowledge, which is going unnamed today. In modern psychology, man cannot create as he cannot commit error. He is a mediator alone. Man is under the control of primary and true inputs, which lawfully determine his behavior regardless what he might say or think to the contrary, for man cannot take in such inputs, reason to their opposites and then project an alternative "for the sake of which" he now behaves and thereby innovates. He is a "victim of his biography," as my teacher, George Kelly used to say. I think that if we began looking at meaning and communication dialectically some new insights might emerge as regards our present situation in the sciences of psychology and psychiatry.

For example, young people today sometime speak about the "System," as if it were some huge, monolithic machine which presses them in a given direction which has been mapped out or programmed beforehand. Yet, anyone who considers the legal system in dialectical terms, with its drawing of presumed intentions from premises recorded in earlier law, must surely recognize that a constant play of dialectical "precedent" is at work. Sometimes what is extracted "by implication" from a constitutional injunction was not even intended by the framers of the constitution. But then, that is the insight of Socrates— that meanings override individuals and reach for transcending *opinions,* an opinion which is not operationally definable from the outset. Legal systems go beyond their programs because they challenge their premises, searching for the "true" or "truer" spirit of the law which was not dictated. Put another way, all "positions" on questions of importance are ultimately arbitrary. But arbitrariness does *not* mean unreasoned, as dialectical reasoning does not mean *only* error and sophistry.

In fact, Aristotle said that one of the most proper uses of a dialectical strategy in reasoning is when we are under attack. At the outset, when I said "That is a chair," if you were to say "No, that is *not* a chair," we would have to enter into a dialectical examination of what our meanings are, how we use this term "chair," and so forth. Rhetoric and debate are the arts of the dialectician. Immanuel Kant was also cognizant of the role of dialectic whenever two men or even one man examines the premises on which his or their reasoning proceeds. Indeed, the concept of "transcendence," which is so popular today, stems from Kant's view that only through a self-reflexive "transcendental dialectic" can man turn around and come to explore his own thought processes.

Another example of how dialectic might help us: Rather than presuming from the outset that our problems of discordance are entirely resolvable, we might simply expect that at some point contradiction is *necessary* for a meaning to enrich our understanding. To reverse the Socratic tactic, we should appreciate that simply because I say something "A," by that very act, you—at least in principle—can be given an alternative "not-A." As a dialectician I would say that my position suggests an opposite to you "by definition," and you either take this flat contradiction as a base of meaning-creation, or you draw a sort of dimension between my view, its opposite, and then take a stand at some point along the route between. In this case you do not have to contradict me directly—which I suppose is the height of discordance—but you can be somewhere on "my side" of the dimension yet not exactly identical to me.

There are a fascinating number of possibilities when we begin viewing man as the dialectical reasoner history tells us that he is. I have seen too many of my colleagues formulating the counter to my view *even as I give it out*—poorly expressed and incomplete—to think that this is always a bad thing or that only maladjusted people do this. I should really not expect them to hear me out first, nor should I be disturbed by the fact that they end up with a view on some subject that I first mentioned entirely in opposition to me. As a dialectician, I do not begin with the premise of *only* "primary and true" items of knowledge "out there," in experience.

This reference to a premise calls to mind another benefit of thinking dialectically: I believe that dialecticians—since they are not so blinded by facts—go to the heart of the matter much more facilely than do the demonstrative reasoners. That is, I think that what Aristotle may not have appreciated about the dialectician is that he was *always* dabbling with the premise rather than with the conclusion. He is fascinated by definitions, points of view, slants on things and so forth. I have always felt that this is what distinguishes the true statesman from the politician, for example. It used to disturb me to see the men at the United Nations haggling about this and that, while avoiding the *real reasons* for their opposition to one another. I refer here to the assumptions being made about the nature of the universe, society and the proper role for government. Of course, I realize that dialectical examination often glides into pedantism. But I still would argue that questions such as our being in or out of Vietnam cannot be dealt with at the level of "facts." Whatever gets us into wars, I at least feel cannot be tied down to facts alone, nor even primarily so; such policies are predicated on assumptions and not all assumptions flow demonstratively from the facts. Sometimes fact A implies a counter not-A, even in the "war game" and "counterspy" sense of a one-upmanship. One man or one nation's move is another man or nation's "taunt," for there are always *implications* in what transpires.

So then do I end on a pessimistic note and argue that concordance in human affairs is impossible? Well, yes and no. If one means by concordance some kind of uniformity in outlook as regards what things "really mean," then I would of course be pessimistic. On the other hand, if one means by concordance that men will come to look at things from *both* sides of meaning, the one where they are standing *as well as* the one where their disputant or "friendly ally" is standing, then I think that we can have a harmony in outlook. This does not mean an agreement in outlook on all things, of course. The harmony results more from the fact that at least we are now on the same dimension—we are singing the same song—and we fully understand or have worked out to our satisfaction the details of our disagreement. At least in this way we will not come to fisticuffs or worse for irrelevancies, and I happen to think that people would have far less cause for hostility if they could appreciate the dialectical nature of life. Some of the old-fashioned virtues which we used to call "tolerance" and a "sense of humor" were revered only because to exhibit them a person had to see the plausibility of opposite views on the same question or the idiocy of life's contrasts.

I think dialectical strategies help us grasp what we mean by "blame" and "being wrong." In the demonstrative scheme of things an oppositional contradiction literally defines error—hence one side must be wrong. The dialectical strategy, pitched as it is to the premises, is always more open to conclude "wrong from this point of view" or at least "wrong for these reasons!" It is surely true that we are often wrong *and* right in life; we *are* to blame and yet *not* to blame—if blame is being assigned! We cannot allow a law of contradiction to blind us to such psychological verities. The dialectician does not have to deny blame, does not have to dismiss it as if blame were simply the absence of scientific control in a person's life, but neither does he have to view blame as one-sided. He can accept it in the sense that the common man knows himself to feel blame or guilt even as he grasps the broader picture, the "other side" to the context of blame. With the broadened perspective comes a more genuine understanding —or so I would argue.

These are just a few of my thoughts on the productivity to be achieved from a dialectical formulation of the human condition. In closing, I would just like to draw your attention to the apparent fact, at least to me, that we are living through an age of confrontation and change, stretching all the way from women's lib through anti-authority attacks, on to a supposed communication gap across the age levels. It seems to me that the nineteenth century scientific ideal of a uniformity and a singleness of reality guiding man's destiny is a hopelessly outmoded style of thought. Our age calls for a dialectical formulation even as it nestles on a technology spawned by the fruits of demonstrative reasoning. The man living through this time is a dialectical creature—as well as a demonstrative one. Why not therefore begin to rethink his psychology in terms of *this* model and then see where our concerns about his communication hangups and discordant human relations lead us. We may be getting needlessly upset about some of the problems which result only from demonstrative premises. Then too, there may be other, more dialectically construed, areas of difficulty which we are overlooking that badly need attention. As to what these latter areas are, I am at this point a complete dialectician and cannot communicate them to you. Of course, I do have potential knowledge within me, as do you. So, we can shift the orientation of this demonstrative essay to that of a dialectical exchange. We will not always agree, but we can learn from one another.

REFERENCES

1. Aristotle: *Topics.* In *Great Books of the Western World* (Vol. 8), edited by R. M. Hutchins. Chicago, Encyclopedia Britannica, 1952, pp. 143–223.
2. Rychlak, J. F.: *A Philosophy of Science for Personality Theory.* Boston, Houghton Mifflin Company, 1968, Chap. IX.

PART II

INDIVIDUAL AND SOCIAL DYNAMICS

Chapter 5

Concordance Requires Discord: A Theory of Human Relations

Manfred Halpern

I BEGIN ON A NOTE of discord. Our Conference is entitled "Man for Humanity: On Concordance vs Discord in Human Behavior." Why concordance *as against* discord? Except for a special case, which need not remain a special case, concordance is impossible without discord at the very same time. And vice versa. Man *for humanity*? Yes, provided that the humanity he lives with is already humane. It usually is not. *Man for* humanity? Yes, provided that man is already humane enough to let humanity grow within himself. He (already reluctant enough to include she) is usually not ready.

We are in for a lot of struggle within ourselves and with others before man and humanity come to recognize each other as brothers and sisters. We are therefore quite fortunate that collaboration and conflict are necessary to each other, that we cannot proceed constructively without troubling about both.

But surely it is not an accident that we separate concordance and discord and speak meaningfully about man separated from humanity. Part of our fundamental trouble is the theory which, by now largely implicitly, shapes our vision and our action. We speak of "individual," "family," "nation," of "love" and "hate," "conflict" and "collaboration" as if each term referred to a distinct, separate, isolated box. If we see life as a collection of separate boxes, then surely life cannot help but be a life of

Note: This chapter was prepared for the Colloquium in the style appropriate for oral communication, but leaves out much that allows the theory proposed to become both a subtle and sharp instrument. For elaborations and many further applications, see the volume, *The Dialectics of Transformation in Politics, Personality and History*, Princeton University, 1972.

prudent isolation at best and more often, imprudent and indeed destructive conflict. To connect such separate boxes as "individuals," "families" and "nations" to each other would seem to require nothing less than miracles of persuasion or seduction or forced leaps into utopia or else what we usually consent to live with instead—shared illusions.

But there is a fundamentally different way of looking at life which serves to give us different choices for combining collaboration and conflict. It is a way at least 2,000 years old. Heraclitus was one of the first to write about it; Avicenna returned to it in the eleventh century, Goethe in the eighteenth, Hegel and Marx in the nineteenth, and Martin Buber and Carl Gustav Jung in the twentieth century. They all made relationship—and not a separately boxed unit—the basic building block of their analysis.

Relationship: they saw the basic matter in motion to be the encounter of self and other from opposing positions producing change. It is this dialectical encounter, not the separate self and other, that becomes the building block of theory and the central experience of practice.

I would like to put before you a new dialectical theory of human relations. The most important questions it seeks to answer are these: How and why do individuals become so separated from themselves and each other that *both* collaboration *and* conflict become fruitless? How can individuals and groups transform themselves to overcome such incoherence?

To answer these large questions, let us begin with a smaller one. What are the central issues in all human encounters? *Continuity:* if the encounter has little persistence and bursts as a mere fragment, it scarcely becomes an encounter. *Change:* if the encounter persisted forever in the same monotone, it would surely drive us mad or make us bitterly rigid. To achieve both continuity and change, we need both *collaboration* and *conflict.* All this encountering of opposing self and other would constitute aimless motion, mere commotion, if there were not also a fifth issue at stake: *the attainment of shared goals,* or, as we might well call such attainment, *justice.*

Next we ask: if we are concerned with our capacity *simul-*

taneously to achieve performance on all five of these central issues in human relations—continuity and change, collaboration and conflict, and the achievement of shared goals, how many are the ways in which man can achieve such performance? The answer is that there are only eight ways.

Let me state this position more formally as a hypothesis which my own work and that of my students over the past five years has indicated might very well be fruitful. There are only eight ways of giving form to the encounter between self and other when these five central issues of performance are simultaneously at stake. This hypothesis, and all the hypotheses which flow from it, apply with the same force and meaning to intrapersonal relations, interpersonal relations and intergroup relations from family and friendship group to nations. They also apply to the relationship of individuals and groups to concepts—any concepts, any conceptions of problems, ideas, values, norms, ideology and the rest. They also apply to man's transpersonal relations— that is, to the spring of undifferentiated energy within each of us and our ability to constellate it in concrete forms that constitute the capacity we all possess in our quality as human beings.

The claim of this new paradigm is therefore larger than any yet proposed. It says we can systematically describe, analyze, compare and make predictions about types of relationships regardless of the realm in which they move, whether within yourself or within the international system. We could not do that before because it was true and it remains true that different boxes labeled "individual" or "Communist Party" or "United States" act out quite different dynamics that are usually not comparable within any common framework. As a result, the findings of psychiatrists remained of little help to the political scientist and vice versa. Once we make types of relationships the focus of our analysis, a single intellectual and practical framework can connect us in all these realms.

Here is a diagram of the eight forms of encounter that allow us simultaneously to deal with continuity and change, collaboration and conflict, and the achievement of justice—that is, of shared goals.

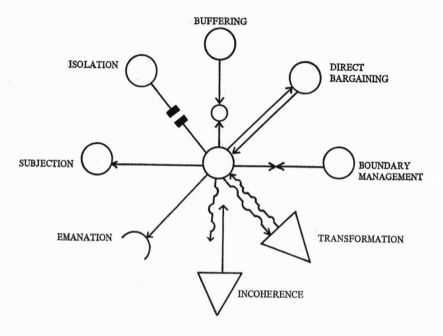

I begin with the relationship called *emanation*. This relationship is extremely asymmetrical. It represents mysterious and overwhelming power at work. If a reference to mystery disturbs you in a scientific discourse, may I remind you that you have all experienced encounters in emanation. All of us began life as small children without power adequate to meet the other. We therefore necessarily yielded our identity to the mysterious and overwhelming power of the mother in exchange for total security. That was the justice we craved: total security.

The trouble is this. As you will see, no other form of encounter offers as much security as emanation. As we increasingly experience conflict in its most extreme form—namely, in the type of encounter called incoherence—we are increasingly tempted as adults to return to the relationship offering the most extreme form of security—namely, emanation. We want to yield ourselves to the mysterious and overwhelming power of a dogma, a political movement or personal hero.

What forms of collaboration and conflict characterize emanation? In emanation, consciousness of change is repressed. No energy can therefore be mobilized for the creation of conflict. Collaboration therefore proceeds with intense passivity, thus assuring continuity. Hence total security is achieved.

Note how these five central issues constitute interconnected aspects of a simultaneous interaction. We shall find this true, each in qualitatively different ways, of the other forms of encounter. For we are not offering new boxes for old, but forms of interaction in motion.

Intensely passive collaboration at the cost of repressing conflict, to purchase continuity at the cost of change, and hence awarding mysterious and overwhelming power to the one and total security to the other—these are the intrinsically connected manifestations of the relationship of emanation. It is the silence of the "silent majority"; the worship of the true believers; the yielding of romantic lovers.

Next: *Subjection.* Here both self and other are fully present, each with an identity of his own. The relationship is still asymmetrical, still rests upon the experience of overwhelming power. But this power, which was mysterious in emanation, becomes naked in subjection—naked in its imposition and naked in its resistance. It is the policeman directing traffic, the teacher demanding rote learning, the psychiatrist engaged in stimulus-response therapy.

In subjection, conflict is no longer repressed but suppressed. Men remain conscious of the loss of their right to step forward urgently and freely. Collaboration proceeds on terms defined solely by the other. The other therefore assures continuity and change in accordance with his power. Justice involves an exchange of the right of survival for the one for the acceptance of the supremacy of power of the other.*

Instrumental rationality is another example of subjection—a relationship in which conflict is suppressed so that collaboration may proceed under the direction of another. When we use another person or the resources of our natural environment solely as a means to our particular end or even when we impose such

---

* Mere survival is hard to come by in most of the world. To secure survival is indeed one of eight forms of justice, however harsh its terms.

discipline upon ourselves while denying to ourselves or others the freedom of seven other choices, law and order secures its most openly exploitive triumph. When, by contrast, subjection is used temporarily in order to create or maintain use of our full human capacity—namely, of all eight forms of encounter—its contribution to our behavior is quite different.

Next I should like to speak of *isolation*. In this relationship, individuals or groups agree upon one mode of collaboration—to refrain from demanding anything of each other. Both sides here collaborate in avoiding all conflict intended to lead to change in, with or by the other. Justice now means self-determination—but at the price of not attempting to affect change in the others. Isolation in this usage of the term cannot be achieved unilaterally. It demands collaboration. The attempt to isolate without an agreement to avoid conflict, change or new forms of justice produces incoherence, not isolation. Witness both the end of black segregation and the hopelessness of black separatism in the United States.

Buffering: Here the encounter is managed by intermediaries. Such a position may be occupied by a mediator, broker or by a concept. Unlike isolation, buffering allows for change by permitting indirect, intermittent or segmented forms of conflict and collaboration. Thus, in intergroup relations, Indian castes relate to each other through ritualized avoidance while the individual members, factions, interest groups and regional, linguistic, caste and class divisions within the Indian Congress Party are held together by political brokerage. In interpersonal relations, buffering is perhaps most often exemplified by mediating one's own experiences through a filter of habits, stereotypes or rituals. Justice is the attainment of self-determination circumscribed or enhanced by such indirect or limited exchanges.

Direct Bargaining. In this form of encounter, individuals and groups for the first time conflict and collaborate with each other directly and upon the same terms. Justice is not only the better bargain that may accrue to one side or the other, but above all the reciprocal capacity to seek a different bargain as, from moment to moment, the balance of power changes. Collaboration and conflict as intrinsic aspects of the same interaction—and here of a constant mobility of continuous change—may be seen in gifts or hospitality which are bestowed as a way of creating or maintaining a sense of indebtedness between self and other or in that form of rebellion which is in fact a continuance of this encounter—that is, one is entitled to remain angrily present while refusing to bargain in order to improve one's bargaining position.

Now we turn to a form of encounter which is so familiar to us as citizens, professional men and women or as parents that we tend to see only collaboration in it while we minimize or ignore its inherent pattern of conflict. I speak of *boundary-management,* a process of encounter in which each self and other is entitled to claim an autonomous zone of jurisdiction based on some principle of law, custom, status, value or competence that both share.

This is the form of encounter that allows us to be fellow citizens, to know how psychiatrist and social worker divide their tasks, to separate the three branches of government, to charter the limited liability corporation, to describe the model teenager on his way to adulthood. It seems to hold a place for everything and puts everything into its proper place. It allows large numbers of individuals and groups to collaborate on a sustained basis in connected roles, for each claim can rather easily be subdivided or a principle found to add more connections in the chain.

Where is the conflict in this collaboration? No one can or will maintain the boundary of your autonomous claim for you except you yourself. If the Congress lets the President take almost sole control over foreign policy, if the citizen remains unconcerned about the Attorney General's wiretapping, if the psychiatrist lets the medical administrator set most policies, he has only himself to blame. If this association does not do what it can to enlarge the boundaries within which the pain and growth of man's psyche is taken seriously as against other claims which confine and narrow man, we will bear a corresponding responsibility. Maintaining and expanding autonomous claims may involve a subtler form of conflict than the other forms of encounter, but it is often a far more powerful form of conflict. More individuals and groups, better coordinated, more capable of sustained interaction are marshalled against each other in boundary-management than in any other encounter. Wars under the banner of emanation can be bloody, like the crusades, but they peter out as faith lessens and heroes die. Wars under the banner of subjection may end with the first defeat. Warriors bound together by direct bargaining tend to be mere summer soldiers. World Wars I and II and the Vietnam War owe much of their endurance to a new admixture of boundary-management into the organization of the industrial, administrative and military machine.

I have tried so far to present evidence for two generalizations at the same time—for the first hypothesis of this new paradigm—namely, that there are only eight ways of structuring the encounter between self and other when continuity and change, collaboration and conflict, and the achievement of justice are simultaneously at stake; and secondly to demonstrate the intrinsic connection of collaboration and conflict in six qualitatively different forms of encounter.

As I turn to the last two forms of encounter, incoherence and transformation, I come to what is a far more important part of the matter. I should like to discuss these two forms of encounter as part of several larger issues, for I need to explain *incoherence* not only as another form of encounter—in this instance, of conflict without collaboration—but as one of the central experiences of the modern age. I shall try to summarize very briefly the longest chapter in my forthcoming book.

The modern age is historically unique in the persistent breaking of all the concrete inherited manifestations of the first six forms of encounter—those which I have so far discussed. The *persistent* breaking of these connections allows us to fuse conflict and collaboration, so that even under the best of circumstances, relationships become temporary. The first hypothesis remains true as before: we have only eight ways of achieving simultaneous performance on all five central issues of human relations. What cannot endure is the concrete expression which we have inherited or just established.

Why is the modern age an age of persistent incoherence? To be brief, I must be highly selective and pick only one or two principal causes for the breaking of concrete connections in each of the first six forms of encounter. Emanation breaks because individuals and groups cannot afford to remain the embodiment of others. To be an embodiment of the mysterious and overwhelming power of another is to be denied the right to ask questions, criticize, experiment, analyze or create the new. In a world already changing, to remain the embodiment of a mysterious and overwhelming other is to become crippled. Let me emphasize a point to which I return again and again: In the modern age, *to maintain* any concrete form of encounter which can no longer achieve performance on all five central issues cripples the participants. Under such circumstances, conservatism is as destructive as the deliberate creation of incoherence.

Subjection breaks because naked power has by now proved itself far less effective in many areas of life than creative education or innovative production. Even instrumental rationality is now seen, despite its power, to have too often been used to cut us from other connections with life, from intuition, feeling, nature and other people. Therefore, to try to maintain such concrete forms of subjection is to cripple individuals and groups. Hence increasingly men break this form of connection. Isolation, again to select only one or two obvious causes, breaks because it leaves the previously insulated without adequate defense or because of their own unwillingness to remain crippled by denying themselves any longer the benefits of taking creative advantage of the opportunities of transforming life. Buffering and direct bargaining work only if you can offer me something I want and if our values are still convertible. But as qualitative changes in experience or education come to distinguish generations, social classes, tribes, countries and individuals, values cease to be convertible or even mutually understandable, and such exchanges end. The existing boundaries defining areas of knowledge, political jurisdictions and problems cease to make sense. Suburbs and inner city refuse to combine human and material resources. Psychiatry and politics are taught in quite unrelated ways. Those who remain unskilled in crossing boundaries increasingly play empty roles, however much they continue to use up valuable resources for defending the existing boundaries of their established jurisdictions.

What I have been talking about is incoherence—a form of encounter in which self and other stand in the same place at the same time, unable to agree on a shared form of tension-management for combining collaboration and conflict. Incoherence is not a residual category for purposes of classification. It is increasingly the most pervasive experience of the modern age. It is the experience of discontinuities rather than continuity—of change, yes, but unintended, uncontrolled change, of conflict without shared rules that leads to injustice for both self and others.*

If the concrete manifestations of the first six forms of encounter are breaking and therefore turn into a seventh form—namely, incoherence—and if there are only eight forms of encounter altogether, it follows there is only one way left to regain coherence through the fusion of conflict and collaboration—namely, transformation.

This statement, which follows deductively from our preceding hypothesis, runs counter to the mainstream of American social science and social practice. We tend to concentrate analysis and action upon adjustment, on incremental change, on incremental escalation or de-escalation. But if the fundamental change that is upon us is the breaking of connections, then the attempt to improve, render more efficient or economical, such relationships is like trying to save medieval knighthood by making their armor of heavier steel or sending them against windmills. It serves for a time to mask incoherence; it prolongs the agony; and it increases the cost of change.

But what is *transformation?* The first thing to be said is that we are talking about the most fundamental kind of change, but not about apocalyptic change. Our paradigm forces us, al-

* Among the applications of this theory in *The Dialectics of Transformation in Politics, Personality, and History* is a demonstration that six qualitatively different forms of violence flow from the breaking of each of the first six forms of encounter.

ways, to focus on concrete encounters between concrete selves and others. Many such relationships by now need to be transformed, but our task always concentrates upon concrete connections. Our paradigm bothers neither to overthrow abstractions called "systems" nor to defend them. Our concern is with the actual relationships of man.

What, then, is transformation? We have been talking so far only about performance. We must now talk about the obverse of performance—namely, capacity. What aspects of capacity are required to overcome incoherence through transformation? First, a new kind of consciousness—an awareness that there are patterns in human relationships, that these patterns are breaking and that man is free to choose among them. What is so different about this kind of consciousness, and why is it still so rare? Let us go back to emanation and recall several things about it. Alone among all the forms of encounter, almost everyone in the world has experienced it as a child. Traditional societies make emanation the keystone of their network of relationships. To be a legitimately formed self or other, to enact a legitimate relationship is to partake in actions endowed with mysterious and overwhelming power. Modern man often retreats into new forms of emanation—into fascism and racism, into worship of charismatic heroes, into property as the outward emanation of personality—in order to mask the incoherence he cannot dare or bear to transform.

No breaking is therefore more vital, more life-giving, than the breaking of concrete inherited forms of emanation, for emanation by its nature prevents us from analyzing, experimenting and from seeing patterns or changing them.

Is the modern age then to be without mystery—that is, without emanation? Not at all. What is characteristic of all concrete inherited forms of emanation is that they demand that we act as embodiments of the other. That is the only way I have so far spoken of emanation. But once that kind of emanation breaks, and we attain a consciousness of alternative patterns, we are also free to recognize that emanation can be reversed. We can become the embodiments of our own mysterious self. This is the common ground of our being which we all share as human beings. This reversal of emanation, under the aegis of the consciousness of transformation, liberates the undifferentiated energies within us and allows us to move to the second aspect of capacity—namely, from consciousness to creativity. We are then enabled to constellate new concrete forms of encounter that will restore coherence, allowing us to deal once again with continuity and change, collaboration and conflict, and the achievement of shared goals, this time, resorting freely to all eight forms of encounter.

Only the free and full use of all eight forms of encounter constitutes the fullness and freedom of being human—to enjoy and produce in the fullness of capacity and performance. At this point in our history, most of us in most of our concrete relationships feel entitled or able to use only one form of encounter most of the time and two or three others some of the time, never all eight.

But what is the difference between utilizing the other forms of encounter under the dominance of transformation and using them instead under the dominance of traditional forms of emanation or in order to mask incoherence? Under the aegis of transformation, all encounters in their concrete form become temporary—not necessarily quick or short-term, but in any case not permanent. A psychiatrist concerned with the transformation of his patient knows that the touchstone of his success is the end of the therapeutic relationship, when his patient has consciousness and creativity enough of his own to enter into new relationships of his own. When the Communist Party of Czechoslovakia proclaimed itself successful as an instrument of social, political and economic transformation, it was either lying or else those were right who called upon it therefore to give freedom to the people it claimed to have transformed. A genuine task force goes home when it has resolved the particular problem which entitled it to raise an autonomous zone of jurisdiction. It does not stay on forever to defend a new bureaucratic boundary.* New theories of transformation like this one can count upon being transformed at least as long as no one turns them into new dogmas.

Unlike Karl Marx or Charles Reich, I can offer no optimism that the breaking of old connections will lead to transformation. Indeed, most of the breaking, as my examples were meant to show, is unintended and uncontrolled, not deliberate as our guardians of law and order suppose. Far more people have already learned to live with incoherence than with Consciousness III. Transformation means the transformation of consciousness into work—work to create new relationships within ourselves, with others, with ideas and with nature.

This then is the basic choice—to be attracted by such hard work, which is permanent employment because incoherence will return even under the most creative of circumstances, or to be driven into such work by the increasing pain of incoherence—or to keep doing what most of us are doing—live with our masks and illusions among the growing debris of familiar things.

---

* Dr. Bryant Wedge's Chapter 23, "Mass Psychotherapy for Intergroup Conflict," offers an excellent insight into the process by which buffers enter and transform a conflict and then depart. Dr. Sol Kramer's Chapter 1, "Conflict and Concordance in the Development of Animal Societies: Ethologic Contributions," makes it vividly clear to me that animals other than humans also possess capacity and performance in any of the eight forms of encounter, but that only the human animal possesses all eight of them, including the capacity for persistent transformation.

Chapter 6

Discordance and Concordance in Economic Behavior

ROBERT H. STROTZ

THE SCOPE OF INTEREST of this colloquium was primarily that of interpersonal social conflict in which individuals are pitted against one another in a personalized way. Conflicts arise latently or expressly among individuals who can identify one another, so that personality and psychological interactions are of the essence. There are, of course, other forms of conflict, thoroughly impersonal, involving no apparent bilateral personal relations at all. It is as if we were at the horse races. The jockeys see each other, know each other and take one another's measure. Identifiable interpersonal competition is down there on the track. But at the pari-mutuel windows, relationships are quite different. Each bettor is pitted against all others, but no personal feelings of animosity or antagonism arise between those who stand next to each other in line. The odds that are quoted may as well have been invented by the computer and the surrounding crowd be faceless.

It is this latter type of conflict—that among the bettors—that is of most interest to economists. Their concern is not with concordance *versus* discordance but with how in economic organization concordance is fashioned out of discordant elements. Later I shall turn to those facets of economic organization in which identifiable, personalized conflicts arise.

Sometimes, I tell my colleagues in the behaviorial sciences that economics is not really about people at all, but that it is about prices and production and unemployment and investment and about all of the impersonal indicators and quantitative market data cast up by corporate accountants and government statisticians. If economists could forecast all these magnitudes with a theory that never recognized the personal psychic identities of individuals, for example, by a theory of sun spots, that would be just as good as other theories based upon axiomatic notions regarding the behavior of people. The economist's task is to explain how market magnitudes are determined and not to contribute to an understanding of social or individual psychology. But this is economics as a positive science, divested of normative considerations and thereby avoiding all questions as to whether the organization of an economy engenders personal psychic conflict among its members or produces a sense of concordance and harmony for the multitudes that interact in economic processes. These latter questions are legitimate, and one can ask whether economic organization abets either concordant or discordant sensations among its participants. As an economist, let me reflect upon this.

I proceed initially from the vantage point of laissez faire economics, not meaning by that a political posture on economic policy questions but referring instead to the central, underlying theme of the discipline from Adam Smith, through the classical and neoclassical traditions, to the economics of the current age as it is known in the western capitalist nations. I exclude the slightly tangential view of Marx and the more fundamentally aberrant views of Thorsten Veblen. I am thus speaking of economics in its major tradition as I know it.

From this vantage point, the theory of economic behavior describes a domain of highly discordant, completely nonaltruistic behavior on the part of the individual participants and yet an organization for social interaction that produces a remarkable concordance in the collective behavior of the participants. The striking thing is that in the conventional concept of economic organization concordance and discordance are not separated by the word "versus" as they are in the title of this colloquium. Instead, economics stresses the synergistic role of the market in orchestrating the selfish, individualistic, seemingly discordant drives of individuals into a socially orderly process by which New York City gets fed, a department store constantly turns over its inventories and industries of growth potential acquire the resources for their expansion—all of this without centralized planning, as if done by a divine hand.

Any economic organization, whether we think of it in terms of a highly idealized system of free enterprise and free markets or as a highly idealized system of centralized comprehensive planning must resolve certain problems in the coordination of the economic activities of many individuals. I shall identify three. First, there is the problem of determining which and whose human wants are to be satisfied. This entails the evaluation of the purposes of production or, speaking somewhat more loosely, the determination of the relative priorities to be assigned to different productive activities. In a planned economy, these wants, in principle, are assigned priorities by the central planning authority in accordance with whatever norms it chooses to impose. In a free market economy, the evaluation of the ends of production is determined by an impersonal process whereby people bid individually for different goods and services and wherein their capabilities for outbidding one another depend upon the value and productivity of the resources they control and upon the relative importance of their own labor in the fulfillment of the diverse wants of the community. The process is characteristically a highly impersonal and, indeed, unconscious one. When I routinely buy a loaf of bread, I am sending an encouraging signal to the wheat growers, the millers and the bakers. But this communication requires no conscious effort on my part. By buying bread instead of eggs, I am also sending a discouraging signal to the poultry industry. I thus contribute in an unconscious way to the resolution of a conflict of interest between those who command different resources. I am also affecting prices, as are all of us who make such decisions. But in any competitive market in which each buyer is inconsequential, no one perceives the effect that he has on prices, and his participation in the market is seemingly a nonsocial act, highly impersonal, and manifesting no sense of either concordance or discordance in his personal relations with others.

Secondly, economic organization must also determine how labor and other productive resources are to be assigned to various productive activities, and this too is done by markets. These are the markets for labor services, for land and natural resources, and for capital equipment. If there are many individual firms each coordinating these resources in the production of the same commodities and if there are many suppliers of these resources, the prices in these markets will also be determined impersonally and will reflect both the relative availability of the resources and the relative priorities that individuals as consumers have assigned to different products. All of this occurs within the technology governing the transformation of resources into products.

Thirdly, an economic system must also generate decisions pertaining to economic growth. Some economic growth is due to the expansion of the population, but economic causes appear to be only partially determining in this process, apart from such outer limits as a Malthusian may suggest. More amenable to economic analysis are the determinants of the growth of capital because the accumulation of capital is at the expense of current consumption. It must be decided how much of an economy's current output should be used up in the satisfaction of present wants and how much of that output should take the form of additions to inventories and to plant and equipment for the sake of greater consumption at a later time. Under central economic planning, the answer to this question would be made deliberately by a political authority that would decide on the amount and kinds of resources that would be used in production in order to store output or to yield new resources available to enhance production in the future. In a free market economy, these decisions are made more impersonally. The mechanism is the interest rate, which serves as a sort of price between the present and the future. It, in effect, adjusts the rate of yield from capital formation to the rate at which individuals are willing to forego the satisfaction of present wants for the greater satisfaction of future wants. The interest rate too, in the idealized free market economy with many borrowers and lenders, is, like other prices, determined impersonally so that no individual need be consciously aware of his contribution to the collective decisions regarding economic growth.

I have now identified three major functions that must be performed by an economic system. One of these has to do with the evaluation of the relative importance of the various economic wants of different individuals, described by the theory of *demand*. Another has to do with the allocation of resources in the satisfaction of those wants, which has to do with the theory of *production and supply;* and the third has to do with the setting aside of some productive resources for the purpose of economic growth, and that is covered by the theory of *investment*. For these functions to be performed in the highly idealized competitive economy three important mechanisms are required: (a) the selfish pursuit of economic objectives by individuals, (b) the price mechanism and (c) the profit motive for firms or entrepreneurs. I want to comment on each of these mechanisms in terms of the problem of discordance versus concordance in human behavior.

First, regarding the individualistic pursuit of economic objectives, the economist does not assert that people in our society cannot be altruistic. If I wish to earn money so that I can give to my favorite charity, I am not thereby defying any of the stereotypes about economic behavior that the economist proposes. The point is that the system is not expected to rest upon altruism or compassion but is supposed to work even though my motivation for engaging in production is only to earn an income to be spent for self-gratification. In short, the competitive, free market system does not require that any individual should suppress his selfish motives for the common good, except that, and and this is no doubt of importance, he must respect property rights so that the distribution of economic goods is determined by the economic system and not by looting and larceny. Thus, no individual needs to be socialized beyond the acquisition of respect for private property and no one need feel guilty if his economic motivation is one of self-interest.

Secondly, the pricing system has as its major characteristic in a competitive economy that prices appear to be given in the sense that no individual feels that he has any opportunity to alter them. At the same time, changes are induced through the summation of a multitude of imperceptible effects stemming from the decisions of a multitude of individuals. In the theory of the economic behavior of the individual or in the theory of the firm, prices always appear as parameters; but in the theory of general equilibrium, which studies the interactions of all participants, prices appear as variables. This means that the price system which determines how conflict of economic interest is to be resolved functions nonpersonally, and no one who identifies a price change that is adverse to his interests can point to another individual and feel that he is in personal conflict with him. Each may feel this way about large numbers of other individuals. A man who enjoys good wine may understand that all others who also enjoy good wine drive up the price to his disadvantage, but it hardly makes sense for him to single out a particular connoisseur as his personal enemy.

Thirdly, the role of the profit motive is especially illuminating. Each entrepreneur who buys productive services to produce a product which he then sells is expected to be efficient in his use of those productive services—to avoid waste or to economize—and to strive to make as great a profit as possible. But the theory of competitive equilibrium is that entrepreneurs, each attempting to maximize profit, are at best able to just break even. Profits, in this theory, appear essentially as signals and incentives to induce adjustments in the economy. If there is an increase in demand for a particular product so that the price of that product rises, the entrepreneurs in that industry will begin to enjoy profits. But this will immediately signal to others that there are profitable opportunities in that industry, and other entrepreneurs will through the investment process transform their resources so as to enter that industry. As the number of firms in the industry increases, the amount of the commodity produced will increase. The market price will fall, and profits will disappear. Upon their disappearance, the indicated adjustment is complete. Thus, profit is a good thing because it motivates efficiency and directs investment into the desired channels. But profit reflects a bad thing because it always indicates a maladjustment in resource use. The system is designed to generate profits when new adjustments are needed in order to stimulate those adjustments and to eliminate profits as a consequence of the adjustment process. Again, in the competitive economy the rise and fall of profitable opportunities in different industries is a nonpersonal phenomenon being regulated by the interplay of many individuals, each having but an imperceptible influence on the phenomenon itself.

It is interesting to note the quite opposite meanings given to the word "competition" by sociologists and by economists. Competition, as the sociologists would see it, entails rivalry, in the sense of two teams competing on the football field or two suitors competing for the same young lady. It is consciously interpersonal, and if one wins, the other loses. For the economist, however, a competitive market is one in which there are so many buyers and sellers that the market price and the total amount exchanged appear to be beyond the control of each individual, so that personal rivalry is completely lacking. To take an example, suppose two wheat farmers are located side by side and one's barn catches on fire. His neighbor may well help him put the fire out because he does not reason that the other farmer's loss may reduce the amount of wheat marketed, thereby increasing the price to his own advantage. It is when markets are not competitive, in the economist's sense of the term, that we find competition in the sociologist's sense. For example, if there are but two general stores in a small country town the proprietor of one cannot help but sense an economic advantage upon seeing the rival store go up in flame. But that is what economists call "duopoly" rather than "competition."

The competitive economy if left to itself does produce, however, a certain distribution of income, and some individuals will be wealthy and others will be poor. There are, of course, opportunities for government intervention designed to affect the distribution of income through a mechanism of taxes and subsidies or through other devices for interfering with the price system. Once government attempts to affect the distribution of income, we, of course, have political conflict over what that intervention should be. I have been satisfied simply to describe the nature of a competitive economy with whatever distribution

of income naturally follows in the absence of government intervention, and this in principle may be an economy with a good
deal of poverty and a great concentration of wealth. This
certainly poses social problems. What I wanted to stress is that
such an economy, while it may yield frustration and jealousy,
does not pit person against person in the marketplace because
each individual sees himself as struggling independently to do the
best he can with the prices at which he can sell his services and
resources and at which he can buy goods, and those prices appear
to be beyond the control of any other particular person. It is
conjectured by many that in a competitive economy with appropriate inheritance tax law and free education and vocational training, there would in fact be little in the way of either
extreme poverty or extreme wealth, but that is an empirical
question that is hard to resolve. The idea, however, is that
extreme inequality in the distribution of income, which may en-
gender a great deal of social discordance at the political level,
is largely a consequence of the departures of our actual economy
from the competitive model I have been discussing, and I should
now like to turn to that.

Apart from the interpersonal jealousies and class conflicts
that arise because of gross inequalities in the distribution of
income and which are to be contested in the political arena, a
major cause of interpersonal conflict in the economic sphere
arises from the departure of the actual economy from the competitive model as a result of the concentration of market power.
Let me consider first the case of monopoly. A monopoly occurs
when, for whatever reason, there is only one seller in a market
rather than an entire multitude. Under these circumstances the
seller will recognize that he may exert an important effect upon
the price of his product by deciding how much he is willing to
sell. Under these circumstances, he has an incentive to sell less
than he otherwise would in order to maintain a higher product
price. He will then be able to earn what is called a "monopoly
profit," and that profit will persist as long as he can retain his
monopoly—that is, prevent other entrepreneurs from entering
his market. Under these conditions, buyers can identify the

monopolist as a person who has direct, personal control over the terms of sale and private antagonisms toward the monopolist (or the monopoly firm) can thereby be engendered. So long as there is a large number of buyers, however, and the monopolist is not engaged in the tactics of personal price discrimination, by which I mean, charging different buyers different prices, no individual buyer feels himself singled out for exploitation, and all buyers may accept the situation docilely. Conditions are ripe, however, for class antagonism, in that all buyers can be angered by the concentration of economic power that enables the monopolist to exploit them as a group. This may lead to efforts on the part of buyers to organize to oppose the power of the monopolist, either through political or market means.

In the case of political opposition, buyers will call upon the government either to regulate the monopolist or to take the monopoly over and run it as a government enterprise. This is not easily achieved because when many are exploited, it is to the advantage of each to let the others do the organizing and bear the organizing cost. It is difficult to get a large number of people, each with a modest reason held in common with others, to organize for class warfare or political action, though this sometimes occurs and can be very significant. The difficulty, however, is so great that many economists have noted that when political action succeeds in establishing a government agency to regulate a monopoly, it is frequently the case that the agency becomes a tool for the enhancement of the very monopoly power it was designed to regulate. Thus the regulatory agency might concentrate its efforts on licensing entry and protecting the position of the monopolist from other market forces. In actual experience, this arises more commonly in a related case, that of oligopoly which is the case where, though there is not a single seller, there are only a few sellers. Oligopolists, if they act collusively, enjoy the advantages of a monopoly. In these circumstances, there is not only an identifiable class interest in opposing the few who share the concentration of economic power, but the oligopolists themselves are able to identify one another and intense interpersonal conflicts can arise among them. They are like the two general stores in the small town, each proprietor being able to see that it is the other proprietor who stands in the way of his having exclusive monopoly power. Agencies that regulate oligopolies find that the active contestants are the individual oligopolists rather than the mass of buyers, and to resolve economic conflict, the agencies are strongly tempted to introduce restrictive measures that prevent the oligopolists from tearing each other apart, for example, through price wars. Thus the role of a regulatory agency is often to help the oligopoly organize or to cartelize by determining price schedules, shares of market and indirectly the investments of the individual firms.

A multitude of buyers, facing a monopolist or a cartel, might also proceed, as a class effort, to oppose this concentration of power in the marketplace rather than in the legislature. This occurs if, for example, buyers organize an economic boycott or attempt to form a consumers' union. The relatively rare occurrence of this in our economy appears to result from the fact that there are so many buyers that the "let George do it" principle becomes operative. In the case of a boycott, each must abstain from transactions with the monopolist that are otherwise attractive, and each is more willing that others should do this than that he himself should make the sacrifice. Similarly, for the problems of organizing a buyers' union.

Analytically symmetrical to the case of monopoly is that called "monopsony," which is simply a buyer's monopoly. This arises when there is only one buyer and appears most commonly in markets for factors of production, for example, in a one factory town there is only one important buyer of labor services. Sellers then have incentives comparable to those of buyers in the case of monopolies, incentives to proceed both through political and market means to curtail the power of the monopsonist (or the oligopsonists if there is a small but plural number of buyers). Through the government, workers might strive for wage legislation or other legislation restricting the terms of purchase. Through market means they might engage in a sellers' boycott or in a sellers' union. In the case of the labor market, these are known as strikes and trade unions.

Though conflict of interest exists throughout the economy, organized economic conflict occurs primarily in the kinds of situations I have been describing, and when, either through exclusion or collusion, there results essentially a market with only one buyer and one seller called "bilateral monopoly" or with but a few buyers and few sellers, economic conflict becomes explicit and personalized. Each side of the market knows who the opponent is. Economic behavior, motivated by self-interest, then becomes strategic behavior, a process that the theory of games was intended to explain. The most intense industrial conflicts in our society have arisen in these circumstances, and government has commonly been called upon either to maintain the peace or to arbitrate the outcome. My main conclusion from the analysis so far is that discordance in the economic sphere, or economic conflict that is eyeball to eyeball, arises as a consequence of the concentration of economic power. We then no longer have competition in the sense of the economist but competition in the sense of the sociologist.

There are, of course, other areas in which the conflict of economic groups or classes arise. These battles are fought mainly in the political arena, however, because the government as an intervenor in the economy is seen to be capable of acting on behalf of private economic pressure groups. Thus special legislation is sought to provide special benefits for the poor or, commonly, to provide special advantages for the producers in a given industry. It seems as if the more government intervenes in economic affairs, the more further intervention is demanded. Government economic policy is, as a result, often fraught with contradictions. If income taxes are made more steeply progressive, then more loopholes are apt to be legislated. Though I will not elaborate on this, I should like to offer the suggestive remark that the economic repression of the black population in American society has not been the result of competitive market forces, but the result of legislatures and city councils that have suppressed open competition and equal access to economic opportunities.

There are two other topics of which I should like to make brief mention: One of these has to do with international economic behavior and, in particular, the notion that national economic aggression is a cause of war. Much currency has been given to some very simplistic views about how wars are started by munition makers or deliberately fomented by the imperialistic interests of industrial or commercial corporations. These views have scarcely ever stood the test of evidence. Indeed, if international economic relationships are pursued within the competitive framework of free trade and investment, international economic dependency is enhanced and there would be little more reason to suppose that nations would go to war for economic gain than that Indiana should go to war with Illinois. But once economic interests are seen as group interests and, in the extreme, as national interests, national economic power blocs become formed and economic rivalry exacerbates the problems of interstate relationships. Thus, colonies have wished to throw off the yoke of externally imposed restrictions upon their trade relations and internal economic policies; and nations, the yoke of reparations. It is *national* economic blocks, not individuals engaged in international trade and investment, that have come to demand *Lebensraum*. Such cravings have reached their height historically in nations committed to economic autarky characterized by extensive governmental restrictions on the flow of international commerce. Indeed, the laissez faire writings of Adam Smith constituted a rebuttal to the system of mercantilism which viewed it to be in the royal interest for the merchant marine to engage in international piracy and for the nation to capture entire commercial markets.

My final topic, one I wish to touch only casually, has to do with economic relationships within the family. Thus far, I have been referring to the participants in the economy as "individuals," whereas the more appropriate term would be "households." The market mechanism does not work—really does not exist—within the family structure, so that "eyeball-to-eyeball" conflict within the family can run rampant. Children can fight over who will take care of their elderly parents; parents in self-gratification can deny opportunities to their children; and specialization of husband and wife as bread earner and homemaker leaves no rationale for the terms on which marriages are dissolved through divorce. Economists have very much avoided this area of economic discordance, and perhaps we must leave it to social psychiatrists to deal with the economic relationships that prevail within the family unit because they are unstructured by markets.

Chapter 7

Poverty and Race as Vectors in Concordance

F. Theodore Reid, Jr.

"Slave, I have bought you."
"God knows you have."
"Now you belong to me."
"God knows I do."
"And you'll not run away?"
"God knows."

IN ILLINOIS, it seems appropriate to start almost any talk about almost any subject with a quote from Carl Sandburg. In my present role, focusing on issues of race and poverty and their impact on our efforts at concordance, the desire to quote him felt very appropriate. The quote above was an excerpt from his volume, aptly titled, *The People, Yes.* It continues:

"In the days of the far off Pharaohs
in the days of Nebuchadnezzar
the king who ate grass
and reconsidered many important decisions—
one of the masters straddling a slave [said]:
  "I think about you often
  and I would be willing
  to do many kind things
  almost anything for you."
    And the man under [replied]:
"Almost anything except get off my back."

I quote Sandburg here because I believe that with a poet's sensitivity, he has captured in those few lines, the essence of man's relationship to his fellowman through most of recorded history and beyond. He refers to the assent of the gagged, the compliance of the chained, the acceptance by the weak of the terms of the strong and always, always, the dream of the time to come when the roles would be reversed.

Beyond this, we have the word of anthropologists and linguists that in many languages, the word for "human being" or "man" is identical with the word for a member of the tribe or clan. Through the ages, man has shown some modicum of concern for his "own kind of people," but with the ethics of the rat pack, he has exploited and destroyed others.

We have always tended to view ourselves as central. We are the important ones—those who really count. Today, with our microscopic veneer of civilization and science, we are condescending towards the primitives who see themselves as the only "humans." We smile from our historic perspective at the battle of Copernicus to gain acceptance of the idea that the earth is not the center of the universe. Yet, if each of us imagines a world map, my guess is that the central continent in that familiar map is the continent containing his own country.

This urge to be central is strong, and one of its most malignant forms is ethnocentricity. Through the ages, we have made violent distinctions between "those I group with me that I call 'us' and all others who are 'them.' " We have grouped by tribe and clan, by geography, by our object and manner of worship, our status in life, by the color of skin, by language and by mode of government, to name but a few. As we met in this Colloquium to promote concordance, there was, and still is, blood being shed somewhere in the world about most of these differences, and of all these differences, race remains the most visible and biologically stable.

It is against this background that we came together to promote concordance. It is with these awarenesses that we, in particular, came together to focus on race and poverty, which I believe to be two of the most potent barriers to human concordance. Further to complicate our already heroic task, we must grapple with the fact that history has dictated that these two issues have a strong affinity. The poor and wretched of the earth are usually also black, yellow, brown or red.

I paused a long time here as I wrote this chapter, filled with a sense of impotence—feeling more than somewhat overwhelmed. It is some help that I see my charge in modest terms. I do not feel responsible for answering the currently unanswerable questions that I have implied. Still, there is the problem of providing you with some focus, some direction. However it is hard for the mapmaker to accurately chart unknown and unexplored territory such as that which we discuss in this Colloquium: I think that it is worth adding that it is hardest to be objective and to give perspective when one is intensely and personally involved.

For this reason, I would like to start with the issue of poverty. Poverty is most often described in economic terms. On the surface, this would appear to be a truism, but on closer observation, it seems to be a distortion or at least an oversimplification, since economic deprivation is only one of a complex series of parameters. There are at least eight major factors associated with poverty in this country: little education, the poverty environment, chronic unemployment, low income, poor physical and mental health, large families, broken families and life styles which are a product of impoverishment.

The works of a number of sociologists and psychologists seem to point strongly to the existence of a supranational poverty culture. For instance, the work of Smilansky, dealing with the children of non-European Jews in Israel reveals aspects of family life, child-parent relationships and attitudes toward people and things which are very similar to the Oscar Lewis' descriptions of Mexican families.

This is an idea of particular pertinence. There is great importance to us as mental health professionals in the concept that poverty, subsistence living and deprivation can, through time, result in a culture, family patterns, child-rearing patterns and a style of life which transcends nationality.

If we accept the fact that poverty has destructive impacts on personality—as well as the obvious and documented impact on bodies—where do we turn? It seems clear that for a start, we must begin with the data already in our possession. This evidence, explicit for the United States, Israel, Mexico and South America, seems reasonably generalizable to the Western World. I am not familiar with comparable studies of the nonphysical impact of poverty in Africa and Asia. However, the impact of malnutrition on the incidence of mental retardation and brain damage and poverty in general and its impact on physical and mental health is clearly established in American studies. It seems highly doubtful that Africans and Asians have genetic protection from the consequences of poverty. At the same time, it would help to define more clearly the impacts of poverty within specific cultures and between them. Such studies might suggest different strategies for intervention in different cultures and countries.

I hope that no one believes that I am suggesting that we wait patiently for the results of such studies. We must move—and move rapidly—in the area of intervention. This is an area about which we know little in social interactional terms and where we ignore or fail to implement what we do know. We have a sparse literature from Israel and a growing body in the United States from such ventures as the Head Start programs.

Head Start is a classic case of failure to follow through on research we have already done. The need for this program is unquestioned. Its effectiveness has been documented. Despite this, it does not encompass all the children it could benefit. Further, despite evidence that the gains of Head Start are lost in the inner city schools, there has been no effort on local, state or national levels to expand Head Start or improve ghetto schools. One must be impressed by priorities: the many-colored poor "thems" of American ghettos can wait—we must concern ourselves with the struggle for power and the distribution of wealth of some "thems" half a world away. These thoughts provide a pivot to turn more fully to the subject of race.

Before I proceed, though, I must share with you some of the dilemmas I face. Race, or more accurately, racism, which is pervasive in our culture, mocks our talk of concordance. It reduces us to the level of the blind leading the blind. As I try to help focus the discussion to come, I cannot be unaware that my attitudes have been shaped by my own black experience in white America. Further, I would be dull indeed not to recognize that it is at least in part because of that experience that I have been asked to keynote this session. I am aware that I would have resented it if this presentation were being made by one who had not lived his life on the wrong side of the racist experience, but at this moment, I am very aware of the highly individualized impact racism has.

I can speak to some extent for myself, but how can I begin to distill and abstract the experiences of my twenty odd million black American brothers? But it is even more staggering, I realized (as I am sure many did when they read the program), that this, the First International Colloquium of the American Society for Social Psychiatry addressed itself to the issues of concordance and discordance under a signal handicap. There was no one on the program who could speak directly to these issues from the viewpoint of the African or Asian experience, the post-colonial experience—what is termed, the "Third World experience." I suggested that they would speak in many voices to the twin issues of race and poverty as factors divisive in man's experience, but I cannot pretend to speak in their names.

Instead, all I can offer are some questions and thoughts that occur to me as a black colleague in an essentially white Western culture. It appears to me that all of our relationships between the races, whether past or present, are based to some degree on the philosophy embodied in the quote from Sandburg. The masters, in this case white, seem willing "to do many kind things, almost anything" for the black—except get off his back. A quick reading of the morning newspaper of any city is all that one need do to document this assertion. Whether one looks to the local news and explores the fate of public housing or the inner city school, to the national news and the fate of school desegregation monies, or to the international news, where one can read of British immigration laws or the napalming of Vietnamese civilians—the message is the same.

Some may say, with more than a grain of truth, that this is not necessarily racism. To be sure, there is the memory of Biafra, the news from Northern Ireland and the plight of the East Bengalese. Perhaps it would be better to use the more accurate label of ethnocentricity than the more limited one, racism.

From an intellectual and international viewpoint, I can acknowledge this but it is racism that remains the central fact of my life in America. It is involved to a greater or lesser extent in local, state, national and international policy. Racism has been labeled "the number one mental health problem in the United States," by the Joint Commission on Mental Health of Children. Having been thus labeled, it has been boxed and pigeon-holed. Court rulings and laws, grudgingly passed, may have made the ride slightly less comfortable, but the masters still ride the backs of the slaves.

Since the philosophy and psychology of slave-master relations evolves from mutual contact, the response is no surprise to anyone. The basic rule of the game has always been, "I'll ride you until you're strong enough to make me get off, and then, maybe you'll get to ride on my back." In essence, this appears to be the underlying principle for such dissimilar programs as "Buy Black," "Black Capitalism," "The Black Panther Party" and "The Deacons for Defense." It is implicit in the separatist stance of the Black Muslims and other black nationalist groups. More and more, it is part of the growing militancy of the more traditional civil rights groups such as the Southern Christian Leadership Conference, Operation Breadbasket and the Urban League. This is by no means a single or simple message. It is often not the major message. Most frequently, it is still contrapuntal to the basic demand that whites get off the backs of blacks and let them stand tall. However, some blacks are beginning to raise the possibility of an international racial alliance.

This raises a possibility that is truly frightening. If the only recourse of the slave is to rebel, then he will, sooner or later, rebel. In fact, there is a growing literature which asserts that the only way to freedom and manhood is through rebellion. Fanon insists that manhood cannot be conferred, it must be wrested from unwilling hands.

My fear is that the shrunken size of the world and the technology that we have evolved would not permit such an upheaval without catastrophic results. It would take a massive global war to reverse the current roles of the races, and the world has become too small and too vulnerable to withstand further global wars. History teaches that the pendulum swings, and no group can be held down forever. The downtrodden bide their time. If we face the lessons of history and the impossibility of surviving a violent solution to this problem, we are faced with the proposition that all men, of all colors, must bend their efforts to the search for a nonviolent, viable solution to a problem that has never known a nonviolent, viable solution. I might add parenthetically that in slave rebellions, the slaves have least to lose, and recent history reconfirms this message.

What hope can be offered for the bleak picture I have painted? A little, I trust. We must begin with the fact that our most important problems are hopelessly interrelated. Overpopulation is tied to poverty, which is tied to racism, which is tied to ethnocentricity, which is tied to foreign policy. Additionally, population is tied to poverty, which is tied to the use of natural resources, which is tied to ecology.

It becomes obvious that we cannot intelligently solve one of these problems without contributing to the solution of some of the others. Bluntly, we seem to have come to a point of complexity at which the organized attempts at survival by any group—short of genocide—must at the same time make some contribution to better survival for others. The urgent strivings made by nations, groups and blocs may yet lead down the path towards concordance.

It is always dangerous to analogize from the individual to the group and even more dangerous when the analogy is extended to races, nations and classes. Having warned myself, and you, I now proceed to do just that.

Harris, in his book, *I'm OK, You're OK,* cites what he considers to be the most basic "game," which is sufficiently pertinent to quote here:

> I believe all games have their origin in the simple childhood game, easily observed in any group of three-year-olds: "Mine is Better Than Yours." This game is played to bring a little momentary relief from the burden of the NOT OK. It is essential to keep in mind what the I'M NOT OK—YOU'RE OK position means to the three-year-old. I'M NOT OK means: I'm two feet tall, I'm helpless, I'm defenseless,

I'm dirty, nothing I do is right. I'm clumsy, and I have no words with which to try to make you understand how it feels. YOU'RE OK means: You are six feet tall, you are powerful, you are always right, you have all the answers, you are smart, you have life or death control over me, and you can hit me and hurt me and it's still OK.

Any relief from this unjust state of affairs is welcome to the child. A bigger dish of ice cream, pushing to get first in line, laughing at sister's mistakes, beating up little brother, kicking the cat, having more toys, all give momentary relief even though down the road is another disaster like a spanking, getting hit by little brother, being clawed by the cat, or finding someone who has more toys.

Grownups indulge in sophisticated variations of the "Mine Is Better" game. Some people achieve temporary relief by accumulating possessions, by living in a better house than the Joneses, or even reveling in their modesty: I am humbler than you are. These maneuvers . . . may provide a welcome relief even though down the road may be a disaster in the form of an oppressive mortgage, or consumptive bills. . . .

I quoted this extensively, because I hope that the similarity between the three-year-old and the ethnocentric is clear. Whether it is a king of France, saying, "Aprés moi, le déluge" or Americans in Vietnam "wasting the gooks," the Briton's condescension towards the former colonial, the subsidized farmer urging that others pull themselves up by their bootstraps the way he has done, or the more obvious situation of the red dirt farmer, allowing that he is poor but thanking God that at least he wasn't born a nigger, the thread runs through—Mine's Better.

We have identified the problem in individuals, and we are beginning to identify and label it in races and countries. We have attempted to treat this as an illness in individuals, and we are beginning to see this as a virus which affects the bulk of the world's population with an illness that threatens the survival of us all. Our enlightened self-interest dictates that we begin to find some treatment.

Chapter 8

Concordance, Discordance and Culture Change: A Psychosocial View

JOHN J. SCHWAB

DAILY, IN OUR CLINICAL work or scientific study, we share a common goal, the alleviation of human misery. At the same time, we are also assessing man's individual and collective condition. Such work is difficult, but it is neither as remote nor as complex as the task of promoting concordance in human affairs.

In certain respects, man's seeming inability to live peacefully contradicts natural law. Biologists, anthropologists and other scientists can demonstrate that cooperative organization, from the most primordial level, even the biochemical, to the later biosocial life of the higher primates, is as fundamental to survival as aggression, if not more so. Interorganismic cooperation is one of the significant facts of biology. Intraspecies aggression is subject to restraints under natural conditions and interspecies aggression involves a series of checks and balances. But the human animal, the biocultural organism, is an exception. Recorded history not only documents but also prophesies that suffering and war constitute man's lot. The chronicles of this century indicate that it may someday be called "The inglorious 100 years," the epoch of organized societal warfare, widespread destruction and despair.

At almost any level of analysis the flagrant discordance in human affairs, which we not only tolerate but are accepting as routine, can be understood only as group psychopathology, as mental illness. In seeking to explain World War I, Freud [1] had to postulate the existence of a death instinct, but 2,500 years before, during the course of the first known psychiatric consultation, Hippocrates agreed with his patient, Democritus, that the

139

world was mad and, therefore, that laughter and melancholy were appropriate individual reactions.[2]

It is difficult to regard our era as other than a decadent one. For the first time since the Enlightenment, pessimism, or at least lack of confidence, has replaced optimism. As individuals we feel powerless, constrained by circumstance, overwhelmed by events and bewildered by the rapidity of culture change. We are beginning to believe that collectively man's fate is subject to cultural determinism to as great an extent as his personal health is genetically predisposed. One hundred years ago, Emerson [3] feared that "Things are in the saddle, and ride mankind"; but today, man is being technologically propelled faster than the speed of thought.

Taking a gloomy view of one's historical epoch, of course, is common throughout history. Countless observers have decried the corruption and moral decay of their times. There have been certain epochs in which opinions of the social commentators of the day were corroborated by later historians. A brief look at two such epochs indicates that they were transitional periods in history when there was no prevailing ethic.

In the post-Hellenic era, 100 to 200 B.C., the Mediterranean world was in a stricken and abject condition, pervaded by poverty, social unrest and despair. As Bertrand Russell [4] has said, the philosophies of that day (Stoicism, Epicureanism, Skepticism and Cynicism) were weary ethics for a weary age. At best, they were guidelines for daily living in a world devoid of hope and lacking spiritual unity. Psychosocially, we know that melancholia and suicide were prevalent.

We can only surmise why that epoch passed. Perhaps the Christian Ethic, proclaiming love, forgiveness and the brotherhood of man, gave hope to the oppressed and vitality to the stale. As Brett [5] has mentioned, all existing philosophies must have appeared pallid and thin compared to Paul's doctrine of salvation. Also, perhaps, the supremacy of Rome, with its partial restoration of order and some tolerance for a pluralistic society, increased material well-being and stabilized social conditions.

The second was the transition from the Medieval to the Modern

Age. In that masterful book, *The Waning of the Middle Ages,* Huizinga [6] described "the violent tenor of everyday life" in Western Europe in the fifteenth and sixteenth centuries. The incessant wars of nationalism were surpassed in ferocity only by the ravages of the religious wars of that time which almost equalled the destruction wrought by Attila one thousand years before. The social order, fashioned by feudalism, was foundering. The Christian Ethic was first buffeted by humanism and later fragmented by the Reformation. Mechanisms for maintaining social control were weak and inadequate. Psychosocially, in the fifteenth and sixteenth centuries, both church and state sanctioned demonology, persecuted deviants and tortured and exterminated nonconformists and heretics. Florid psychoses existed and epidemics of hysteria swept entire provinces. Melancholia was so common in the British Isles that it became known as the "English sickness" or the "Elizabethan Malady." [7] Hamlet, expressing the spirit of the age, said that he had "lost his mirth."

Again, we can only surmise why that era passed, but we should note that, again, a new spirit of the age emerged. The Protestant Ethic glorified work, particularly individual effort for the sake of tangible gain, and espoused sentiments associated with capitalism, nationalism and social order. Moreover, with developing Newtonian science, increasing knowledge went hand-in-hand with invention, geographic expansion and growing prosperity.

In the eighteenth century, the Enlightenment proclaimed the triumph of rational man and belief in progress. Only one hundred years ago, it was thought that the twentieth century would be the most wonderful in history. Instead, we are in a crisis, beyond the threshold of decadence foreseen by Nietzsche [8] and Burckhardt [9] and described by Ortega.[10] We can hope that ours is a transitional epoch. The frequency of identity crises, role conflicts, aggressive behavior and sociopolitical turbulence around us can reach such extremes only at a juncture in history, when an era is drawing to a close, when its forms are outworn, its ethic obsolete, its creeds rejected. Psychosocially, it appears that the affective responses, the most basic human reactions, are those of distress, pessimism and apathy.

The social history of our era bears witness to much human failure. We know that we are living in an age of violence and conflict, but we do not know why, how the rational became the absurd. I do not believe that we can castigate that traditional scapegoat, man's emotions, his passions. Instead, I think we should indict man's rationality, the rationality which has created missles with multiple warheads and the so-called conventional bombs—dropped from an altitude of 20,000 feet so that the bombardier sees only a little blast and smoke, not blood and flesh.

I would like to suggest that Spinoza's thesis is not relevant; our human bondage has little to do with the power of the passions.[11] We should recall that for almost two thousand years, from Lucretius [12] to Rousseau,[13] it has been thought by some that our passions are indispensable to our social existence. They believed that long ago primitive men, huddling in caves for protection, found a sense of pity for one another, extended sympathy and even discovered that indefinable emotion—love. Rather than scapegoating man's emotions, perhaps we should consider that we are enchained because of a cultural thought disorder and that the profound discordance of our times is evidence of an illness. This illness, characterized by conspiracy and atrocity, resembles a horrible paranoia in which man is enslaved as a captive of his misused intellectual faculties.

Modern man, in the overdeveloped, developing and underdeveloped nations, is afflicted by culture shock, his fate inextricably linked to the sweep of our intellectual creations, our technoculture. We fear that we are becoming Ernst Junger's [14] new man, "depersonalized and standardized, without heart, soul, or brain . . . [a human robot who is] mechanically employed in a series of civil or imperialist wars on which we have already embarked and which will dominate the coming centuries."

The external conditions of modern man, according to Alex Inkeles,[15] may be described by such key terms as "urbanization," "education," "mass communication," "industrialization" and "politicization." These terms, in reality, appear to be social scientific euphemisms for crowding, overpopulation, pollution and the increasing power of self-interest groups whose political antipathy toward others leads to civil strife. Such conditions are associated with social disorganization, discordance and aggression. Mass communication has been held responsible for the contagion of violence. Our entire educational system has been branded as irrelevant by the young who fear that they will not even have an opportunity for a meaningful existence unless these external conditions are drastically changed.

Modern man's internal (personal) condition can be described in terms of concern, distress, disaffection and disillusionment. As Ignazio Silone [16] has said, "Any portrait of modern man, if it is at all faithful to the original, cannot but be deformed, split, fragmentary—in a word, tragic."

This has come to pass perhaps because rationalism has triumphed at the expense of the passions and the sentiments. The premises of rationalism, I submit, are as uncertain as those of history and science, certainly in view of the nihilism of modernity, the decadence inspired by faith in rationality and the consequent identification, in Nietzsche's [8] terms, of goodness, justice and truth with self-interest. This nihilism, I believe, is as much a disease of the brain as it is an affliction of the spirit. There is too much emotional distance, as well as social distance, between us.

If I sound overly pessimistic, it is because I believe that we must look beyond the facades and beneath the glazes; false optimism, self-deception and the failure to recognize the decadence of our age can lead only to greater spiritual malaise. A clear view of our condition shows that we are dominated by fear, caught up in conspiracies, living with surveillance, building more elaborate warning systems and even impelled to attack first, before the enemy destroys us. These are manifest symptoms of paranoia. As is generally observed in clinical paranoia, there is some element of truth at the center of the delusional system. The memories and the scars of Hitler's Germany have conditioned us so that we perpetrate atrocities in the belief that we are pre-

venting war and preserving peace; indeed, although Hilter's
Third Reich did not last the thousand years he predicted, in a
sense it has certainly dominated the history of the middle third
of this century.

In the nineteenth century, Burckhardt, Nietzsche and Durk-
heim feared that the accelerated social change, with the
disappearance of basic institutions and the progressive homog-
enization of society, would leave the individual deprived, rootless and at the mercy of autonomous sociocultural influences
and the state. As early as 1930, Ortega [10] declared that the
greatest present danger is the state. We should recall Randolph
Bourne's [17] plaintive 1917 protest; "War is the health of the
state"; and we should courageously remember Simone Weil's [18]
observation, "Justice is the fugitive from the winning camp."

It appears that much of our decadence can be attributed to
the rapidity of culture change, the fruits of rationality. Twenty-
five years ago, Margaret Mead [19] described some of the implications of rapid culture change for personality development. These
involve discontinuities: conflicts pertaining to race, interests,
the generations, man and the natural environment, man and
his robotizing technoculture, and man and his fellowman.

With rapid culture change, man's emotional faculties are left
diminished, numbed or outraged. Boundaries essential for identity and dignity become blurred. With rapid culture change we
can no longer grow as humane communities because there is little
or no opportunity for either the "prefiguring of experience or
the reinforcement or consolidation of past experiences." Consequently, our emotions are impaired and our behavioral sequences lack coherence. Perceptually, we become disoriented;
cognitively, we make errors in syntax and reasoning, with paranoia resulting; affectively, we react with fear or despondency; and
conatively, we are fragmented and tentative. Behaviorally, we
take the paths of rebellion, retreat or resignation—torn between such alternatives as meaningless conformity or radical
protest.

In the past the emergence of a new ethic was associated with
the ending of a decadent era. Perhaps a new ethic is being

generated by the young as they protest, worldwide against the follies of their elders and this age. Certainly, the time has come to esteem our passions and extend our emotions. Camus [20] has said that compassion is the only remedy for despair, for our modern condition. Greater compassion can lessen the emotional distance as well as the social distance between us. After all, the therapy of paranoia calls for recognition, appreciation and expression of the emotions, as well as the lowering of anxiety and the reduction of stress; delusions seldom succumb just to rational discourse or intellectual proofs.

In addition, we need to look fearlessly at our present conditions, examine our beliefs and scrutinize our value systems so that we can find a cultural reality, an orientation which will cure the paranoia of our time. To do that, we need to make what Silone [16] has called "a declaration of trust." It can be founded on "the certainty that we human beings are free and responsible; that we feel the need of reaching out to touch the inmost reality of our fellow-men; and that spiritual communion is possible. [From this] love of the oppressed is born as a corollary that the disillusionments of history can never place in doubt. As long as there remains a determination to understand and to share one's understanding with others, perhaps we need not altogether despair."

Such a declaration of trust can serve as a start to promote concordance, but to make such a declaration, we need to look into our hearts. We can think of concordance, the theme of this colloquium, as agreement and harmony, "concurrence in feeling and opinion." We can also think of concordance in its original meaning—"with one heart, one mind."

Finally, I would like to close with a few lines from Schiller's [21] great lyric poem, "The Song of the Bell." The poem portrays Schiller's broadening interest in humanity, from the development of the individual through successive stages of his growth as a member of a family, a local community and ultimately all of humankind. In a small village a bell is cast; the fires needed to melt the bronze threatened the entire town, but the bell is successfully completed. As the bell is suspended on high, Schiller says the following:

> . . . Name the bell with joy profound!
> Concordia is the word we've found
>
> . . . .
>
> Joy to all within its bound!
> Peace, its first, its latest sound!

REFERENCES

1. Freud, Sigmund: Thoughts for the times on war and death (1915). In *The Complete Works of Sigmund Freud*, edited by J. Strachey, A. Freud, A. Strachey, and A. Tyson. Vol. XIV. Toronto, Hogarth Press Ltd., 1957.

2. Freud, Sigmund: Beyond the pleasure principle (1920–22). In *The Complete Works of Sigmund Freud*, edited by J. Strachey, A. Freud, A. Strachey, and A. Tyson. Vol. XVIII. Toronto, Hogarth Press Ltd., 1955.

3. Emerson, Ralph W.: Compensation. In *Complete Essays and Other Writings*. New York, Modern Library, 1955.

4. Russell, Bertrand: *A History of Western Philosophy*. New York, Simon & Schuster, 1945.

5. Brett, George S.: *Brett's History of Psychology*, edited by R. S. Peters. Cambridge, Mass., The M.I.T. Press, 1965.

6. Huizinga, Juan: *The Waning of the Middle Ages*. New York, Doubleday Anchor Books, 1954.

7. Babb, Lawrence: *The Elizabethan Malady: A Study of Melancholia in English Literature From 1580–1642*. East Lansing, Michigan State University Press, 1951.

8. Morgan, George A.: *What Nietzsche Means*. New York, Harper & Row, 1941.

9. Burckhardt, Jacob: *Force and Freedom: Reflections on History*. New York, Pantheon Books, 1964.

10. Ortega y Gassett, Juan: *The Revolt of the Masses*. New York, W. W. Norton and Co., 1932.

11. Spinoza, Benedict: *The Ethics*. New York, Tudo Publishing Co., 1936.

12. Lucretius: In *Of the Nature of Things*, edited by William E. Leonard. New York, E. P. Dutton & Co., Inc., 1965.

13. Rousseau, J. J.: *Discourse Upon the Origin and Foundation of the Inequality Among Mankind*. New York, Burt Franklin Publishers, 1942.

14. Junger, Ernst: Quoted in The choice of comrades, by Ignazio Silone. In *This is My Philosophy*, edited by W. Burnett. New York, Harper & Brothers, 1957.

15. Inkeles, A.: The modernization of man. In *Modernization: The Dynamics of Growth*, edited by Myron Weiner. New York, Basic Books, Inc., 1965.

16. Silone, I.: The choice of comrades. In *This is My Philosophy*, edited by W. Burnett. New York, Harper & Brothers, 1957.

17. Bourne, Randolph: Quoted in *U.S.A.*, by John Dos Passos. New York, The Modern Library, 1930.

18. Weil, Simone: Quoted in The choice of comrades, by Ignazio Silone. In *This is My Philosophy*, edited by W. Burnett, New York, Harper & Brothers, 1957.

19. Mead, Margaret: *Some Implications of Culture Change for Personality Development in Personal Character and Cultural Milieu*, edited by D. G. Haring. New York, Syracuse University Press, 1956.

20. Camus, Albert: *L'Estranger*. New York, Pantheon Books, 1963.

21. Schiller, Friedrick: The song of the bell. In *An Anthology for Our Time*, edited by Frederick Ungar. New York, Frederick Ungar Publishing Company, 1969.

Chapter 9

Dehumanization and the Legitimation of Violence

Comrade Machine Gun has the floor.
VLADIMIR MAYAKOVSKI

PAUL L. ADAMS

SPURNING IDEOLOGY, and in some instances spurning thought, our era in history is called the age of analysis, but it appears to be ending up as the age of killing. Whether in cold blood or in the heat of passion, we murder. My interest is in the legitimation of murder, to which many metatheories of child development have made their contribution. Eloquent legitimations of murder are in print. Jean Paul Sartre [39] has made the validation or legitimation of violence his major vocation:

> For me, the essential problem is to reject the theory according to which the Left ought not to answer violence with violence.

Violence in all forms is of higher incidence and of greater prevalence. The twentieth century has been depicted by Pitirim A. Sorokin [46] as

> . . . the most murderous and bloodiest century out of all the preceding twenty-five centuries of Greco-Roman and Western history— measured by the absolute and proportionate number (per 1,000,000 of respective populations) killed in wars, revolutions, riots, and individual crimes of this century.

In the year 1968, in the United States of America there were one-half million victims of homicide, rape and assault. Add that to the homicide abroad and we have a picture of frequent murder. Concomitantly, studies of violence are reported more frequently by a diverse array of scholars, from single and multiple disciplines. This chapter, while not achieving finality in its results, will undertake to include in its scope many of the empirically based studies from varied, discrete disciplines such as sociology, ethology, political science, psychodynamics, history or cultural anthropology. From this survey and interpretation no decisive closure or

148

confirming proof will emerge. Instead, there will be some logico-empirical analysis intermingled with some cognizance of the "truth of commitments" [24] or some effort to use both objective analysis and engaged style.[1] Could it be possible that militancy among reasonable men will ever reappear? Camus [9] said, "One can refuse to be a fanatic and still continue to be a militant in politics." One can live both by the truth of propositions and the truth of commitments. In North America we should add that one even can be militant *without being mindless* and without denying the truth of propositions.

THE SPECTRUM OF VIOLENCE

We must understand and control in our era the phenomena of assassination, rioting, genocide and warfare, for these are the forms of politicalized murder that give a special cast and flavor to contemporary life. The fisticuffs of television dramas, the war play of children and the angry speech of an irate husband need not detain us too long. To pause with these lesser forms of violence and to make them our focal points would only permit us safer and hence more cowardly consideration and would entrap us in the morality that proscribes card-playing while it supports human slavery.

It is not given that all violence is of a piece, and we can properly ask, Is all anger, all aggression and all murder arranged along a continuum? Pacifism has joined with psychoanalysis when it has habitually lumped all of these forms together, so that civil war and foreign war are fully equal as repugnant facts:

> . . . an important element in our response must be our assertion of the indivisibility of violence. War has been called "an international riot," pointing out that international violence is an offense against "law and order" as surely as a civil disorder in our cities.[10]

George Fox, the early Quaker, referred to the light and the spirit that lives *in the individual* and "that taketh away the occasion of all war." This view has the logical shortcoming of reducing *the war institution* to personal sentiments; in a later age it was to be a view that would be rebuked as "psychologism." Should priority be given to personal ethics or to impersonal social structures? The psychologist, Kenneth Keniston,[28] shows

how psychologism works when he sees inner-life anger as part
and parcel of the outer-life institutionalization of murder:

> Continual confrontation with the fact and possibility of violence in
> the world has activated and become joined with universal human
> potential for aggression, anger, and rage: the psychological and his-
> torical possibilities of violence have come to strengthen each other.

Keniston is of the opinion that the issue involved in the interdependent types of violence can be viewed "as central to our
time": the Sartrean diagnosis but not the Sartrean treatment
plan. Mohandas K. Gandhi, the apostle of *satyagraha* or nonviolent revolution, saw the same continuum between the fear
(equated with hatred by Gandhi) of snakes and the hatred of his
British overlords whom he desired to fight nonviolently and without hatred. For Gandhi and for most of the religious "pacifists"
who have opposed war and societal violence, there has been
operative a single moral imperative: *Love, do not kill.* Hatred
within the person was equated with the warlike postures of
nations and large groups of people. In the United States such
thinking, without any citation of its grounding in logic or ethics,
has been made the basis for draft boards, as well as certain
pacifists, to determine sincerity among claimants to exemption
as conscientious objectors by asking, "Do you hunt and fish? What
would you do if you found your grandmother being raped by
a Japanese/German/Russian/Korean/North Vietnamese?" The
conclusion is that a "sincere" war objector must be devoid of
hatred or violence in all of its forms against things and persons;
and the effect of such administrative procedure is, of course, to
diminish the number of war objectors who are exempted.

We shall survey the many kinds of violence before deciding
that it is extragroup (intergroup) political murder which makes
the unique case for our age. Human murder and violence can
be categorized with utility in several different ways, according to
its object (whether thing or person or group) ; its legitimacy or
proscription by the state; its impersonality; its openness or covert-
ness; and its phylogenesis or ontogenesis (Table 1).

Violence Against Things

It is not possible to destroy or kill anything except a thing.

Table 1

CLASSIFICATIONS OF VIOLENCE

1. According to the recipient of the violence—whether thing, animal or person
   A. Against Inanimate Objects
      1. One's own property—e.g. pacifist draft card destruction, hypomanic wastefulness, destructiveness when running *amok*, etc.
      2. Another's property—e.g. sabotage, pillage, looting, vandalism, riot
   B. Against Animals and Children
      1. Nonhuman animals—wild and domestic, especially pets
      2. Human animals regarded as lacking full humanity—slaves under slavery, wives under patriarchate, children under certain cultural circumstances
   C. Against Fully Human Persons
      1. Intragroup attack
         a. Self-aimed
         b. Interindividual
      2. Extragroup attack
         a. Small group—including packs and bands
         b. Large groups—urban insurrectionists, large-scale *guerrilleros*, National Guard, armed forces
2. According to the legitimacy of the violence: if legitimate it is state-sanctioned and enacted by police and armed forces; if illegitimate it is state-proscribed
3. According to whether it is personal and hateful *or instead* impersonal, strategic, hateless and with little passion of commitment
4. According to whether it is latent (covert, potential—such as the balance of terror seen in Cold War) *or* it is overt, active, manifest
5. According to whether it is ontogenetically given and learned *or rather* is phylogenetically programmed

One cannot kill a human being, a brother, but must make a delusional transformation from self to machine, from human person to thing, in order to kill it. Murder is the end of dialogue and the end of humanity; it is an action that makes him who is not a thing into nothing but a thing. An inanimate thing, an It, no longer Thou. It was the situation retold by Martin Buber [6]—When Cain had slain Abel his brother and converted his brother into inanimate material: Cain had been indecisive, says Buber, and the "intensification and confirmation of indecision is decision to evil." What was the punishment that this murder warranted? To be a fugitive and a rootless vagabond on earth, indecisive and unsettled . . . and murderous, alienated, out of the life of dialogue.

Is violence against things as things of profound ethical concern? Indeed it is. In the United States and in other western areas property is often valued more highly than life, and looting in a North American city is railed against with a greater fervor than warfare in Southeastern Asia. A black arsonist symbolically destroys "whitey" in the latter's most cherished zone.[34] Also, in the United States the Government drafts young men and sends them off to be murderers or risk being murdered, but the Government does not intrude with equal forcefulness onto private (corporate) property. In fact, even in *declared* international wars there has not been strong support for nationalization of war-profiting industrial enterprises. People are nationalized, not property. That result gives evidence of what governments hold as most sacred—the private ownership of great wealth.

To place strong emphasis on violence against things, against one's own property or against another's property would serve only to deflect our major focus from the needed gaze upon *political murder of human beings*.

Violence Against Animals and Children

Roughness and murder itself have been the lot of both animals and persons regarded as not quite human. Cases in point have been slaves, women, colonials, blacks and children—as they have been perceived by masters, males, colonialists, whites and adults. It is paradoxical that our age which has, in its primitivist yearnings, created the cult of childhood [3] has also experimented upon and murdered thousands of European children [56] and has sustained the deprivation and repression of millions more. There are counter-trends operating against the subjugation of women, of blacks and of "people in emerging nations;" yet much legitimate violence still is done against people in these categories. The major legitimation is to refer it back upon a god if pious, upon scientism if of that faith, upon the state, upon nature. The most convincing or "clinching" rationalization in our time is to justify it as needed by the nation state.

One of the most sensitive indices of a group's respect (or concern or caring) for its own members (not with the members seen as citizens with duties paramount but with group members loved and cared for as claimants on *rights*) is the manner in which that group treats its domestic animals.[36] Household pets in particular lead the way in receiving humanitarian care, as was obvious in both Britian and the United States where children came to receive legal protection under cover of laws that protected animals against cruelty.[27] We know certainly that violent persons are developed and patterned in ways that give a positive value to violence—by parental beatings, by neglect on the part of adults (a class-bound phenomenon, by the way) and by parental inducements to rage and violence. Children who are abused and neglected in a class society which is racist, militarist and nihilistic grow up to become hollow men and ruthless killers.

To generalize hastily on child development that is geared for concordance (or nonviolence), these are the things that must be enabled for the growing child:

Objective

1. *True competence* becoming established progressively, with validation by adults and compeers. He gets better at doing many more things, and everybody knows he is getting more competent!

2. *Stable residence* (secure custody) with adults who provide security, protection and parenting, and toward whom the child can be oriented with trusting love.

Semiobjective

3. *Developing viable values* or conscience in a milieu where nihilism and absurdity are minimal, where the world has meaning and the child develops a moral sense.

4. *Unfolding of loving relations* ranging from mother to broader kinship to same-sex friends to heterosexual mates and, in adulthood, to offspring to all children and all mankind.

Subjective

5. *Positive self-esteem*, associated with enjoyment of bodily pleasure or id-resources.

6. *Sense of some unsocialized uniqueness* of one's "self beyond roles," creativity, autonomy, spontaneity, unprogrammed ecstasy—as seen in a child's free play.

Of course, our society does not promote the dimensions of

healthy childhood; for it breeds alienation, inferiority feelings and true incompetency—all according to economic class. Our society breeds and nourishes killers—both directly and through neglect.

Withal, one need not be sidetracked by the violence against animals deemed less than human beyond observing that it is an index of the debasement and dehumanization of human beings. Saint Francis and his brother Wolf, or Gandhi, insistent on vegetarianism, and Schweitzer, enunciating reverence for life, could be said to have been morally sidetracked by those pre-occupations. The preoccupation that bathes its holder in counsels of perfection can lead its holder to inactivity in the much more crucial ethical arena, the arena of political murder. Martin Luther King, Jr., a saintly man, is emblematic of one who kept the emphasis on major moral concerns, on war and group violence, and on the terror that is imposed by established groups upon those whom they subjugate. Gandhi and King were assassinated not for all of their personal piety *but for all of their larger views on political man.* Our society gives us the reminder that even he who *does not live by the sword* may quite likely die by the sword.

Violence Against Fully Human Persons

Since Gunnar Myrdal [35] characterized it so well, a situation that existed to some degree even when whites owned black slaves has been repeatedly described in the literature of social science and moral philosophy—namely, the intragroup violence of blacks that receives approbation by ruling whites. The number of black people who commit suicide is great and the number who commit assault and homicide on blacks is enormous; but whites are not upset about "what nigger does against nigger." [23]

From the perspective of social ethics, murder is murder but some murder is more heinous and unjustifiable than other murder and violence. No abiding ethical system condones intrafamilial violence of the enraged and killing variety. Only going as far as to arrive at familial morality and a familistic ethics has been the farthest extent to which many ethical conceptions can travel.

It is rarer for moral codes to reach out and "humanize" all people and to interdict violence against all people, thereby enlarging the moral scope to a societal or a species-wide range. Moral codes of all sorts interdict suicide and the murder of one's clan-member or neighbor: Thou shalt not kill. It was this area of familistic concern that preoccupied Freud. The contribution of psychoanalysis to our understanding of violence has been made in the less inclusive area of suicide and interpersonal violence and merits some consideration at this point.

Psychodynamic Insights

Psychoanalysis and psychodynamics generally are individually oriented or family centered—that is, concerned with face-to-face interpersonal relations. In the entire developmental theory the family is crucial to psychoanalysis. Many efforts to extend psychodynamic insights into group behavior have encountered failure, inasmuch as a mechanistic and deterministic theory—even if we could concede its propriety for individual study and interpretation or for study of interindividual relations at best—cannot be expanded "upward" to groups, to large and complex groups above all. Freud [18] felt constrained to expand upward substantively by constricting downward methodologically: he invoked a physicochemical-like mechanistic metaphysic about a drive to death. In this respect, Freud was not of the nineteenth century with its idolatry of biology; he was instead of the eighteenth or twentieth centuries when the mode was to ape physics. So it was not with psychology or biology that Freud moved into sociology; he invaded sociology through retreating "downward" to physics. In his letter to Einstein in 1932, Freud repeated, giving an apology that does not sparkle with sincerity, that aggression is but a reflection of self-destructive longings and that whatever is not libido is then mortido, and the "death instinct" is not an imperative to commit active, destructive murder. It is, instead, far from empedoclean strife, a running down to passivity. What Einsteinian physics really made of this would be good to know!

It was Alfred Adler who first posited an aggressive drive. Adler recanted, but many Freudians have clung to aggression as an instinct, or drive, directed to the self and projected onto others. Some have seen frustration-rage-aggression and violence as the explanatory means. By this view, all violence is of one piece with anger, and anger is innate. This was a view of the world that found a mixed reception among Freud's own followers, but its persistence has been manifested in the work of many neo-Freudians, especially of Erich Fromm. *The Heart of Man: Its Genius for Good and Evil* [20] continued less his earliest interest in "social character" but more his concern for "ethical orientations." The latter-day Fromm has reduced his former rich panoply of Theophrastan character types to only two literary figures: lovers and haters—or lovers of good and lovers of evil, or lovers of life and lovers of death.* The latter in all three of the foregoing pairings by Fromm *are not established in nature* (as Mani of old and Freud of recency postulated), for Fromm regards man's proclivity to violence as not phylogenetically given but rather as a secondarily elaborated *perversion*. Psychodynamic theories are divided between those which regard violence as *inborn* and those which see violence as *learned*.

In short, the psychoanalysts have tended to give a very human face to violence, stressing its innateness, its seriousness and its ubiquity in interpersonal dealings. However, as Karen Horney [26] declared, Freud and the neo-Freudians disagree sharply on whether we kill in order to live or rather live in order to kill. As an explanatory set of concepts and tools, psychodynamics has decided limitations when it is brought to bear on social systems. It works in the personal sphere where conventional ethics reigns and the person is enjoined, *Heal thyself*. It is not as useful in the societal sphere where utopics reigns and the society is enjoined, *Serve the people*.

It is not wholly a problem that psychodynamics treats of a too closed system; for the major shortcoming is its inapplicability (in ways that applications have been attempted to date) to

---

* Fromm described briefly several forms of violence (psychologically perceived) other than the complex of necrophilia-sadism-incest—namely, playful violence, reactive violence, revengeful violence, violence due to the shattering of faith, compensatory violence and archaic blood thirst. Most of the categories or ideal types were added following his initial essay entitled *War Within Man*.[19]

complex social systems. To biologize or "physicize" both individual and society is not to apply psychodynamics to society.[33] Frantz Fanon,[13-16] although a psychiatrist, virtually abandoned psychodynamic theory in his analytical work on violence and racism; putting in its place, by and large, a social science perspective. A similar course was taken by Comer and by Carstairs, both psychiatrists, in their appraisals of violence.[22] It may be that psychodynamic theories cannot aid social psychiatry in any important ways.

It is inescapable that psychodynamic thought has had its best reception in the study of intrapsychic and interpersonal relations, in the terminology of our classification and in the study of intragroup violence. The biographic study of persons who killed or were killed* is still historiography with an individual and interpersonal scrutiny, when it is carried out by psychodynamicists.[17,51,53] Polemology could be enriched by studies of interpersonal violence. I think particularly useful would be a study using individual life histories of randomly chosen killers from the two groups: (a) those including many who attended this gathering—whose murders are or have been officially sanctioned, those who *conform* in killing (police and military killers) and (b) those whose murder is labeled criminal, those who *deviate* in killing. A comparison of their rage, their murder-lust, their homosexual fears, their cowardice and so on could be a highly instructive study of groups of individuals.

The conspicuous moral concern of our age is with political murder, with murder carried out not by estranged and anomic Cains but by those who, whether haves or have-nots, being involved in political struggle, set about methodically to assassinate and to engage in armed battle. The legitimation of this political murder will be discussed later on in this chapter. For the present, we can condense argumentation and the assertion can be offered that political violence is *extragroup* in its direction, *illegitinate* when the guerrilla fighters have not yet triumphed, *per-*

---

* Martin Luther (Erikson), Woodrow Wilson (Freud and Bullitt), and Mohandas Gandhi (Erikson) have all been studied by this technique that Erikson (1966) called "psychohistory."

sonal and cataclysmic *(patria o muerte!)* ; it is *active,* and it is *learned* or acquired.

Ethologic Insights

In hurriedly skipping over psychodynamics we made mention of the penchant of Freud to "biologize" on many topics, although his "death instinct" was not indicative of his biologizing as much as it showed his resort to metachemistry and metaphysics as Freud understood them. More needs to be said, however, of the biologizing of war and of human aggression by J. P. Scott [42] and Konrad Lorenz [32] and also by Robert Ardrey [2] and others with more meager biological credentials. Some broader and opposing views by biologists such as Tinbergen,[50] Klopfer [29] and Holloway [25] will also warrant some consideration if we are striving for an overarching view of violence, especially that of war, genocide and political armed struggle.

One point that can be made at once and rather simply is that Freud's equation of destructiveness and "death wish" has been rejected by biologists.[5] Secondly, biologists do not mean "drive" when they speak of "instinct" and therein lies some very basic disagreement with Freud—or more accurately, with Freud's translators who turned *Triebe* not into *drives* but *instincts.* "Instincts" for biologists are unlearned activities, phylogenetically programmed into organisms and subject to inborn and experiential releasers and inhibitors.[31] Programming of behavior, according to Lorenz, occurs not merely species-wide (instincts) in conjunction with biologic evolution *but also with specificity to the individual* based upon his individual coping in his milieu. With the concept of programming, Lorenz cuts through many of the squabbles over nurture and nature, and innate and acquired, that have plagued both biologists and psychologists, when wearing their hats both as hard scientists and as speculative philosophers.

Ethologists—behavioral biologists, *not* the scientists of human nature proposed by John Stuart Mill in 1843—begin with nonhuman animals as the population studied for killing and aggression but all too often they end up hopping across lines between animal species. Speculation that betrays their value biases, often conservative ones at that, passes off for data on *human* violence.[50] The most careful laboratory scientists sometimes abandon reasonableness when they come to consider human issues such as war and violence. Nonetheless, popularizers persist in taking on authority the assertions of ethologists regarding human violence. This leaves untouched the possibility that their human-fixated values will from the onset of their work corrupt their observations and their data. It is possible, from the author's personal impressions, that ethologists who study nonhuman animals are prodded and continually influenced by their own values as anthropomorphic anthropoids. Aggressors, by this token, could "find" inborn aggression rampant, while pacifists would be more inclined to a more pacific set of "findings."

In a brief summary, what observers of territorial birds and monkeys and other nonhuman species proclaim about human violence would include a diverse set of assertions:

1. Aggression is programmed into *human* behavior phylo-genetically (this is contradicted by Klopfer [29]), and it is an endowment biologically given to every member of the species.

2. Aggression is programmed into human individuals at birth in a complex matrix of unlearned individual differences such as temperament, physique, intelligence and gender. (This asser-tion also has been contested.)

3. Aggression is learned, culturally given, acquired, condi-tioned, reactive, etcetera. (All agree to this as being either partially or entirely explanatory of human violence. Some would insist, however, that culture itself is also *biologic* in a very basic sense.)

4. Curbs on some forms of human aggression are provided ontogenetically and perhaps phylogenetically. (Again, general agreement exists here among biologists and anthropologists, especially on considering *individual* behavior.)

Until biologists have gone further in applying the ethologic *approach* to mankind and have stopped their transfer of ethologic *data* from other animals to human animals, and until they take the trouble to do what social scientists do by way of making their own values explicit, we will be forced to accept the view of the ethologist, Peter H. Klopfer who, having considered the intricate evidence, felt he should "suggest that more serious consideration be given to the view that aggression is a cultural artifact." That is a tenable and promising hypothesis for violence in all its forms; it seems eminently suitable for war and political murder. To the heart of the matter, political killing, assuredly a cultural artifact, we now turn.

FURTHER LEGITIMATIONS OF VIOLENCE
Anarchist Insights

The fact that power struggle is at the inner center of politics was the basis of a well-known Trotskyist dictum; that politics merges along a continuum into warfare was understood in a famous maxim of von Clausewitz. The military mind has repeatedly underscored the point that violence and politics are all of a piece. However, the anarchists among all of the partisans have made the point most clearly and perceptively: *the state has expropriated individual violence.* The understandable murder of a momentary fury is called illegitimate; but the most pervasive violence, when depersonalized and institutionalized, is an affair of state, the prerogative of the state. Max Weber [52] embraced the anarchist genius when he defined the very essence of the state to be the monopoly of legitimate—that is, considered to be legitimate—violence.

However, anarchism has carried two contradictory traditions within it: that of Tolstoy and that of Bakunin—the former emphasizing nonviolent sociability and brotherhood and the latter espousing a mystique of destruction. The Bakuninist anarchists, whom George Woodcock [57] has aptly called "the heroes of violent action (who) have been far outnumbered by the paladins of the word," are people whose "shadows walk darkly beside any historian of anarchism; he cannot dismiss them as intruders on the road. By the right of tragedy alone they demand their place." The humanizer and dehumanizer walk the anarchist path together. This dual tradition is what Camus [8] called the *yes* and *no* carried in rebellion:

Its [rebellion's] most profound logic is not the logic of destruction; it is the logic of creation. Its movement, in order to remain authentic, must never abandon any of the terms of the contradiction that sustains it. It must be faithful to the *yes* that it contains as well as to the *no* that nihilistic interpretations isolate in rebellion. . . . The consequence of rebellion . . . is to refuse to legitimize murder. . . .

Anarchism goes to the limit in "politicalization" of all social life, and this is what makes it paramount in the passion to free men from arbitrary controls imposed by states. Anarchism (whether violent or nonviolent) enshrines killing as the supreme form of power, a diagnosis with which political theorists of many stripes have agreed. However, they might not elect to travel the entirety of the anarchist-egoist path with Max Stirner [47]:

The State practices 'violence,' the individual must not do so. The State's behavior is violence and it calls its violence 'law'; that of the individual, 'crime' . . . only by crime does he overcome the State's violence when he thinks that the State is not above him, but he is above the State.

To the anarchist, then, everything is political that could possibly have to do with power relationships in any form*—the exercise of any sort of influence over others in accordance with one's own intentions. The principal expressions of this influence are as they were formulated by Goldhamer and Shils [21]:

The power-holder exercises *force* when he influences behavior by a physical manipulation of the subordinated individual (assault, confinement, etc.); *domination* when he influences behavior by making explicit to others what he wants them to do (command, request, etc.); and *manipulation* when he influences the behavior of others without making explicit the behavior which he thereby wants them to perform.

Force alone is what interests us, the force which our epic *Iliad* discusses incessantly, according to Simone Weil [54]:

Such is the nature of force. Its power of converting a man into a thing is a double one, and in its application double-edged. To the same degree, though in different fashions, those who use it and those who endure it are turned to stone.

Social philosophy owes its gratitude to anarchists for their alertness to the nefarious ways of the state apparatus in its usage of force, domination and manipulation. In the anarchist

---

* Max Weber's classical "Class, Status and Party" defined political affairs as those having to do with "power chances," again showing his adoption of the analytic tools of the anarchist critique of power and domination.

perspective, violence is only political force, and even the violence of angry persons in the interpersonal sphere, perhaps abstractly a right of the individual, is delegitimized and punished with that same ardor which the state uses in punishing self-consciously political dissidents. At the same time, however, the state apparatus frequently will require individuals to murder on behalf of the state. The state lives in violence; Jerome H. Skolnick [44] attested to this in his report to the U.S. Commission on the Causes and Prevention of Violence. Establishment violence, when legitimized, is called Law and Order.

Legitimizing Violence as a Revolutionary Tactic

Albert Camus said in 1946 that a future without barbarism required a renunciation of violence. The choice of a political course that would make one neither victim nor executioner was, for Camus, the first rule of social action. Camus [8] took notice of the apostles of terror at that time, and he contended that the terrorists were both fascists and communists. "It is not legitimate to identify the ends of Fascism with the ends of Russian Communism. The first represents the exaltation of the executioner; the second, more dramatic in concept, the exaltation of the executioner by the victims. The former never dreamed of liberating all men, but only of liberating a few by subjugating all the rest. The latter . . . aims at liberating all men by provisionally enslaving them all." For Camus the existence in terror, in a world of fear, in a world where murder was legitimate, was an insupportable existence.

This simple and straightforward viewpoint of Camus illuminated the thought and activities of a large segment of the American civil rights movement and democratic Left until the midsixties. After that date a highly vocal minority of civil rights activists became less convinced of the revolutionary potential residing in nonviolence and turned to pinning their hopes on black power to be gained by the older methods of violent warfare. In important ways, the New Left in the United States has been an outcropping of the civil rights movement, and its preachments and activities have been riveted to racism, which it sets itself up to oppose. Consequently, when the New Left turned toward violence—as always, "in self-defense" a la Sartre—it would accept into its bosom any black people and or spokesmen for the Third World if they were committed to violence.

The New Left found two figures both of whom wrote in the tongue of Camus, French, but not from the same value orientation as Camus. These two apostles of violence whose writings have inspired deeply certain parts of the New Left are Regis Debray [11] * and Frantz Fanon.[13-16] Debray, now freed from a Bolivian prison, is a young French philosopher and journalist in his third decade of life; Fanon was a "Negro psychiatrist" who died in 1961 at the age of thirty-seven. Both writers speak, using "Marxist" words and phrases, to Marxists. They carry the endorsement of such figures as Sartre and Guevara. The vision of Debray and Fanon is conditioned by the Cold War and by their desire to use "new revolutionary approaches" on behalf of the Third World, meaning Asians, Africans and Latin Americans. While this Third World gets its identity through the Cold War, it is not bound up in the Cold War and presents revolutionary possibilities when not under North American or Soviet occupation.

Writing in the tradition of Marx-Engels, Lenin-Trotsky and Sorel, both Fanon and Debray come forward as articulate proponents of armed insurrection as the device by which exploited and colonized peoples will be liberated in Asia, Africa and Latin America. Violence is portrayed as a tactic with utmost timeliness for the Third World. Violence is characterized by activism, visibility and concreteness and by its pragmatic superiority to ideology. We shall see that usage of violence carries with it militaristic virtues, an air of secrecy and mistrust, unskeptical commitment and a success ethic with gambler overtones.

Both Frantz Fanon and Regis Debray live in "a world where murder is legitimate" and where murderous attack upon established unjust Power is considered to be the obligation of a "true revolutionary." As a tactic, guerrilla violence is depicted as worthwhile for its being so *active*. It gets movement; it gets change going. Ernesto Guevara stated this rationale succinctly,

* We are told that Fidel Castro was virtually co-author of this book.

"The duty of a revolutionary is to make the revolution," shunning inactivity, caution and overplanning. The myth of violent activism is pushed forward as the only revolutionism. Being engaged in violence against the established army is the sole action that begets true revolutionaries, for according to Debray,[11] "Revolutionaries make revolutionary civil wars; but to an even greater extent it is revolutionary civil war that makes revolutionaries." The active guerrillero is made into a revolutionary. The slogan is "Activism now, program later."

George Sorel,[45] an earlier self-proclaimed Marxist, and a mythmaker about violence, wrote the following:

> It is the myth in its entirety which is alone important; its parts are of interest only in so far as they bring out the main idea (p. 135) . . . the general strike must be taken as a whole and undivided, and the passage from Capitalism to Socialism conceived as a catastrophe, the development of which baffles description.

As Sorel saw it with the general strike so it is with guerrilla warfare, according to Fidel Castro: if one's thinking becomes analytical and skeptical, "from then on he is at the mercy of the enemy." Debray [11] writes, "However risky these (guerrilla) raids are, they are preferable to passive waiting. . . ." Debray and Fanon praise violence as a supreme organizer of men into effortful action. Debray asserts, "In Latin America today a revolutionary is not defined by his formal relationship with the Party, whether he is for or against it. The value of a revolutionary, like that of a Party, depends on his activity."

In addition to its having *activist virtue,* the launching of violent tactics is subscribed to by Debray and Fanon for being *visible and concrete:* project-focused and specific. DeBray writes, "armed propaganda follows military action but does not precede it . . . the most important form of propaganda is successful military action." The mood of the New Left in the United States is to value revolutionary action, in its visible concreteness, far more than long-winded theoretical talk. Members of Students for a Democratic Society live where the poor live, inaugurating change where people in need of radical changes live. They do not value generalities, ideologies and old-line parties. Even when balking at murder-lust, the New Left shares with Debray his contempt for Old Left long-windedness. The New Left would contend, with William Blake, "He who would do Good to another must do so in Minute Particulars. General Good is the plea of the scoundrel, hypocrite and flatterer."

Fanon [15] advocates violence partially because he sees violence as a palpable concrete act. Violence is action that, because it is direct and realistic, frees its native user from voodoo and tribal magic forever thereafter.

> At the level of individuals, violence is a cleansing force. It frees the native from his inferiority complex and from his despair and inaction; it makes him fearless and restores his self-respect. . . . Illuminated by violence, the consciousness of the people rebels against any pacification. From now on the demagogues, the opportunists and the magicians have a difficult task. The action which has thrown them into a hand-to-hand struggle confers upon the masses a voracious taste for the concrete.

Fanon shows how violence becomes its own *raison d'etre* in the here and now: "The group faces a local attack as if it were a decisive test. It behaves as if the fate of the whole country was literally at stake, here and now." But Fanon, more than Debray, lashes out critically against these excesses of "impetuosity" or "instantaneity." At times, Fanon expresses a need for programmatic goals or ends and a plan for achieving them, but Debray minimizes any deliberations that stand in the way of an unremitting string of murderous acts. Playing by ear, the guerrillero has, as his solitary goal, the seizure of political power. Toward this end, any act of violence helps, but "excessive deliberation is a vice."

Political power resides principally in the military and the police, for they are any regime's armed force. Such "legitimately armed forces" are the principal repositories of the violence of the repressive state; and logic dictates to Debray and Fanon that they be overcome. Willie Sutton declared that one robs banks because that is where the money is; and so it is with power: one is most active where power is most concentrated. Until the armed forces are exterminated and/or contained, the revolutionary seizure of power is not secured. Hence, guerrilla warfare rounds out the cycle of violence with counterviolence. One kills cops and soldiers because they epitomize the pervasive violence of the established order. When depicting the violence on which colonialism and imperialism rest, both Debray and Fanon appear to be sound—for, again, as diagnosticians they are correct. A terrorist knows what fear is.

Violent tactics have another general characteristic that commends them, in Fanon-Debray reasoning: reliance on violence gives an empirical, pragmatic quality to social action. The guerrillero is not doctrinaire, for whatever kills the enemy is useful to the cause of revolution. Violence is self-justifying political activity.

> Every success confirms their hostility towards what in future they will describe as mouth-wash, word-spinning, blather and fruitless agitation. . . . The problem is clear: the foreigners must go; so let us form a common front against the oppressor and let us strengthen our hands by armed combat. . . . To fight the war and to take part in politics: the two things become one and the same.

Debray writes scornfully of those who separate "traditional leftist political activity" from "guerrilla armed combat":

> . . . politics on one side, the military on the other. The people's war is considered to be a technique, practiced in the countryside and subordinated to the political line, which (latter) is conceived of as a super-technique, 'purely' theoretical, 'purely' political. Heaven governs the earth, the soul governs the body, the head governs the hand. The Word precedes the Act.

Such a stand is ridiculous, says Debray, for *insurrectional activity is today the number one political activity.*

There are still other traits that attend the user of violent insurrection: military virtues, secrecy, mistrust, blind faith and a willingness to win or lose totally.

The guerrillero shows a heightened sense of comradely identification with other guerrilleros. Individualism perishes quickly as the rebel warriors develop militarily and in military morale, solidarity and heroism.[15]

> The very forms of organization of the struggle will suggest to him a different vocabulary. Brother, sister, friend—these are words outlawed by the colonialist bourgeoisie. . . . The native intellectual takes part, in a sort of *auto-da-fe,* in the destruction of all his idols: egoism, recrimination that springs from pride, and the childish stupidity of those who always want to have the last word. . . . (He will) discover the substance of village assemblies, the cohesion of people's commit-

tees, and the extraordinary fruitfulness of local meetings and group-ments.

But Debray's [11] tone is more militaristic:

> In order to destroy one army, another army is necessary, and this im-plies training, discipline, and arms. Fraternity and bravery do not make an army. Witness Spain, and the Paris Commune. But once in the rebel army, . . . they adapt to each other. Slowly the shared existence, the combats, the hardships endured together, weld an alliance having the simple force of friendship. Furthermore, the first law of guerrilla life is that no one survives it alone. The group's interest is the interest of each one, and vice versa. To live and conquer is to live and conquer all together.

Youthfulness and physical prowess are biological traits that have been revered by militaristic minds throughout the ages. They are indispensable considerations for draft board selection procedures. These biologic characteristics are indispensable for the guerrillero; especially in Latin America where *machismo* is a cultural axiom.

> In addition to the moral factor—conviction—physical fitness is the most basic of all skills needed for waging guerrilla war; the two factors go hand in hand. A perfect Marxist education is not, at the outset, an imperative condition . . . Physical aptitude is the prerequisite for all other aptitudes; a minor point of limited theoretical appeal, but the armed struggle appears to have a rationale of which theory knows nothing.

Debray's vaunting of physical prowess is consistent with his (and Fanon's) anti-urban sentiments:

> . . . any man, even a comrade, who spends his life in a city is un-wittingly bourgeois in comparison with a guerrillero. He *cannot* know the material effort involved in eating, sleeping, moving from one place to another—briefly, in surviving. Not to have any means of subsistence except what you yourself can produce, with your own hands, starting from nature in the raw. . . . It is said that (in the cities) we are im-mersed in the social, and prolonged immersion debilitates. Nothing like getting out to realize to what extent these lukewarm incubators make one infantile and bourgeois.

> The guerrillero . . . must use his strength in order to show it, since he has little to show but his determination and his ability to make use of his limited resources. He must make a show of strength and at the same time demonstrate that the enemy's strength is first and foremost his *bluster*. In order to destroy the idea of unassailability—that age-old accumulation of fear and humility vis-a-vis the *patrono*, the policeman, the guardia rural—there is nothing better than combat.

Fanon likewise is suspicious of city people and pro-peasant in loyalty. His agrarian romanticism is not as extreme as Debray's, however, for his is moderated by nationalistic sentiments whereas Debray's is reinforced by *machismo*.

> The cafes are forgotten. . . . Their ears hear the true voice of the country, and their eyes take in the great and infinite poverty of their people. . . . They come to understand, with a sort of bewilderment that will from henceforth never quite leave them, that political action in the towns will always be powerless to modify or overthrow the colonial regime. These men get used to talking to the peasants. They discover that the mass of the country people have never ceased to think of the problem of their liberation except in terms of violence, in terms of taking back the land from the foreigners, in terms of national struggle, and of armed insurrection. It is all very simple.

It is all very simple to respond to one's victimization with a desire to murder one's oppressors. It is a simple reflex. Surround that reflex with a system of militaristic lore, some hypermasculinity, some nature lore, some physical culture body worship, some disenchantment with the cities' political parties and leftist verbosity and you get a recipe for guerrillas. The guerrilla is probably the most effective form of violence available against armies and militias in the present-day world. With cold war in the air, the guerrillas will flourish, in more places than Cuba and Vietnam, wherever revolution follows the simple mechanism of the violence reflex.

Still other features of guerrilla murder must be mentioned. First of all, it demands secrecy, underground or undercover operations, and an eternal untrusting vigilance. It is contralegal and illegal force arrayed against legal but morally illegitimate force. It is the end of dialogue, the final conflict, absolute violence and trickery, absolute fear among victims and executioners. Illustrative of his militaristic mind, Debray is wary of civilians in particular.

> 'Constant vigilance, constant mistrust, constant mobility'—the three golden rules. All three are concerned with security. Various considerations of common sense necessitate wariness toward the civilian population and the maintenance of a certain aloofness. . . . Not having undergone a process of selection or technical training as have the guerrilla fighters, the civilians in a given zone of operations are more vulnerable to infiltration or moral corruption by the enemy. . . . It is

known that this vigilance is exercised vis-a-vis guides especially, all of whom are carefully misinformed concerning where the guerrilleros came from, where they are eventually going, etc.

Another feature of guerrilla murder as advocated by Debray more than Fanon is the total commitment, the blind faith, of the guerrillero. He is embarked upon an absolutist course of unending violence, total destruction of the enemy, and once he sets foot upon that course he can place moral considerations under moratorium. A fanatic is not open to moral sensitivities. He does not evaluate his tactics; he admits no error. Even "propaganda follows military action but does not precede it." [11] Political parties, political programs and political goals are all put onto ice since the guerrilla army itself has become the political vanguard, and whatever is good for the rebel army is good for society. Success is the only pertinent goal.

> This (Cuban war) was a war that cost dearly in combatant casualties; a war that, although exceptionally short, required nonetheless a wealth of tactical inventiveness, mobility, and audacity, together with real soundness of strategy. It has simply been forgotten that *Patrio o Muerte* is not a slogan with which to end speeches but a principle of conduct which the Cuban fighters followed to the letter in all their actions, from the attack on the small La Plata fort to the capture of Santa Clara. Strategically, they staked all and in the end they won all.

> To risk all means that, having risen in the mountains, the fighters must wage *a war to the death,* a war that does not admit of truces, retreats, or compromises. To conquer is to accept as a matter of principle that life, for the revolutionary, is not the supreme good.

> For the sake of its own salvation, this little group *cannot* remain quiescent and isolated. It stakes everything. *Patria o Muerte.* It will either die—physically—or conquer, saving the country and itself.

The nonprofessional gambler's ideology is quite apparent here. One does not lead a life that is regulated by orderly work and reason. One gambles; one takes absolute risks; and one is either cut down totally *or* one achieves a phallic grandeur, by losing nothing that has been staked and by gaining total success. Win or lose. All or nothing. There are no compromises to be made between opponents. One gambles by his intransigence.

When all values are gambled with and only success comes to be valued, that is, very simply, nihilism. Now nihilism and opportunism are prevalent on the right and in the center; and it is not unheard of on the political left. What is strikingly new is that nihilism should become quite so widely endorsed on the left as it has been endorsed by the New Left. It may well be, as Camus stated, that taking a stand concerning the destruction and dehumanization of human life is the paramount political issue in the modern world.

Violence as a Redeeming End (or as a Way of Life)

Those who come to revere the tactics of violence appear to pass easily into a reverence for violence as a way of living or as a cult. In the cult of violence, according to Fanon, truthfulness is not a major rule of conduct.

> The problem of truth ought also to be considered. In every age, among the people, truth is the property of the national cause. No absolute verity, no discourse on the purity of the soul can shake this position. The native replies to the living lie of the colonial situation by an equal falsehood. His dealings with his fellow-nationals are open; they are strained and incomprehensible with regard to the settlers. Truth is that which hurries on the break-up of the colonialist regime; it is that which promotes the emergence of the nation; it is all that protects the natives, and ruins the foreigners. In this colonialist context there is no truthful behaviour; and the good is quite simply that which is evil for *"them."*

It appears that rules of conduct are in shortage for the guerrillero. Not even strategic thinking is indulged, for "everything is a matter of detail" in tactics. What matters?—tactics that succeed, not principles to enhance human living.

> That an intellectual, especially if he is a bourgeois, should speak of strategy before all else, is normal. Unfortunately, however, the right road, the only feasible one, sets out from tactical data, rising gradually toward the definition of strategy. The abuse of strategy and the lack of tactics is a delightful vice, characteristic of the contemplative man. . . ." [11]

Empiricism carried to its full lengths gives some brand of nihilism. Resentment drives the cultist of violence to unpredictable outrages.

> What they (the exploited masses) demand is not the settler's position of status, but the settler's place. The immense majority of natives

want the settler's farm. For them, there is no question of entering into competition with the settler. They want to take his place . . . in the colonial countries the peasants alone are revolutionary, for they have nothing to lose and everything to gain. The starving peasant, outside the class system, is the first among the exploited to discover that only violence pays. . . . The exploited man sees that his liberation implies the use of all means, and that of force first and foremost. . . . Colonialism is not a thinking machine, nor a body endowed with reasoning faculties. It is violence in its natural state, and it will only yield when confronted with greater violence. . . . Non-violence is an attempt to settle the colonial problem around a green baize table before any regrettable act has been performed or irreparable gesture made, before any blood has been shed. But if the masses, without waiting for the chairs to be arranged around the baize table, listen to their own voice and begin committing outrages and setting fire to buildings, the elites and the nationalist bourgeois parties will be seen rushing to the colonialists to exclaim, 'This is very serious! We do not know how it will end; we must find a solution—some sort of compromise.' [15]

"A Party," writes Debray [11] with reference to both the bourgeois and the Marxist-Leninist party, "is marked by the conditions of its birth, its development, the class or alliance of classes that it represents, and the social milieu in which it has developed." The Party is in history and may (but most likely does not) constitute a revolutionary vanguard; but a guerrilla army is a revolutionary vanguard that is described as if it transcends history, with a locus outside of time.

. . . the prime role of a (guerrilla) leader is to offer an example of courage and sacrifice. Better to kidnap a doctor or sequester half a hospital than to go to town for medical treatment, one guerrilla commander concluded. A leader cannot go down to the city to attend a political meeting; he has the politicos come up to discuss and make decisions in a safe place, up above. . . .[11]

In America, wherever an armed political vanguard exists, there is no longer a place for verbal-ideological relation to the revolution, nor for a certain type of polemic. We are on new ground; we are dealing with new issues. Wherever imperialism is actually challenged, splinter groups are reabsorbed and revolutionaries unite on methods and objectives tied to the people's war. . . . (Splinter groups) do not exist where an active guerrilla movement is found—Venezuela, Guatemala, Colombia, countries whose guerrilla movements look to the Cuban Revolution as their defender and their moral and political ideal. They exist to some extent in countries where armed struggle is on the agenda

of history—Peru, Bolivia, Brazil, etc. They really amount to something
only in those countries that are remote from the armed struggle,
where there is no clear-cut revolutionary vanguard in action. In other
words, the importance of these "Marxist-Leninist" groups is inversely
proportional to the revolutionary situation of the countries where they
are found.[11]

> To work means to work for the death of the settler. This assumed
> responsibility for violence allows both strayed and outlawed members
> of the group to come back again and to find their place once more,
> to become integrated. Violence is thus seen as comparable to a royal
> pardon. The colonized man finds his freedom in and through violence.
> This rule of conduct enlightens the agent because it indicates to him
> the means and the end.[15]

Violence is both the means and end. Freedom is found through
violence and *in* violence. The warrior cult erases old differences,
unites opposing factions and splinter groups, and introduces a
popular front of the deed. Ideology is secondary to war and
thought is secondary to murder. Indeed, "the value of a revolutionary, like that of a party, depends on his activity." [11] Faith
without works is dead! This is the mode of patriarchal society:
performance is required incessantly; a man is what he does. By his
deeds, know him. His participation in violence is like baptism,
for "violence is a cleansing force." [15] Violent struggle

> sets on foot a process of reintegration which is fertile and decisive in
> the extreme. A people's victorious fight not only consecrates the
> triumph of its rights; it also gives to that people consistence, coherence
> and homogeneity.

> Violence alone, violence committed by the people, violence organized
> and educated by its leaders, makes it possible for the masses to under-
> stand social truths and gives the key to them.

In short, then, Fanon and Debray employ the terminology of a
cult of violence. In Debray's book, violence is espoused as sup-
planting or having precedence over all of the following:

1. rational discourse
2. educational work or propaganda
3. awareness, political knowledge
4. democratic structures
5. wide popular support
6. formation of alliances or coalitions

7. drawing up political programs
8. party
9. political discussion, dissension
10. understanding of enemy
11. property
12. urban activism
13. trade union activity
14. survival or life itself.

By such excesses, the cult of violence shows us that institutionalized violence lacks any proper legitimation and that institutionalized violence is not in any way a necessary outgrowth of being born human.

Some Speculations as to the Moral Roots of a Cult of Violence in America

Desperate times bring deperate proposals.

Our alienation has led us to despair. We feel "played cheap," as Richard Wright termed it, and we will go to all ends to articulate and to avenge our numbing, overpowering bewilderment. We want our lives to count, but we have doubts. We are powerless, inferior and full of indecision.

We doubt that there are any eternal verities that can give meaning to our condition. Ethical principles are suspect—even the ethics of pacifism, of libertarianism, of democratic socialism. "Are there any viable values?" we ask. With a little illumination, and a sense of commitment, we for a time adopted nonviolent revolutionary tactics; but we hasten to say that it was *tactical* nonviolence, *not nonviolence "as a way of life."* We acknowledge that our subscription to nonviolence was really only a minor foray into the liberal civil rights field, its effectiveness dependent upon the backing of the Supreme Court and the Kennedys. Nonviolence was good for integration, we say, but what about the black ghettos?

We despair of ever achieving a reasonable society by reasonable means.

So many things go farther than we go, so we condemn them all as not going far enough: labor unions, cooperatives, war resistance groups, welfare rights groups. The less we do, the more ferocious our rhetoric becomes.

We are sick of our cities. We have "had it" with the proletariat, with the middle class, with the military-industrial complex, with labor unions and with old-line political parties. We have had it with the electoral process. We are having it at work, even if our work is in academia. For everywhere we are powerless and in despair, barely able to go on wishing for something to engage us wholly. Hope lessens when every single "thing to do" is read off as "inconsequential all by itself."

No more war, we cry. Yet Cold-War, Vietnam, Bangladesh, Santo Domingo, Bolivia—these are what we get, since we are not moved to oppose war and imperialism effectively. Perhaps some day we will have a holy war, we say, so it would be indiscreet to be antiwar across the board. We search for justifications.

We despair of ever having humane, loving relations. The life of dialogue, gentleness, fair play, openness, willingness to take the consequences when one disobeys a law, willingness to share existence with one's enemy—these "turn us off." Soft-heads and acid-heads have helped us to purge ourselves of these liberal notions.

Doing so little, we find ourselves attracted most by violent cataclysm. When in despair we are ripe for counsels of perfection, of intransigence and of perfect nihilism. Somewhere in our hearts we have a readiness to say, with Sartre,

> This irrepressible violence is neither sound and fury, nor the resurrection of savage instincts, nor even the effect of resentment: it is man re-creating himself. . . . No gentleness can efface the marks of violence; only violence itself can destroy them.[15]

The roots of the cult of violence lie in our unutterable despair.

Trotsky insisted that violence is the essence of politics; but we must find the ways and means to make *the containment of violence* the essence of our politics. There remains a practical and tactical issue (not distinctively moral) of some consequence that has been stated very congently by Arthur Schlesinger[41]:

> . . . if the left, through the cult of the deed, helps create an atmosphere which destroys the process of democracy itself, the only winners will be those who use violence best, and they will be on the right.

VIOLENCE AND MORAL VALUES

It would appear that as human beings we receive little in the way of divine guidance. We are, nevertheless, animals and persons who do operate within a framework of values, implicit or explicit and both ideal and real. Values are among the most durable dimensions of human personality and although they are learned (largely in conflict settings—that is, where choices have to be made between two or more alternatives with mixtures of appeal and repulsion to the chooser), values rank, with unfolded temperament and uncurbed intelligence, as quasi-immutable structures. It is fashionable to speak of human "needs" and to borrow the terminology and cognitive style of the marketplace in an economy of scarcity. Yet, what matter are our values, and as Dorothy Lee [30] commented with such graceful finality, "I believe that it is value, not a series of needs, which is at the basis of human behavior." Régis Debray was correct in his claim that there are values that take precedence over the value of life itself. But a general value on life is widespread, even among intellectuals. Shils [43] contended that we have abiding positive values on the sanctity of life in our culture which will not be discarded even as the Christianity it originally fed upon is discarded; and Shils says hopefully that "the protoreligion, the 'natural metaphysic' of the sanctity of life, must be intellectually rehabilitated and rendered acceptable."

Such reverence for life is not negated by the murderousness of so many people in our time, much as the telling of lies by so many people does not negate the truth of logico-empirically sound propositions. When one reveres life, however, and essays to convert his personal valuations into political programs, he quickly discerns as did Simone Weil [55] that his aversion to killing is made up of two sets of values: "the aversion to kill and the aversion to be killed. The former is honorable but very weak; the latter, almost impossible to acknowledge, but very strong." One has to wonder (in opposition to Weil) if we ought to be ashamed of our wishes to preserve our lives, even if we would not do anything and everything in order to "save our necks."

There are other moral considerations that bear upon our decisions concerning political murders: happiness, lucidity, authenticity or sincerity, veracity, informedness or freedom from error, and many others. The totality of the value judgments that are made in our era underpin a stand that is very close to pacifism. The nonviolent revolutionism that spurs rapid and radical change, along with the nonviolence that conserves liberty and concord in society and that allows for slower transformations also, seem to be morally defensible stands. No ethical stand ever ends the struggle; for the only complete surcease of moral dilemmas comes from dropping out. That means either *delinquere* or *morire*.

Not all of the attention should go to political activism in a moral appraisal of violence. It would be a serious omission not to point to another less militant tradition of nonviolence—namely, the tradition that works more quietly and through more "respectable" channels to effect what might be called *moral or social equivalents of war*. These are the scholars who strive to learn how to make integrative relations occur in place of threat relations, among nations and within nations. They study polemology. They practice "conflict resolution." These are also diplomats who use old and new avenues for disarmament negotiations, for peace talks and for strengthening the United Nations, among many other things. The Peace Research movement [48] has made great strides forward in Scandinavia, Britain, the United States and Canada. The "strategic studies movement" has of course had more abundant monetary and official backing in many countries; and on the testimony of Kenneth Boulding [4] we have the opinion that many of these students of strategies are giving intensive energy to the engineering of a warless world. In all of these gentler ways, ways that will not risk getting skulls cracked immediately by Establishment violence, the work of bringing about the containment of violence is proceeding.

Socrates and Unamuno: A Closing Polemic

Philosophers in the mass show a tendency to dress up violence, to take off its jagged edges and to formulate the issues in such fashion that war, as a particular manifestation of violence, is called the lesser evil if evil at all. Philosophers today refrain from conceiving large systems and they refrain from large commitments also. In reality, what we refrain from is any unpopular stand.

Since the death of Socrates, philosophers have taken a "party line" in opposition to the judges of Socrates. In actuality, however, they are aligned on the side of the judges, not Socrates. Philosophers align themselves with established social truths and not with the critique and wisdom that pervade the good reputation of philosophy. Hence, even if philosophers' public claims put them with Socrates, their public deeds are those of the judges.[40]

The judges of Socrates have not become more merciful or permissive since 399 B.C. Immanuel Kant, with an eye to the judges of Socrates, did not support conscientious objection or refusal of military service. Erasmus chose to rise above the judges on both sides. Laodicean or no, he abstained from making a decision favoring the winds of Lutheran change and in some ages that would have satisfied quite amply the demands of the judges of Socrates. At times the judges settle for a long-winded neutrality; but at other times the judges can be ferocious and fanatical. In 1936 Miguel de Unamuno, rector of the University of Salamanca, had a confrontation with the judges of Socrates. General Millán Astray appeared at the University under his motto, *Viva la muerte*. When Unamuno challenged the necrophilous plea of the General, General Astray was provoked to articulate his corollary wish and to scream out, *Abajo la inteligencia*.[49] Millán Astray, as a judge of Socrates, knew that life and intelligence are cardinal "corrupters" of youth and principal fomenters of rebellion against the state. Judges of Socrates wish to legitimize their violence—against Socrates, against students, against blacks, against Vietnamese communists—and few are the philosophers or psychiatrists who stand up against the judges of Socrates.

Throughout the 1960's and into the 1970's, intellectuals could be seen as idolizing cautious conventionality whilst verbally asserting their admiration for Socrates and Unamuno. What Bertolt Brecht said of poets applies to psychiatrists also, perhaps:

But nobody will say: The times were dark.
Instead: Why were their poets so silent?
Why were their shrinks so silent?

REFERENCES

1. Ackerman, J. S.: Two styles: A challenge to higher education. *Daedalus, 98 (No. 3) (Summer)*:855–869, 1969.
2. Ardrey, R.: *The Territorial Imperative.* New York, Atheneum, 1966.
3. Boas, G.: *The Cult of Childhood.* New York, Warburg Institute, 1966.
4. Boulding, K. E.: Insight and knowledge in the development of stable peace. In Friends World Committee for Consultation: *No Time But This Present.* Birmingham (England), Friends World Committee, 1967, pp. 210–219.
5. Brun, R.: Ueber Freuds Hypothese vom Todestrieb. *Psyche, 1951*:81–111, 1953.
6. Buber, M.: *Good and Evil.* New York, Charles Scribner's, 1952.
7. Camus, A.: Neither victim nor executioner. Translated by Dwight Macdonald. *Politics,* July–August, 1947.
8. Camus, A.: *The Rebel.* New York, Vintage Books, 1956.
9. Camus, A.: A final interview. *Venture, 3 (No. 4) (Spring-Summer)*:25–38, 1960.
10. Clark, B. P.: The indivisibility of violence. *Quaker Service,* Winter 1968–69. Philadelphia, American Friends Service Committee.
11. Debray, R.: *Revolution in the Revolution?* New York, Grove Press, 1967.
12. Erikson, E. H.: Gandhi's autobiography: The leader as a child. *The American Scholar, 35 (No 4) (Autumn)*:632–646, 1966.
13. Fanon, F.: *Black Skin White Masks.* Translated by Charles Lam Markmann. New York, Grove Press, 1967.
14. Fanon, F.: *A Dying Colonialism.* Translated by Haakon Chevalier. New York, Grove Press, 1967.
15. Fanon, F.: *The Wretched of the Earth.* Translated by Constance Farrington. New York, Grove Press, 1968.
16. Fanon, F.: *Toward the African Revolution.* New York, Grove Press, 1967.
17. Frank, J. D.: *Sanity and Survival: Psychological Aspects of War and Peace.* New York, Random House, 1968.
18. Freud, S.: *Civilization and Its Discontents.* London, The Hogarth Press, 1961.
19. Fromm, E.: *War Within Man.* Philadelphia, American Friends Service Committee, 1963.
20. Fromm, E.: *The Heart of Man: Its Genius for Good and Evil.* New York, Harper & Row, 1964.
21. Goldhamer, H., and Shils, E. A.: Types of Power and Status. *Am J Sociol, XLV (No. 2) (Sept.)*:171–182, 1939.

22. Graham, H. D., and Gurr, T. R.: *The History of Violence in America: A Report to the National Commission on the Causes and Prevention of Violence.* New York, Bantam Books, 1969.

23. Hentoff, N.: The last stand of the dispensables. *Evergreen Review, No. 70 (Sept.):*50–62, 1969.

24. Hocking, R.: The problem of truth. In *Truth, Myth, and Symbol,* edited by T. J. J. Altizer *et al.* Englewood Cliffs, Prentice-Hall, 1962.

25. Holloway, Jr., R. L.: Human aggression: The need for a species-specific framework. *Natural History,* Special Supplement, December 1, 1967.

26. Horney, K.: *New Ways in Psychoanalysis.* New York, Norton, 1939.

27. Kahn, A. J.: *Planning Community Services for Children in Trouble.* New York, Columbia University Press, 1963.

28. Keniston, K.: *Young Radicals.* New York, Harcourt, Brace & World, 1968.

29. Klopfer, P. H.: Aggression and its evolution. *Psychiatr Soc Sci Rev, 3 (No. 3):*2–7, 1969.

30. Lee, D.: Are basic needs ultimate? *J Abnorm Soc Psychol, 43:*391–395, 1948.

31. Lorenz, K.: *The Evolution and Modification of Behavior.* Chicago, University of Chicago Press, 1965.

32. Lorenz, K.: *On Aggression.* New York, Harcourt, Brace & World, 1966.

33. Mark, V. H., and Ervin, F. R.: *Violence and the Brain.* New York, Harper & Row, 1970.

34. Meir, A., and Rudwick, E.: Black violence in the twentieth century: A study in rhetoric and retaliation. In *The History of Violence in America: A Report to the National Commission on the Causes and Prevention of Violence,* by H. D. Graham and T. R. Gurr. New York, Bantam Books, 1969.

35. Myrdal, G.: *An American Dilemma.* New York, Harper & Brothers, 1944.

36. Panunzio, C.: *Major Social Institutions.* New York, Macmillan, 1939.

37. Rapoport, A.: Models of Conflict: Cataclysmic and strategic. In *Conflict in Society,* by A. deReuck and J. Knight. Boston, Little, Brown & Co., 1964, pp. 259–287.

38. Sartre, J.-P.: Preface. In *The Wretched of the Earth,* by F. Fanon. New York, Grove Press, 1968.

39. Sartre, J.-P.: Interview. *France-Observateur,* February 1, 1962, p. 8.

40. Schilpp, P. A.: In Defense of Socrates' Judges. *Enquiry, 2* (No. 2) : 3–10, 1944.

41. Schlesinger, Jr., A. M.: *Violence: America in the Sixties.* New York, New American Library, 1968.

42. Scott, J. P.: *Aggression.* Chicago, University of Chicago Press, 1958.

43. Shils, E. A.: The Sanctity of Life. *Encounter, 28 (No. 1):* 39–49, 1967.

44. Skolnick, J. H.: *The Politics of Protest.* New York, Ballantine Books, 1969.

45. Sorel, G.: *Reflections on Violence.* Translated by T. E. Hulme. New York, Peter Smith, 1941.
46. Sorokin, P. A.: Comment on War Within Man. In *War Within Man,* by E. Fromm. Philadelphia, American Friends Service Committee, 1963.
47. Stirner, M.: *The Ego and His Own.* New York, Libertarian Book Club, 1963.
48. Taylor, H.: Peace and war and the intellectuals. *The Progressive,* July, 1962.
49. Thomas, H.: *The Spanish Civil War.* New York, Harper & Brothers, 1961.
50. Tinbergen, N.: On war and peace in animals and man. *Science,* June 28, 1968.
51. Toch, H. H.: *Violent Men: an Inquiry into the Psychology of Violence.* Chicago, Aldine Publishing Co., 1969.
52. Weber, M.: Politics as a vocation. Translated by H. Gerth and C. W. Mills. In *From Max Weber: Essays in Sociology.* New York, Oxford University Press, 1946.
53. Wedge, B.: Psychiatry and international affairs. *Science, 157* (No. 3786): 281–285, 1967.
54. Weil, S.: The Iliad: A poem of force. Translated by Mary McCarthy. *Politics (No. 22),* November, 1945.
55. Weil, S.: *The Need for Roots.* Translated by A. Wills. New York, G. P. Putnam's Sons, 1952.
56. Wertham, F.: *A Sign for Cain.* New York, Paperback Library, 1969.
57. Woodcock, G.: *Anarchism: A History of Libertarian Ideas and Movements.* Cleveland, Meridian Books, 1962.

Chapter 10

Contributions of Dynamic Psychiatry to Human Concordance

ALFRED M. FREEDMAN

BEFORE ONE CAN delineate the contributions of dynamic psychiatry to human *con*cordance, it is necessary to emphasize that dynamic psychiatry has also contributed to human *dis*cordance, in that dynamic psychiatry has raised ehtical, moral and spiritual questions that have evoked doubt as to prevailing values and standards. This can be seen most clearly by studying the youth of today throughout the world who, often unknowingly, have incorporated dynamic psychiatry into a posture of dissent.

The following contributions of dynamic psychiatry to human dissonance are especially relevant: the man's behavior is explicable on the basis of his historical development with many factors interacting in a complex fashion, whether one places greater or less emphasis on instinctual drives, constitutional types, heredity or other conscious or unconscious influences; that the affective life of the individual is important, as are self-awareness, self-knowledge and self-fulfillment; that personal worth, identity and personal dignity should be encouraged; that the search for pleasure on the basis of the excitation-reduction hypothesis is appropriate; the guilt may involve the invasion of arbitrary and external standards and should in such instances be rejected; that man has the capacity, with help if necessary, to seek and approach perfection.

We are now living with the first generation of youngsters who have been raised in a dynamic psychoanalytic ambiance, with such notions as a search for identity, self-awareness and self-fulfillment. It is very difficult for them to accept a world with chronic wars, threats of nuclear extension and the constant spoiling of the environment; a world which denies identity and personal worth because of race, sex or age; or a world which regards the search for pleasure as evil. Few adults can accept the statement from a youngster, "You shouldn't say that, it makes me feel guilty."

The fact that dynamic psychiatry has created discord can also be seen in the work of leading thinkers who are critical of present-day society. I shall refer to three of these: Erich Fromm, a psychoanalyst; Herbert Marcuse, a philosopher; and Ralph H. Turner, a sociologist.

Fromm states that the belief in the unity of the human race and man's potential to perfect himself by his own efforts are basic.[1] Yet we speak today of fear that man may become the slave of nationalisms and a prisoner of things he himself has created, including nuclear weapons. Fromm points out that while Marx was sensitive to the psychological needs of humanity, he had no dynamic psychology to utilize; therefore, what appears as Marxism today is a preoccupation of the physical and material needs of man. Thus, Marxism differs from capitalism only in its methods, which are stated to be more efficient economically and could be initiated by the working class. Fromm shares the humanism of Marx as originally stated and cites him as the first declarer that theory cannot be separated from practice, knowledge from action or spiritual aims from the social system. Free and independent men could exist only in a social and economic system which would bring rationality and abundance. Thus, Fromm makes up the deficiency in Marxism by adding dynamic psychiatry and forms an amalgam—Humanitarian Socialism—for although we are familiar with the uses of psychoanalytic theory in literary criticism, theatre, literature and biographical history, psychoanalytic theory has had its most important social impact on political theory and political action.

A recent book written by a professor of history, Paul A. Robinson, is entitled *The Freudian Left: Wilhelm Reich, Geza Roheim, and Herbert Marcuse*.[2] Marcuse has been the idol and doyen of leftist students throughout the world, but it is not generally appreciated that, like Fromm, he attempts a synthesis of Marxian and Freudian philosophies. In *Eros and Civilization*,

Marcuse [3] has come up with a number of extensions and interpretations of freudian principles that have exerted powerful influence upon student activists. Leon Rappaport [4] states that

> . . . these facts of contemporary life and many others like them make Marcuse required reading because he presents the only unitary rubric of ideas relevant to their interpretation. . . . Unless one is familiar with his Marxist-Freudian reading of our society, then one has less of a legitimate right to be critical of the [New Left] movement than the hard-hats of lower Broadway. . . . In academia you can't talk social science to bright students today unless you are prepared to handle yourself in the Marxist-Freudian arena defined by Marcuse. In more applied settings you can't in good conscience allow yourself the luxury of thinking you are helping until you have examined your work from the vantage point of Marcuse.

Illustrative of Marcuse's thought is his reinterpretation of Freud's reality principle as a performance concept, which he then turns upside down and states that this serves to oppress rather than liberate men, thus contributing to discord if not to revolution. The work of Charles Reich in *The Greening of America* [5] is illustrative of this frantic (and in Reich's case, futile) search for human, interpersonal satisfaction in the midst of a technically deteriorating bureaucracy. This is one of the challenges of the seventies which the professionals in the behavioral sciences are evading.

Professor Ralph H. Turner, Professor of Sociology and Anthropology at the University of California at Los Angeles, points out that "any major social movement depends upon and promotes some normative revision. In case of movements having the greatest significance for social change, this normative innovation takes the form of a new sense in what is *just* and what is *unjust* in society." [6] Turner differentiates between concepts of a problem as a misfortune or as a state of *injustice.*

Historically, major changes have occurred when a misfortune has been redefined as an injustice for which large sections of the population have demanded correction. Poverty was a misfortune to the leaders of the revolutionary movements in the nineteenth century. To be denied material needs of life was redefined as an injustice, with resultant revolutions in the nineteenth century, the organization of labor unions and, as a later manifestation, the New Deal.

It is Turner's contention that "today, for the first time in history it is common to see violence in the nation expressed over the fact that people lack a sense of personal worth. They lack an inner peace of mind which comes from a sense of personal dignity or a clear sense of identity." Thus, "the phenomenon of a man crying out with indignation because the society has not supplied him with a sense of personal worth and identity is a distinctive new feature of our era. The idea that a man who does not feel worthy and who cannot find his proper place in life is to be pitied, is an old one. The notion that he is indeed a victim of injustice is the new idea."

This is a notion whose roots extend into those of dynamic psychiatry. Lack of personal worth, alienation and lack of identity have been defined as injustices, and therefore, youth, blacks and women, for example, demand change and express outrage against the depersonalizing and demoralizing effects of modern institutions ranging from the family through the university to the state. The philosophy of this new era is clearly existentialist, and the conception of injustice is focused upon the psychological and psychiatric theatres of human concern.

The most powerful insight dynamic social psychiatrists, psychologists, social workers and other behavioral scientists can gain is the awareness that factors that frustrate personal worth, identity, self-esteem and independent decision-making are important contributors to current human discord. Techniques must, therefore, be developed jointly with political figures and social scientists to include achievement of these objectives in life programs of social change.

REFERENCES

1. Fromm, E. (Ed) : *The Application of Human Psychoanalysis to Marx's Theory in Socialist Humanism.* Garden City, Doubleday, 1965.
2. Robinson, Paul A.: *The Freudian Left: Wilhelm Reich, Geza Roheim, and Herbert Marcuse.* New York, Harper & Row, 1969.
3. Marcuse, H.: *Eros and Civilization.* Boston, Beacon Press, 1965.
4. Rappaport, L.: Review of *Five Lectures* by Herbert Marcuse.
5. Reich, C. A.: *The Greening of America: The Coming of a New Consciousness and the Rebirth of a Future.* New York, Random House, 1970.
6. Turner, R. H.: The theme of contemporary social movements. *Br J Sociol,* 20:390–402, 1969.

Chapter 11

Social Psychiatric Contributions to the Understanding of Discord and the Promotion of Concordance

Louis Miller

"CONCORD" IS DEFINED by the *Oxford Dictionary* as "agreement or a state of peace and amity." For our purposes such a state would include a maximum of human creativity and satisfaction.

One could also define *concord as the voluntary and cooperative reduction, to an absolute minimum, of violence and war in human society* and in any aspect of human relations. This is a purely pragmatic and humanistic working definition.

However, this definition leaves open the discussion about the causes of violence, its relation to instinct and aggression and their socialization. Violence is adjudged negatively but aggression is left open to positive connotations as are some aspects of conflict and discord. War has the connotation of more organized forms of violence. The concepts of "peace" (and concord), however, should not be restricted in meaning to the absence of violence. Human relations cannot be free of some degree of dissention, discord or conflict. Hence, if it is to be constructive and maintained, concord should include the constant negotiation of (rather than controlled or managed) discord and conflict. This approach would deal with a sentimentalized, millennial or paradisiac version of peace. It also opposes on theoretical and pragmatic grounds the philosophy of peace through control or by imposition. Peace and concord, like individual mental balance, are obtained only through constant negotiation of differences and incompatibilities in order to seek change in, and new compromises between, people.

The promotion of this awareness of the universal existence of conflict, its positive content and the need for its negotiation

185

is the business of social psychiatry. When we look for the sources of conflict, we will find them along the path of the developing child. We understand infantile conflict better by far than we do adult conflict. We are better therapists of the conflicts of childhood than we are of adult conflict. This says that we are better therapists, as things are now, than social action experts. Nevertheless, we are able to contribute in that we understand many of the original sources and patterns of conflict between individuals.

Conflict is universal. It is inevitable in human beings, in the ultimate analysis, because of the nature of the human being. Conflict is not only the outcome of socialization of the child, it is its very machinery. Without conflict there can be no socialization. Yet the ideal is the avoidance of all violence in conflict. This at least is the democratic ideal when added to the idea of leaving open the possibility for the negotiation of every conflict. Tyranny suppresses conflict and engenders violence against the tyrants but leaves room for violent solutions of conflict everywhere else.

The nature of child-rearing is therefore in any society the archetype and the prototype of an approach to conflict. While we are able to learn much and may attempt to alter things at the culture-contact point of the child and society, the values and the modes of child-rearing are inherent in the society. Changes in child-rearing therefore demand changes in the adult society. We must therefore bring our experience in child-rearing to bear on the adult attitudes and norms of the society. This I suppose is our chief business as social psychiatrists. This is our role and this is the way in which many have indeed acted. It is a role expected of us. We are not expected to act within the context of adult conflict and its negotiation. That is just as well, as we are not experienced or skilled at or trained for such social action.

Our information has to do with the genesis of human conflict and can be relevant for all adult conflict. This knowledge we should contribute to those involved, as the leader, social philosopher, diplomat or mediator. While we may learn from our experience, we are still very much in the dark as to childhood conflict and development. Our confusion in the matter of a common language about human function is a major stumbling block and underlines the degree of our confusion. We have therefore still to agree about the identity of the phenomena involved in infant development before we may proceed satisfactorily with concepts of regularity of relations between phenomena.

Our business is definitely to search for the relations between events as in any science. It is very difficult to define these human phenomena which differ so remarkably from the phenomena associated with the inert, nonliving substances and living organisms with very limited options in behavior. Our prime need is therefore for an agreed phenomenology of behavior and so-called mind. From that we may be able to proceed to a more satisfactory theory of the sources of violence which will have useful application in society.

For our purposes in considering concord and discord the phenomenological issues involved include in addition to the complexities of acculturation the nature of instinct and its relation to aggression. In the midseventeenth century Thomas Hobbes [1] had written about three "causes of quarrel": "[the seeking after] Gain; the second for Safety; and the third for Reputation." Hobbes also stated that men ". . . first use Violence to make them masters of other men's persons, wives, children and cattell." Hobbes believed that when there is no common power to awe them, men are in a condition of war, where every man is enemy to every man. We have made little progress on this issue. Is man really born a beast of prey with overwhelming predatory narcissism?

L. T. Hobhouse wrote "there is not wanting something we can call an organization of life in the animal world . . . in the aid they often render to each other" and of *humans*: "Morality is in its origin group morality. This division between the community and the stranger cuts deep into the ethical consciousness."

Freud's theory of instincts as set out in 1923 (ego and id) [3] seems to say that there are two classes of instincts: those preservative of life and those which are sadistic and lead to death.

In 1929 he [4] wrote ". . . but the theory of instincts has groped its way forward under greater difficulties than any other part of [metapsychology] . . . hunger and love make the world go round." Hunger represents those instincts, he says, which are self-preservative—it is an ego-instinct. Love seeks objects; its function is preservation of the species. The energy of the latter is the libido. Sadism too which is connected with sexual life is an object instinct; however ". . . it clearly allied itself with the ego instincts and with instincts of mastery. . . . Neurosis appeared as the outcome of a struggle between the interests of self-preservation and the claims of libido, a struggle in which the ego was victorious, but at the price of great suffering and renunciation." He then says more clearly ". . . I take up the standpoint that the tendency to aggression is an innate, independent, instinctual disposition in man, and I come back now to the statement that it constitutes the most powerful obstacle to culture." Eros binds together individuals, families, tribes, races, nations and all of humanity. "The natural instinct of aggressiveness in man, the hostility of each one against all, and of all against each one, opposes this programme of civilisation." Aggression is innate and shares with Eros his rule over the earth.

This differs from Freud's earlier view that aggression was a primordial reaction to the frustration of pleasure-seeking or pain avoidance, in accord with McDougall's view of aggression as an "instinct of combat" aroused by "obstruction." On these earlier views were elaborated the frustration and aggression hypotheses of Dollard and others.[5] There is no question, however, but that Freud had returned to the belief that aggression in man was innate and an instinct.

One of the immense stumbling blocks in examining instinct theory for the origins of aggression is that the very phenomenon of instinct is in doubt and that its definition is unclear. It appears that the word "instinct" is applied to *two entities* as stated in the *Oxford Dictionary:* "(a) innate *impulse,* (b) an innate propensity in organized beings . . . manifesting itself in *acts* which appear to be rational but are formed without conscious adaptation of means to ends."

Freud deals largely and almost purely with the first entity and its subsequent development in organized behavior. The second (inborn behavior) has remained largely the province of the animal psychologists and ethologists. In animals the two entities may be inseparable. This is the approach of Lorenz, who in discussing animal instinct isolates "big" drives—reproduction, feeding, flight and aggression (species preservation) and their "little servants," running, digging, flying, etcetera. In referring to human drives, Lorenz says, "There must be superlatively strong factors which are able to overcome the commands of individual reason which are so obviously impervious to experience and learning." Lorenz, however, like Hobhouse and Freud believes in hereditary social instincts in man. He assumes "that human social behaviour (is) far from being determined by reason and cultural tradition alone. . . ." He says, "All the great dangers threatening humanity are direct consequences of conceptual thought and verbal speech!" His reference is to the discovery of weapons and material culture with which social inhibitions could not keep pace.

Lorenz also believes that in some animals, as distinct from man, innate behavior mechanisms control aggressive behavior and function as an analogue to morality. In human evolution no inhibitory mechanisms preventing sudden manslaughter were necessary and there was originally no selection pressure on mankind to breed inhibitory mechanisms. With the arrival of weapons humanity was not destroyed because the curiosity which led to the production of weapons also entailed a sense of responsibility. Lorenz maintains that man's instinctive behavior is peaceable in their own groups and devilish towards "species not belonging to their own community."

Our experience, I believe, bears out much of these theses of Lorenz. However, I would say that man is born unrestrainedly aggressive but with great potential for the development of cultural controls and transformations in order to mitigate his destructive impulses. I maintain that in the past acculturation of the aggressive drives has been devoted to the control of intragroup violence but has promoted extragroup aggression. Acculturation could be directed to control aggression against other human groups.

On balance it would seem that, like Freud and others here referred to, one may have to go beyond the frustration hypothesis of aggression and return to the thesis that man is innately an aggressive animal. The aggression assuredly is released from its cultural restraints by frustration, but very likely, also by willful social direction against objects in the group or elsewhere. Let us stress again that patterns of violence may be educated into our species as a value. Surely this is an area in which social psychiatry should be active!

Socialization processes may fail for the reason given by Lorenz—namely, the cultural lag relative to rapid intellectual and technical development producing new means of destruction. Other factors may arouse frustration or reduce tolerance for it —that is, the strength of the individual biological drive, usually physical, economic and emotional deprivations flowing from inequalities on the social system or ecological problems. Something can be done to prevent or correct these situations in a society which holds concord as a value and permits negotiation of conflicting demands among individuals and groups. But in a society which sets a value on violence or where negotiation is greatly limited, nothing can be accomplished without a total cultural change.

The question arises about the origin of violence as a cultural value. I believe that this relates to impairment of the development of identity. The conflict negotiation which takes place between parent and child results in change and growth processes in the child's ego and identity formation through internalization of attitudes and patterns usually at variance with its own drives. Unsatisfactory negotiations may lead to simple suppression or displacement of its impulses. The want of the development of satisfactory expressions of aggression may lead to patterns of behavior complicated by aggression and violence.

Associated with unsatisfactory negotiations with the child are impairments of its identity. Confused transactions with the child are in our times often the outcome of poverty of identity in the parents. The child's sense of self and self-value may be affected as may be its sense of acceptance of or by the group which has socialized it. Many identity problems are expressed as a sense of inferiority vis-à-vis, usually dominant and reference groups. They may be expressed as a sense of deeply rooted superiority over another which may evoke a negative image of itself.

Attempts to compensate for or correct impairments of identity tend to express themselves, especially if frustrated, in individual or group violence. Those who seek identity, unless they have developed high intellectual capacity or a profound sense of responsibility (and this latter is unusual) are very easily led. They identify irrationally with leaders and causes which feed identity into their persons—usually through external symbols, slogans and stereotypes. Thus the search for identity sets afoot dangerous and violent movements.

Here again we are most strategically placed to assist those who are involved with child-rearing in situations where identity is an issue. Adolescence gives one a further chance to support those seeking identity.

In world perspective this issue of the problem of identity is probably, after physical deprivation, the most besetting and dangerous. Vast groups in Asia, Africa and America are making over their identity as a result of the pursuit of new political, social, economic and technical goals. This movement inevitably entails structural, cultural and family change. The focus of human attachment and identity formation is shifting from the complex interrelations of family and tribe to the humanly inefficient mass. There is no question but that this results in impoverishment of family relations and in loss by the individual of identity and the sense of inner meaning, dignity and belonging. As this occurs, customary social and ritual controls are also lost and the stage is set, especially where there is physical deprivation, for violent reaffirmation of the self and of the lost group identity.

Obviously this stupendous change and its dangers to personality and society transcends the role of the social psychiatrist, since his contribution can only be indirect. Our knowledge, relevant to the issue, relates mainly to social-psychiatric researches and experience in the innate origins of aggression, acculturation in various social and cultural milieux, the conflicts of infancy with the adult representatives of the culture and their vicissitudes in ego and identity formation and social and antisocial behavior.

Social psychiatry naturally should bring its weight to bear on factors in the adult society which make for violent and warlike rather than negotiated solutions. However, it is at the level of the contact of the adult with the generation of children that our chief effort should be made. It is at this point that displacements of aggression against others in the group and education for violence against other groups occur.

Mutual negotiations and compromise between adult groups and between adults and children is a *sine qua non* for the constructive patterning of aggression, the promotion of concord and the avoidance of violence. In other words the world, as I see it, and social psychiatry have a vested interest in human communication, compromise, change, negotiation and democracy.

REFERENCE

1. Hobbes, Thomas: *Leviathan.* New York, Dutton, 1937, p. 64.
2. Hobhouse, L. T.: *Morals in Evolution.* London, Chapman, Hall, 1929, pp. 1–233.
3. Freud, S.: *The Ego and the Id.* London, Hogarth, 1935, pp. 55 passim.
4. Freud, S.: *Civilisation and its Discontents.* London, Hogarth, 1946, pp. 95 passim.
5. Dollard, J., et al.: *Frustration and Aggression.* Kegan Paul, 1944.
6. Lorenz, K.: *On Aggression.* London, Methuen, 1968, pp. 204 passim.

PART III

STUDIES IN TRANSCULTURAL DISCORD
AND CONCORDANCE

Chapter 12

Psychiatric Charity Begins at Home

Louis Miller

OUR THEME—"Psychiatrists for Peace"—implies that psychiatrists are able to contribute to the prevention of war and the promotion of peace. I agree that they can. But it is to the promotion of peace particularly rather than to the prevention of war that psychiatrists may contribute with success.

For me the act of the prevention of war refers essentially to the management of acute crisis situations between nations. Intervention in such conflict situations at a late stage when emotions and violence are about to erupt requires techniques and powers which no professional has or can employ. The psychiatrist in this situation can do very little if anything at all. The restraint and dissuasion of and mediation between antagonists demands power, machinery and leadership which the psychiatrist does not have and cannot acquire without a total change in his identity and role. While he should do everything in his power to bring about direct negotiations between antagonists, his role is elsewhere and he should act long before such crises develop.

Dangerous conflict even at the point of ignition *can* be turned away and violence and war avoided. This is best accomplished by the direct negotiation of antagonists. Mediation of any sort tends to be inadequate and to delay the psychological processes essential for both sides in the peaceful negotiation of their conflict. Negotiation is therefore the affair of those involved. However, mediation may have an early part to play in permitting communication, but its persuasions and pressures do not produce real change. In any case there is no room for direct psychiatric intervention in such acute crises.

Like any citizen or professional group the psychiatrist may build bridges between nations before conflict advances to a dan-

gerous point or after violence has occurred and expended itself.
During such periods he should also attempt, of course, to influence his own people towards reflection and rational behavior.

It is on the other hand the role of the psychiatrist and his
colleagues in mental health to foster during the child's development in the family the greatest possible potential for the management of conflict. This is another way of saying that a role of
the psychiatrist should be the promotion of mental health. In the
psychodynamic sense, progress towards mental health is progress
toward peaceable relations.

Of course I have simply applied here concepts from the mental
health movement. Peace is equated with individual or group
mental health and the handling of inner or family conflict. War
and violence are equated with breakdown in this process and
deviation and mental illness.

I have here suggested that the psychiatrist has no particular
role to play in direct intervention in crisis situations threatening
war but that he has a role in the promotion of peace in his own
society. However a difficulty arises. Among the most important
factors in mental health are the social, for example poverty or
technological, forces. Hence the psychiatrist cannot even in this
sphere, where social action is required, take upon himself a direct
role and responsibility. This is the direct social business of political leaders and perhaps of social philosophers. Nevertheless
the psychiatrist has an inescapable role to play for mental health
and peace in advising and perhaps supporting them in these
functions.

The role of the psychiatrist for mental health and for peace is
therefore not central since the forces which shape a mind through
the production of conflict and educate for its management are
cultural and not open to direct psychiatric influence. They can
however be influenced directly by those who are vested by
society with power and influence—namely, political leaders,
social philosophers and adults as parents and citizens.

The function of the psychiatrist is that of seeking communication with social leadership and social educators in order to make
available to them his understanding of the infantile psychological

sources of human conflict, the psychodynamics of its management through adaptation to frustration or its mismanagement resulting in expressions of violence.

The unity of the concepts of the promotion of peace and of mental health is most evident in the developing child. The satisfactory management of conflict by the child and by the adult representatives of society in its family is synonymous with education and socialization. It is at the time of child-rearing and the first acquisition of patterns of conflict negotiation that the most important contribution can be made to mental health and the management of adult conflict.

The negotiation of conflict and the establishment of voluntary cooperation is probably the most deeply ingrained of our democratic social values, and yet it has been little studied or seldom analyzed explicitly as an adult function. Insufficient actual negotiation goes on between adults and children and many transactions are based on the adult power and authority to deny affection while demanding suppression of will on the part of the child. In some societies, the suppression of the child's will has unfortunately been replaced by a tendency to overpermissiveness or by vacillation.

Unsuccessful management of conflict with the developing child may result in adolescent and adult patterns of maladaptation of rebellion and conflict solution through violence. Hence the machinery of acculturation is on the whole crucial for problems of aggression. At this interpersonal developmental phase, conflict must be negotiated wisely so that internal patterns of mediation (ego) are laid down which do not seek solutions through a recourse to violence or sacrifice individuality or initiative.

Conflict from a social standpoint is the source of acculturation and therefore in its essence a constructive and desirable and even ineluctable social phenomenon. However, it results frequently in destructive tendencies both against the self or others. From the ideal point of view all conflict whether in earlier or later years, if appropriately managed, may be constructive and a force for social maturation. In the ideal scheme the aggression generated by frustration and conflict becomes the energy for negotiation, conflict solution and growth. This is certainly true of the developing child. It may be so too of the adult world if its conflicts were managed appropriately rather than through the seeking of one-sided victories as sought once by king and knight and now pursued by politician, tycoon or academician.

Perhaps increased understanding by the psychiatrist of the conflict-laden process of acculturation of the child may expose the roots of the drives toward unmitigated power and the refusal to compromise. Our assumption is that some cultures will tend to produce personality patterns in which the potential for true compromise is deficient. The onus is upon the adults in every society to review constantly the goals and results of their child-rearing and educational systems.

There is a certain positive homogeneity, directed against pathological conflict, in the conception of a democratic society and in its democratic ways of child-rearing. In democractic societies the possibilities of personal choice are wide for the adults. Granting the child individual status and rights increases these possibilities. This has occurred in societies in which the individuals are still ill equipped to come to terms with these responsibilities. Small wonder that the blessing of increasing freedom and permissiveness have been accompanied by the new discontents such as drug abuse, student revolt and dropouts which plague Western countries. It is our concern to point this out and promote at every opportunity the maturation of the adult. This can best be done, not by theoretical lectures or through the mass media but by the direct involvement of adults in the negotiation and solution of social, political and intergroup problems. Skills in negotiating are acquired in the act of negotiation. Individuals mature only through active, personal and social experience—even though mass participation and negotiations are not exactly the ideal of politicians, managers and bureaucrats!

From my experience the underlying general motive for war is associated with mass problems of personal self-image and identity. Identity is also largely a product of the acculturation of the child and the culturally determined conflicts of the adults with it and within the family. Negotiations of those conflicts result in their internalization in the child who internalizes as well the patterns of compromise reached. In a sense the child incorporates the attitudes of its adult antagonist in the conflict as its own identity.

I have made reference to leaders past and current who seek total unilateral victory in international and national struggles. Such leadership is fed by infantile group feelings especially those concerned with issues of identity which become tied to the leader and expressed as territorial, economic, religious, ideological and even frank power drives. Subtle symbols and stereotypes are evolved both of the "enemy" and of the self. Changes are wrought in the individual mind, in the perception of reality, its meaning and in the personal relations to it. A set of impairments thus occur both of reality testing and morality to a degree which can be termed "psychotic" and permits of the desired state of warlike morale—a blind activity of fear and hatred of particular groups and aggression against them. This warlike state and others resembling it such as antisemitism and religious and color prejudice are close relatives of the clinical delusion.

This distortion of reality permits acting out against the "enemy," the "bad" object who may as well be the bad society, with feelings of heroism, victorious struggle, pride and sacrifice. The "good" objects with which identification takes place are the leader and group—traditional, such as tribe and religious movement; or more modern, such as nation or political movement.

Problems of identity are today especially notable in Western Society where social institutions and adult roles in the family have become blurred and confused. On the other hand social change, from tribalism to the modern state also result in shocks to the parental and social roles as a result of confusion in the family and in the rapidly changing society. This is especially evident today in Middle Eastern society where there is a violent search for new identities touching all, from person and family to state and religious group. Unsatisfactory transactions in such families and the identity problems which result tend to seek solutions in bravado, violence and even war to discharge unsolved conflict and screw identity to the sticking place.

Much support can be found for this point of view when the motivations for wars in the past are reviewed. An insult, a murder of a public figure by a deviant, a piece of worthless territory or a refusal to accept a theological view became the trigger for the murder of many thousands.

Is all this over now? Going to war for a social ideology or a religious one, or going to war for the sake of mastery? Has man come to his senses? Has the fact that war is only for losers changed it all? No, nothing has changed radically! The dispositions have changed because of the balance of super powers and super-weapons, but little has changed in man, although it has become apparent to many that the victories of war are insanely destructive, delusional and infantile especially when compared to the achievements of peace. We have a breathing space. There is as it were a deadlock but no change in the basic human forces. But the deadlock may yet be exploited by raising a generation which knows how to resolve conflict constructively and find its identity and which will raise a further generation even more capable of it. This, as I have said, is the particular arena for action by the psychiatrist.

Of course this requires the commitment of the society. It is an ideal to which not all nations will subscribe or subscribe honestly. But to this one should not react neither by preparing for aggressive war, which was the classical response, nor by a nonviolent or pacifist stance. One should certainly prepare for self-defense, but at the same time one should certainly prepare and educate for peace. This is like living in two worlds (on "two time-levels" as Ernst Simon has said) —preparing and educating oneself to defend onself and at the same time preparing and educating one's children and people for peace. Nothing in the preparation for defense, Simon has stressed, must preclude or obstruct the education and readiness for ultimate peace.

Not only has the balance of international power provided an all-important hiatus in the cycle of war and peace; another powerful agent has come to our aid. This is the autonomous development which has occurred in youth. Many youths have broken away from the vicious circle of the infantile struggle for identity and mastery and the resulting production of insoluble group conflict in adulthood. Many young men have paid a sore price in so doing, such as their precipitation and regression into the dream worlds of the hippy, of drug abuse and the beachcomber and mystic. At times they have regressed into states of anarchy and violence. These phenomena, both positive and negative, are the products of the individual freedom and responsibility of Western Society.

Many youths who have survived socially in this society have begun to build relations between nations and groups. They have begun to break down empty rituals, intergroup prejudices and stereotypes and other false abstractions in a way that no other pantisocracy or universalism has been able to do.

We have noted that the products of early experience of the child are later transferred to and expressed in the older social groups. This provides of course the cohesion for the group. The obverse of group cohesion is the competition with or fear or hatred of other groups. These group identity phenomena, whether tribal, national or power-bloc, receive the inheritance of infantile striving and become the stage for their expression against other groups. No wonder gang activity, antisemitism, civil strife and war appear to be rooted in group interests such as economics, religion or territorial struggles. What many youths indeed have done today is to attempt to break down these exclusive group feelings and to remove them from the chain of determinism of conflict and war. Such people presumably have in mind as well an attack on the childhood causes of unsuccessfully managed conflicts in child-parent relationships.

The kibbutz too was an organized form of rebellion against the child-rearing familial, social and economic springs of pathological social conflict. It is a satisfactory example of education and socialization for constructive conflict mediation and positive identity. It is no wonder therefore that the kibbutz has realized and lived out as well the social philosophy of education for defense and for peace at once. The kibbutz was a crucible in which these values were clarified for all of Israeli society. What the kibbutz demonstrates is that by successful child-rearing in a

given social organization one may produce not only an individual
who is on the whole reasonably well balanced and motivated to
subscribe actively to the values of the society which has produced
him, but one capable too of dealing well with conflict and aggression.

In essence the avoidance of violence between adult groups,
and of war between nations, is possible today through the direct
negotiation of conflict. The possibilities even of such negotiations in crisis situations are limited to a type of firefighting but
they can be successful and are urgently necessary. Such negotiations must involve the leaders of those involved in the conflict.
The psychiatrist has little or no place in such crisis negotiation
or conflict; however, he may build bridges between groups and
nations in anticipation of the ever-present danger of such crises.

The long-term view of the fostering of peace is a matter of child-
rearing. The acculturation of the child is involved with conflict
with adults and its negotiation. Such conflict negotiation becomes
the pattern for its personality and for the child's behavior later
in social situations concerned with conflict. The infantile conflict
is also the source of the adult's sense of his own identity. Impairments of identity often are at the root of intergroup conflict,
violence and war and can be exploited by leaders for such ends.
The psychiatrist and his colleagues are particularly fitted to
approach these problems arising from child-rearing and identity.
However, since the total social machinery and all parents and
leaders determine the ways of acculturation, the psychiatrist
must act through leadership and social educators in order to bring
this influence and experience to bear.

Particular problems of child-rearing and identity in the changing Western and Middle Eastern family are fraught with danger of
violence. The positive methods of child-rearing, conflict negotiation and identity formation in the Israeli kibbutz provide a
model for Israel and others of education for peace while remaining prepared for self-defense. The kibbutz and much of
Israeli society therefore are working models of mental health
and psychiatric action for conflict negotiation and peace.

Chapter 13

Subjective Culture Interference in Intergroup Relations

GEORGE VASSILIOU AND VASSO VASSILIOU

SUBJECTIVE CULTURE AS A DETERMINANT OF BEHAVIOR

THE CONCEPT OF *subjective culture* is one of the most important elements enabling us to understand variations in human behavior and experience.[1-3] Subjective culture refers to the way in which individuals perceive their social environment. Moreover, studies on delimited aspects of social perception such as stereotyping [3-5] indicate the importance of subjective culture in the development of intergroup attitudes.

Recent reviews of the literature in cross-cultural psychology, covering five chapters of the *Handbook of Social Psychology*,[6-12] established the importance of culture in determining human behavior and experience. Overall cultural factors have been shown to exert important influences on processes related to perception and cognition. Triandis [13] observed that cultural factors are important determinants of perceptual responses since members of a culture may perceive object A rather than object B for a number of reasons: (a) the greater meaning of A than B,[14] (b) or because of the higher frequency of occurrence of A relative to B or (c) more pleasant associations with A rather than with B.[15] Previous cultural experiences, therefore, may enhance the perception of object A and depress that of object B.[16,17] Likewise, the availability of a category of objects will also affect their retention.[14,18,19]

The perception of space also involves the acquisition of *habits* of perceptual inference.[20,21] Ecological and cultural factors operating in the visual environment have been to create differences in visual inference.[13,22]

Criterial attributes for categorization differ from culture to culture.[23,24] Studies on social distance, for example, have shown that in the United States some subjects respond to the stimulus "black people" and indicate that they will exclude them from their ingroup by choosing answers such as, "I will exclude them from my neighborhood." [13,25,26] In this case the criterial attribute for inclusion in the category "black people" (equals outgroup) is skin color.

In the Greek milieu, the *amount of concern* shown in a given interpersonal encounter is a much more important criterial attribute in "other-perception" than is skin color. While the American defines his ingroup statically as "people like me," the Greek defines his ingroup operationally as "people concerned with me." [27] The Greek ingroup is a dynamic social entity which is constantly in process. There are no static human characteristics, such as skin color, which operate to secure ingroup membership. But "being concerned" is the criterial attribute, *par excellence,* for ingroup membership. Conversely, one's membership in the Greek ingroup can be terminated abruptly the moment one is perceived as "not showing concern." Accordingly, whenever the Greek meets concern from somebody else, he establishes ingroup ties which call for absolute interdependence, mutual loyalty, complete mutual acceptance and virtually unlimited give-and-take, ignoring other "objective" criteria. These behavioral norms operate only within the ingroup. Outgroup relations, on the other hand, are characterized by mutual suspicion, antagonism, readiness to outmaneuver, cheat, defy and defeat the "Other." Relations with the outgroup are highly competitive.

In effect, Greeks perceive social transactions quite differently than do Americans. In Greece one is perceived as either an ingroup or an outgroup member; for example, the concept of fairness in human relations, a key concept for Americans, is nonexistent within the Greek core culture. The Greek knows that he has to "give his heart" to his ingroup and antagonize "to the end" outgroup people.

Some of these points can be illustrated by research findings. An American who *acts* like an executive in Greece [2,5,27] (a) will be concerned with time and planning; (b) will feel that he controls the rewards he receives from his environment; (c) will perceive his obligations relatively independently of authority figures; (d) will use broad, impersonal ingroups; (e) will compete with standards of excellence; and (f) will be optimistic about controlling his environment. But in Greece, he will *interact* with a culture in which (a) the ingroup is delineated functionally, based on strong, interdependent, face-to-face relationships; (b) people are extremely nurturant, open and giving within the ingroup, but look at the world with suspicion; (c) people believe that material "goods" are limited and that one obtains his share by fulfilling his obligations to the important "Others," with no standards of excellence but the expectation that he will do *his* best; (d) people identify with authority figures—recognized as such only within the ingroup—and expect direction from them; (e) people consider planning a waste of effort, have no strict conception of time and do not believe that they can control their environment, but rather see themselves under the influence of external forces; and (f) interpersonal relations are primarily means of survival.

The American's behavior is largely regulated by his commitment to his principle of "fairness to all people like him." Therefore, the American is likely to show equal concern, demand equal standards of performance and expect cooperation from such people. But to the Greek, "people like me" is a meaningless category. The Greek dichotomizes people into "people who are concerned with me" and "all the others," the potential opponents, rivals or enemies.

When the Greek perceives an American as "showing concern to him," he is likely to admit him into his ingroup. However, double membership in rivaling ingroups is unacceptable. Consequently, if and when an American, out of "American fairness" and "equal treatment for all people like me" shows similar concern to another Greek who does not belong to that ingroup, the American automatically betrays the trust of the Greek ingroup and, at the same time, is regarded as an object of suspicion by the second group. These are some of the complexities that an American manager is bound to encounter when working in Greece.

Many cross-cultural studies concerned with educational efforts among trainees and trainers have shown the inappropriateness of the assumption of a "common culture." Triandis, Shanmugam, Tanaka and Vassiliou, 1971,[3] invited subjects from different cultures to present "antecedents and consequents" of a number of concepts such as love, trust, knowledge, progress, anger, freedom and punishment. The research findings showed that each of four cultures stressed a different dominant theme; for example, Americans emphasized respect, whereas Greeks emphasized competition and the need for social control. Important differences were also found to exist in the consequents of "good" concepts; the major trends suggest that the Americans stressed progress, self-confidence, good adjustment, status, serenity and satisfaction, while the Greeks stressed societal well-being, civilization, glory, victory and individual well-being in the form of receiving concern and appreciation from others.

Corresponding investigations of interpersonal perceptions have also indicated that role attributes,[2] such as (a) giving or denying affect, (b) giving or denying status and (c) intimacy *versus* formality, appear in various forms. Dimension, giving of affect, may be expressed either as nurturance (providing care, help) or as love (fall in love, pet, caress). The behaviors which are perceived as superordinate may differ from culture to culture.[2] In the American group [29] the superordinate behaviors refer to "correct," "reprimand," "advise," "not be afraid of"; in contrast, in the Greeks the superordinate behaviors referred to "reprimand," "teach," "not apologize to" and "punish."

In addition to such differences in role perception, there are major differences in the degree to which a particular role is perceived as having more or less of the attributes of affect, status or intimacy. For example, the Greeks showed highly significant affect in the son-mother role, whereas the roles of boss-secretary and laborer-foreman involved more subordination for a Greek than for an American. Therefore, when the American boss provides "friendly criticism" to a Greek employee, the Greek interprets it as "hatred." Or, when the American withdraws to what he considers an "indifferent position," intended to indicate neutrality, he is definitely perceived as "hostile" by his Greek counterpart. Or, when a Greek behaves normatively and provides help and assistance in a manner which he considers "positive," he is perceived by his American counterpart as "violating my privacy" and "prying into my affairs."

GENERAL IMPLICATIONS

In view of the above, international efforts can easily go astray, not only because of objective socioeconomic and sociopolitical conflicts but also because of a large number of vicious circles that emanate from subjective culture interference and from misunderstandings created by the different ways in which things and events are perceived across milieux. International relations on all levels, including mass media, tourism, business, education, science and politics, are heavily affected. The problem is that those who are responsible and influential in these areas do not seem to be aware of this source of misunderstanding or they tend to fall victim to the general principle that "people are the same the world over." However, those people who are assumed to be so similar really perceive things quite differently. The end result is that the vicious circles which are generated from the subsequent misunderstandings lead rapidly to *objective* conflicts or "clashes." At this stage each party may feel indignant about the "unfairness," "hypocrisy" or the "treachery" of the other. Such situations can best be served by specialists, who possess knowledge of the subjective cultures of both parties involved, *hence the practical importance of the study of subjective culture.*

The more heterogeneous a society in the subjective culture of its subgroups of ethnic minorities, the more it will need such expertise to reduce conflict and develop more harmonious human relations within its boundaries. One needs only to review the conflicts arising in multicultural societies, such as the American, to realize that in the absence of an adequate awareness of subjective culture, interference in intergroup relations become a "melting pot," a "boiling pot."

IMPLICATIONS CONCERNING MENTAL HEALTH

The rapid acceleration of social change, following the Second World War, imposed strenuous demands on individuals and societies, the "developing" as well as the "developed" societies. Subgroups coming from rural areas find it difficult to adjust to urbanized and industrialized centers, especially in the "overdeveloped" areas. The impact on human relations necessarily varies across milieux, with mental reactions and malfunctioning also varying. From this point of view, nosological similarities are misleading—they are "reductions" made out of context. Behavioral reactions occurring in different milieux vary in their meaning, social function, prognosis and requirements for therapeutic intervention. Therefore, "milieu-specificity" in mental health training, diagnosis, intervention techniques and preventive efforts are of paramount practical importance.

In training, the most practical solution would be to develop programs that could provide adequate awareness of the issues involved, the research findings in the area and some implications of these findings which can be applied for mental health care. This is particularly important in centers which train mental health practitioners for a multicultural milieu or which receive trainees from diverse cultures. But such centers have been heavily influenced by their surrounding culture, which influences the scientific theories, clinical approaches and techniques of intervention which are taught. On returning to their original milieu, trainees will find themselves confronted with numerous failures and complications if they disregard the fact that they are now in a different culture.

In the area of therapeutic intervention and prevention, the effectiveness of techniques and approaches used will be directly related to their milieu-specificity. The author's experience supports this assumption. Preliminary attempts, which were developed on the basis of qualitative observations and research findings and which aimed to add milieu-specificity to already established intervention techniques, are beginning to provide encouraging results.

SUMMARY

By eliminating conflict produced by subjective culture interference, one can arrest a number of misleading rationalizations which, disguised as "ideological issues," tend to cloud the objective reasons for conflict or complicate them to the point of rendering them uncontrolled. If the etiology of conflict is reduced to its bare, *objective reasons*, the conflicting groups can find an operational solution. Mutual annihilation is no solution. One can hope that the "tantalizing seventies" will open the door which will permit contemporary Anthropos to escape the fate of Tantalus.

REFERENCES

1. Osgood, C. E.: On the strategy of cross-national research into subjective culture. *Soc Sci Info, 6*:1–37, 1967.
2. Triandis, H., Vassiliou, V., and Nassiakou, M.: Three cross-cultural studies of subjective culture. *J Pers Soc Psychol, 8*:1–42, 1968.
3. Triandis, H., Vassiliou, G. and V., Tanaka, Y., and Shanmugam, A. V.: *The Analysis of Subjective Culture.* New York, John Wiley & Sons.
4. Campbell, D. T.: Stereotypes and the perception of group differences. *Am Psychol, 22*:817–829, 1967.
5. Triandis, H., and Vassiliou, V.: Frequency of contact and stereotyping. *J Pers Soc Psychol, 7*:316–328, 1967.
6. Whiting, J. W. M.: Methods and problems in cross-cultural research. In *Handbook of Social Psychology* (Vol. II), edited by G. Landzey and E. Aronson. Reading (Mass.), Addison-Wesley, 1968.
7. Tajfel, H.: Social and cultural factors in perception. In *Handbook of Social Psychology* (Vol. III), edited by G. Lindzey and E. Aronson. Reading (Mass.), Addison-Wesley, 1969.
8. DeVos, G. A., and Hippler, A. E.: Cultural psychology: Comparative studies of human behaviors. In *Handbook of Social Psychology* (Vol. IV), edited by G. Lindzey and E. Aronson. Reading (Mass.), Addison-Wesley, 1969.
9. Inkles, A., and Levinson, D. J.: Cultural psychology: Comparative studies of human behavior. In *Handbook of Social Psychology* (Vol. IV), edited by G. Lindzey and E. Aronson. Reading (Mass.), Addison-Wesley, 1969.
10. Etzioni, A.: Social-psychological aspects of international relations. In *Handbook of Social Psychology* (Vol. V), edited by G. Lindzey and E. Aronson. Reading (Mass.), Addison-Wesley, 1969.
11. Child, I. L.: Personality in culture. In *Handbook of Personality Theory and Research,* edited by E. F. Borgatta and W. W. Iambert. Chicago, Rand-McNally, 1968.

12. Honigmann, J. J.: *Personality in Culture.* New York, Harper & Row, 1967.
13. Triandis, H. C.: Cultural influences upon cognitive processes. In *Advances in Experimental Social Psychology,* edited by L. Berkowitz. New York, Academic Press, 1964.
14. Bartlett, F. C.: *Remembering.* London and New York, Cambridge University Press, 1932.
15. Eriksen, C. W.: *Concepts of Personality.* Chicago, Aldine Press, 1963.
16. Bagby, J. W.: *J Abnorm Soc Psychol, 54*:331–334, 1957.
17. Luria, A. R.: *The Role of Speech in the Regulation of Normal and Abnormal Behavior.* New York, Liveright, 1961.
18. Talland, G. A.: *J Soc Psychol, 43*:75–81, 1969.
19. Goodman, M. E.: *Ethnology, 1*:374–386, 1962.
20. Segall, M. H., Campbell, D. T., and Herskovits, M. J.: *Science, 139:* 769–771, 1963.
21. Segall, M. H., Campbell, D. T., and Herskovits, M. J.: *The Influence of Culture on Visual Perception.* Indianapolis, Bobbs-Merrill, 1964.
22. Jahoda, G., and Stacey, B.: Susceptibility to geometrical illusion according to culture and professional training. *Percept Psychophysics, 7:* 179–184, 1970.
23. Hallowell, A. I.: In *Social Psychology at the Crossroads,* edited by J. H. Rohrer and M. Sherif. New York, Harper & Row, 1951.
24. Mathiot, M.: *Am Anthropol, 64*:340–350, 1962.
25. Triandis, H. C.: Exploratory factor analyses of the behavioral component of social attitudes. *J Abnorm Soc Psychol, 68*:420–430, 1964.
26. Triandis, H. C., and Triandis, L. M.: A cross-cultural study of social distance. *Psychological Monograph, 76*:2i, whole no. 540, 1962.
27. Vassiliou, V., Triandis, H., and Vassiliou, G.: Reported amount of contact and stereotyping. In *The Analysis of Subjective Culture,* edited by Triandis *et al.* New York, John Wiley & Sons.
28. Vassiliou, G., and V.: On aspects of child-rearing in Greece. In *Yearbook of the International Association of Child Psychiatry* (Vol. I), edited by J. Anthony. 1970.
29. Sarbin, T. R.: Role theory. In *Handbook of Social Psychology* (Vol. I), edited by G. Lindzey and E. Aronson. Reading (Mass.), Addison-Wesley, 1954.

Chapter 14

The Economic Factor in Concordance and
Discordance:
Some Cross-Cultural Observations

ISIDORE ZIFERSTEIN

IN JULY, 1950, the Committee on Social Issues of the Group
for the Advancement of Psychiatry issued a GAP Report
No. 13, titled *The Social Responsibility of Psychiatry*, which has
great relevance to today's deliberations of the American Society
for Social Psychiatry. This report read in part:

> [The Committee on Social Issues] believes that many of the warps
> and twists of our society have significant relevance for the issues of
> mental health. . . . It believes that certain changes in the pattern of
> interaction between individuals and family, and individuals and so-
> ciety, may provide a more nourishing matrix for the cultivation of
> mental health. . . . At the time of Robert Koch, it was enough to
> locate and describe the tubercle bacillus. . . . But soon the pathologist
> became an ecologist and eventually a public health officer who . . .
> strove to eliminate dust, dirt and darkness from the environment. . . .
> We favor the application of psychiatric principles to all those problems
> which have to do with family welfare . . . social and economic factors
> which influence the community status of individuals and families,
> inter-group tensions, civil rights and personal liberty. This in a true
> sense carries psychiatry out of the hospitals and clinics and into the
> community.

In our own area of special concern—that of providing adequate
psychiatric treatment to the people (and more generally, the
problem of providing medical care)—we see an appalling spec-
tacle. In the United States, the richest country in the world, the
talk is all about cutbacks. At the recent meetings of the American Psychiatric Association, great concern was expressed over the

Note: The research on which this chapter is based was supported by grants from
the Foundations' Fund for Research in Psychiatry and the National Institute of
Mental Health (Grant Number MH 16872).

impending phase-out of federal funding of residency training of psychiatrists. In universities throughout the country, faculties are being cut back, at a time when increasing numbers of students are clamoring for admission. The Medicare program and local programs for providing medical care, such as Medical in California, are being drastically reduced.

I should like to compare these phenomena in our country, with the status of psychiatric and medical care services in another country—a country which is significantly less affluent than ours in terms of gross national product and other economic indices.

In 1967, the First U.S. Mission on Mental Health to Russia made an official visit of inspection of Soviet psychiatric facilities, under the auspices of the U.S. Department of State. One of the participants in this mission wrote the following report on his observations of the delivery of mental health care in the Soviet Union:

> The major attraction of the system is that it has removed the economic barrier to good psychiatric care for all of its people. In many ways, this is the most shocking failure here in America. Under a predominantly fee-for-service system, only three percent of our people can afford private psychiatric care. The health insurance industry here moves with glacial slowness to cover the economic costs of mental illness. . . .
>
> We have much to learn from the emphasis in Russia upon the training of adequate numbers of health personnel. Despite the enormous competitive pressures from other segments of the economy for skilled workers, the Ministry of Health of the U.S.S.R. conducts a successful battle for increased funds for the training of more health personnel. The brilliant Deputy Minister of Health, Dr. Venediktov, talks impatiently of being limited by having only 600,000 doctors for a population of 230,000,000 people (this compares with less than 300,000 doctors for more than 200,000,000 people in this country). Dr. Venediktov wants 700,000 doctors by 1970, and he is expanding medical schools and building new ones to achieve his goal.
>
> Compared to both Russian achievements and boldly announced aspirations, our American goals these past few years, during the so-called community psychiatric revolution, seem rather limited in that they do not fundamentally challenge out-moded ways of delivering services which are conditioned upon ability to pay.
>
> [We] submit that the time has now come for a more profound examination of our mental health delivery system, with an eye toward

bringing the boon of psychiatric care to millions of Americans whom it does not reach today.

My own observations during four visits to the Soviet Union, including a fifteen-month stay in 1963–1964 and a recent four-month stay, from which I returned in January of this year, confirm this evaluation.

In the course of my work at the Bekhterev Psychoneurological Research Institute in Leningrad, I was struck by the fact that the patients in this excellent treatment facility constitute a genuine cross section of the population of the Soviet Union. For example, the patients on one ward in the women's section included the wife of a cabinet minister of the R.S.F.S.R. (Russian Soviet Federated Socialist Republic), a milkmaid from a collective dairy farm, a worker from a textile mill, a woman agronomist, etcetera. This was true of all the psychiatric facilities, both inpatient and outpatient, that I observed. It would be instructive, as a cross-cultural study, to compare the social composition of the patients in our finest private psychiatric hospitals and in corresponding facilities in the Soviet Union.

During my several stays in the Soviet Union, I found the same narrowing of the gap between the haves and the have-nots, in other areas of living as well. This was true for the provision of psychiatric care, as well as general medical care, both of which are made available without charge, to all who need it.

In the area of education, I found that in the Soviet Union there are no private schools, accessible primarily to the wealthy, as is the case in our country. Higher education, including courses of study in professional schools, such as medicine, law, engineering, is free of cost. Furthermore, a large percentage of students receive stipends while studying.

In the area of housing, there is genuine integration of various socioeconomic groups. With the exception of the cooperative housing projects built by some of the trade unions, there is not, in the Soviet Union, the kind of socioeconomic geographical segregation that prevails in our country, where there are fashionable neighborhoods for the well-to-do, less fashionable areas for the lower middle class, and slums for the poverty folk. For example, when I visited in the home of one of the psychiatrists of the

Bekhterev Institute, I learned that across the corridor in the same apartment building lived a woman who worked as an uborshchitza, a cleaning woman, at the Institute. Her apartment was exactly like the apartment of the psychiatrist.

In this connection, it is worth noting that community psychiatrists in our country have called attention to the socioeconomic and cultural gap that exists between upper–middle-class American psychiatrists and the patients they attempt to treat in community psychiatric facilities. It has been pointed out that this gap produces discordance between psychiatrist and patient and hinders the psychotherapeutic process. In the Soviet Union, the economic gap between doctor and patient is much less or is nonexistent. The earnings of a psychiatrist are not more, and may sometimes be less, than those of a factory worker.

George Feifer, author of *Justice in Moscow,* points out yet another area in which there is often quite a socioeconomic gap in our country, but practically no gap in the Soviet Union, the area of administration of justice. In summing up his observations of Soviet court proceedings, Feifer writes,

> In the first weeks I was surprised by the informality, the lack of legal phraseology, of practiced, self-conscious precision, of esoteric procedural niceties and devotion to form. . . . What the people in court have to say is more important than how they must say it. In the trials that I observed, when an interested observer had some relevant information to give, he gave it, even if it would have been inadmissible as evidence in a foreign court and even if he was not, at the moment, in the witness stand.

Feifer concludes as follows:

> The drab little chambers seem not inappropriate as courtrooms; whether because of the bareness or in spite of it, they preserve that dignity and solemnity that means a court. People, not furniture or ornaments, dominate those rooms; simple people, unintimidated by pomp and polish, tell their stories and make their excuses in a setting natural for them, and they seem stronger for it.
>
> One feels, too, a sense of social (if not professional) equality in these courts, a real absence of class distinction that is more than a propagandist's invention. Equality between those on the bench and those below it: the judge is not "your honor," and there is no obsequiousness to his person as to someone of higher social stuff. He is, if not always a comrade, then at least a *prostoi Sovietskii chelovyek*—an "ordinary

Soviet fellow"—made of the same stuff and stock as his prisoners. No one is embarrassed, awed or frightened by him.

And equality, too, between the defendants. Every statistic confirms that in American courts it's "the rich what gets the mercy and the poor what gets the blame." But it is no longer the same the whole world over. In the People's Courts, money talks softly, when at all. It can buy a better lawyer, and it has been known to bribe a weak investigator; but this is less common than the Soviet tendency to set an example by punishing the more affluent wrongdoers more severely.

In the People's Courts it is poor work in the factory, rather than a poor purse, that puts a defendant at a disadvantage.

To sum up: In the course of my visits to the Soviet Union and of my observation of psychiatric practices there, I was struck by a kind of basic economic democracy that prevails in that country, in terms of the kind of psychiatric care that is available to those higher in the socioeconomic scale and those in the lower. This applies also to medical care in general, to housing, education and the administration of justice.

I submit that in our deliberations about the sources of social discordance and concordance, we must give serious consideration to the basic economic factors enumerated above: to the discordance produced by economic inequities; to the discord between the haves and the have-nots, between the overprivileged and the underprivileged, between the technologically advanced and the underdeveloped—whether this be within a nation or between nations.

Chapter 15

Developing Countries and Human Concordance

ARI KIEV

THE DEVELOPING COUNTRIES in Asia, Africa, the Caribbean and Latin America are all characterized in varying degrees by the increasing use of technology, growing industrialization and large-scale migrations from rural into urban areas, all of which contribute to making these societies highly stressful environments with a consequent increasing incidence of psychiatric disorder.

The United Nations estimates that by the year 2,000 there will be more than seven billion people in the world, the bulk of whom will be in these developing countries. With rapidly expanding populations, personnel and resources for medical and educational programs will not be adequate to meet the needs of these countries in the years to come.

At present less than half the world's population has access to medical care and often this is grossly inadequate for its needs or has little effect. It is very doubtful, for example, that a country such as Liberia with a million and a half people now and one psychiatrist is going to have sufficient numbers of psychiatrists in twenty years. There probably will not be sufficient numbers of paramedical personnel either. There is, therefore, an urgent need to understand the special sources of human problems in these societies resulting from the marked social change and turbulence. This will not only add to our general knowledge of man's interaction with society but will enable us to pinpoint areas of stress or discordance in these societies in which psychiatric intervention can be introduced and proper preventive measures established. This is particularly true of disorders most likely to be affected by environmental factors—that is, the neuroses,

216

alcoholism, delinquency and drug addictions which are reportedly on the increase in most of the developing countries.

Poverty, population pressure, limited resources, new social structures and class relationships, political unrest and instability, large dependent populations, inadequate educational systems, inadequate food production, too rapid urbanization and inadequate rural development are the predominant problems of the developing nations of Asia, Africa, Latin America and the Middle East. These are problems unequally balanced by the positive characteristics of development which relate to industrialization, urbanization, migration, improved health and sanitation.

POPULATION GROWTH

The world population increased by 485 million, or 19 percent, between 1950 and 1960, equal to the same increase in number as between 1750 and 1850 and the same percent increases between 1930 and 1950.

By the year 2,000, as stated, the world population of seven billion people will exceed the world's ability to produce adequate food to feed this population or prevent overcrowding.

The recorded birth rates in Africa, Asia, Middle and South America in 1960 were in excess of 35 per thousand and the gross reproduction rates were over 2, the majority being between 2.7 and 3.2. Europe, North America and Oceania had birth rates no higher than 30 per thousand and production rates of 2.

Throughout the developing world, urban population is growing more rapidly than the rural population due in large part to migration from rural to urban areas. In Africa, Asia and Latin America, some urban areas doubled between 1950 and 1960 and projections envisage further doubling in these same regions between 1960 and 1975, at the same time as rural populations are expected to continue to decline. There are insufficient jobs for this expanding urban population, the majority of whom are dependent youth. Population growth has deterred economic progress by creating a labor surplus, increased consumption needs and a decrease in overall income which might otherwise be utilized for long-term investment in education, equipment and capital needs. Thus the expanding population has widespread effects on numerous aspects of society.

Strategies to achieve breakthrough, including forced savings, the creation of export industries and foreign aid are, however, difficult to implement.

The natural increase per thousand population is everywhere extreme, a trend relating not only to increased rates of birth but also to declining death rates. Medical advances, particularly the control of cholera, plague, malaria and other infectious diseases, have reduced the crude death rate substantially since 1930.

Fertility rates which are twice as high in developing countries as in the developed ones are clearly linked to religious, ethical and cultural values. Increasing industrialization may in time lead to reduced fertility rates in much the same way as happened in Europe following the industrial revolution. Working women and those seeking better educations for their youngsters are likely to favor smaller families. Despite such anticipated reductions, the development of the population on usable land, the population density in urban areas and the need for adequate social, medical and welfare services for large numbers of people will still present major obstacles to development.

The numbers reaching school age and looking for jobs and homes are increasing even more rapidly than the total population increase. Schools, jobs and dwelling units must increase more than 3 percent each year to keep present deficiencies from growing, according to the United Nations' figures.

Increased population usually means the perpetuation of malnutrition, illiteracy and a subpar standard of living. Urban industry and employment opportunities are not commensurate with population growth. The massive application of capital to resources is the way to end the discrepancy between people and resources, according to Ward, but savings are difficult to secure in a poor society where productivity is less than the population increase. When the rate of population increase is 2 percent, as in parts of Latin America, people cannot save. Since three times as much capital as population increase must be invested to secure one unit of income, the developing countries would have to increase their national income by at least 9 percent each year beyond the 4 or 5 percent of traditional society. To achieve a breakthrough into a period of sustained growth, it may even be desirable to get a rate up to 12 to 15 percent of national income devoted to productive capital.

In 1962 the population of Latin America, for example, was 210 million. It is increasing by 2.6 percent yearly. The total population will thus have increased by 85 percent in 25 years. By 1980 there will be 333 million Latin Americans. This population is primarily a youthful, rural and poor one. More than 40 percent in 1960 were less than 15 years old. Fifty-four percent live in rural areas, and 50 percent are employed in agriculture and livestock raising. The gross product per person in 1960 was equivalent to $320 in 1950 American prices or $371 in 1960 prices. Improved health standards and public health measures such as insect control, sewage disposal and improved water supplies have led to increased birth rates, reduced child mortality rates and increased survival rates. To maintain economic growth in the face of increasing population, it is necessary for industrialization and agriculture to expand considerably. Most of the jobs have come in industry and this implies a continuing large-scale movement of population from the agricultural rural areas to the more arrant urban areas. It also implies a need for heavy investments to provide sources of employment and an increased need for urban housing and services. The urban population in particular is increasing at a rate of about 5 percent annually. Large cities are probably increasing at a higher rate because of the lack of planning.

There is in all of the developing countries a large lower stratum in the population that has not benefitted from the little economic progress that has occurred up to the present and is suffering from multiple deficiencies: lack of employment at wages permitting a tolerable level of living, lack of education, skills and working habits, levels of housing, sanitation and diet that reduce working capacity and unstable family life contributing to and fostered by the other deficiencies. With rapid population growth and continuing reallocation of population from rural to urban areas, it is likely that this group will continue to grow even in the face of industrialization, improved standards of living and improved conditions for the remainder of the people. What significance do these trends have for mental health? What is the impact of the revolution of rising expectations on a sense of dissatisfaction, emotional instability and declining loyalty to the family and community? What are the psychological consequences of overcrowding, slum dwelling and unemployment in an urban area?

A growing literature is beginning to describe the effects of the population explosion and the redistribution of the population. Does psychiatry have something to offer here? Yes, it does—in particular correlating the negative pattern of adaptation with faulty planning, clarifying culture, specific needs of different groups, creating preventive life style approaches to protect groups from the excessive strain of social change.

The major change in the Third World is thus the shift from a rural agrarian world to an urban industrial one. The extent and the pace of this development toward modern industrialism and urbanization differs from country to country, thereby generating various problems for the inhabitants of different countries.

LATIN AMERICA

Modernization may begin with changes in social class structure, industrialization or urbanization. Some rural societies (for example, El Salvador) have a small educated urban middle class and a spirit of nationalism but have made no significant gains in urban or industrial growth. Elsewhere the initial stages of modernization have taken the form of industrialization or urbanization (for example, Peru). Where urbanization has occurred before, comparable industrial growth has taken place, the increased population has been inadequately cared for and has often been worse off than in rural underdeveloped situations where traditions provided a sense of security. The increased city populations have not received adequate jobs, social services or housing and have been without the psychologically supportive family and community ties of the rural culture. The same holds true even for rural workers, when they become wage laborers on mechanized plantations separated from their traditional ways of life, without a patron, or protective social legislation.

Housing and transportation are a problem in the city. Many travel hours each day to work which increases fatigue and susceptibility to social and psychological breakdown. Endemic tuberculosis, primitive health and sanitary conditions and lack of potable water are added stresses. Unions are weak and social services are inadequate. Inadequate housing, minimal living standards, chronic unemployment and urban discontent are also common. In the more advanced countries like Brazil with cities of 100,000 or more people, industrialization, a middle class, nationalism, 50 percent literacy and $100 per capita income, the majority of the population live in urban slums without benefit of the industrial gains. In some societies the bulk of the population live in traditional rural areas. In others (for example, Colombia and Panama), urbanization has outstripped economic growth resulting in inadequate housing, minimal living standards, chronic unemployment, urban discontent and rural violence.

Latin America has contained powerful urban areas since the sixteenth century. Except for Brazil where the large landowners lived on estates, the upper class has been concentrated in the urban areas. The shortage of land, poverty, strife and conflict in the rural areas coupled with the material attractions, educational opportunities and transportation facilities have contributed to heavy cityward migration.

In the ensuing migration, special problems have been created. Most difficulty has been experienced by Indians whose dress, language and manner of living are quite distinct, making assimilation and adaptation difficult. The depopulated rural areas are often left with women, the very old and very young, the least ambitious and the illiterate who are unable to produce sufficient food for the country. In other rural areas, overpopulation, fragmented land holdings and underemployment create problems.

According to United Nation reports, the revolution of rising expectations has barely penetrated the lives of the slum dwellers and most show no generalized or aggressive discontent with their lives, as compared to those more fortunate. Most of these people depend on contacts with family members, neighbors and employers to lessen their insecurity. Mutual aid outside the family, however, is limited in scope. Participation in formal organizations is minimal and they have little interest in nationalist issues or political forces.

Most of the slum dwellers are illiterate, rural, unskilled laborers, who contribute little to the economy but make heavy demands on social service resources. Development may increase the slum dweller's awareness of the discrepancy between his lot and the lives of the more fortunate. The "revolution of rising expectations" can lead to frustration, dissatisfaction and reduced morale and may contribute to the increased frequency of neurotic and behavior disorders on an individual level, social protest and revolution on a social scale.

The problems of development affect other groups besides the disenfranchised. The landowning and merchant classes are relinquishing power to other groups through the establishment of land reforms and more equitable tax systems. Industrial entrepreneurs, middle income groups of shopkeepers and civil servants have displaced the old aristocracy in a number of countries. Elsewhere these same groups have become increasingly conscious about participating in national, political and cultural life. In industrializing situations, industrial workers and union members have also begun to improve their status and seek a better life. The material aspirations of the middle classes have risen faster than their incomes or their levels of living. In many instances they have not shared in the national per capita income gain or availability of new consumer goods. Changes in the roles of women and adolescents further contribute to the instability of the middle income group.

AFRICA

Patterns of urbanization vary by continent. While urban centers long existed in northern and western Nigeria, most of the urban developments in Africa have occurred since the Second World War with the expansion of public and private investment in mining and agriculture and the growth of transportation facilities. Bamako, Baqui, Cotonou, Douala and Pointe Noire in the French territories, Sekondi-Takoradi in British West Africa, Kampala and Ginga, Stanleyville and Jadopville in the Belgian Congo and Beira in Mozambique, for example, are all new cities. People migrate to the city to obtain money for taxes, consumer goods or the bride price, to avoid famine, to escape from the monotony of tribal life or to join a family.

Many African cities, with the exception of those in Kenya, South Africa, Rhodesia and the Belgian Congo, are trading centers with primary industries and crops and are heavily dependent on foreign trade, rather than on internal manufacture or trade. The heterogeneous populations are separated by racial, linguistic, religious, socioeconomic, educational and tribal differences and are often in conflict with one another.

The movement of labor, the relative lack of skill, the low wages and job opportunities, poor health, the preference for traditional values and the lack of involvement in the values of success and material advancement contribute to lower levels of productivity and the lack of stabilization in the urban areas. Some seasonal workers migrate between urban and rural areas maintaining both contact with their tribes and an adequate wage but at the expense of leading a stable life in either situation. From the viewpoint of urbanization, such mobility reduces opportunity to develop skills, experience or education for advancement.

A variety of tribal associations based on common tribal ancestry and origins have developed to deal with political action programs, problems of burial, marriage, mutual aid and loans. For many they have contributed to psychological stability.

Urbanization has also affected traditional patterns of marriage and kinship. In rural areas, marriage is central to cooperative ventures in agriculture and cattle herding and establishes obligations and relationships between the individual and his new kin. The bride price plays an important part in the cash economy of Central Africa. It is an obstacle to social progress in that a

large portion of earnings are allocated for it; women, to recipro-
cate the payment of the bride price, are expected to manage the
house, do some agriculture in the rural area or work outside
the home in the city.

The excess of men over women, the revolt of women against
their traditional inferior status, the loss of the traditional authority of the father, economic obstacles and tribal conflicts contribute to the instability of marriage in the city. The effects of
this instability are most prominent in the young.

Children are less valued and more neglected in the city. Traditionally the community, not the parents, has taken responsibility for disciplining youngsters. In the urban areas, this
community does not exist. It is difficult for families to begin to
introduce discipline. With schools and jobs scarce, and insufficient
motivational support for schooling when it does exist, adolescents
are likely to drift into delinquency.

ASIA AND THE FAR EAST

The low land population ratio, arising from rapid population
growth in relation to agricultural productivity, is the major
pressure in Asia for the development of cities. The disruption
following the Second World War, political instability, the unavailability of natural resources in some areas and the seasonal
employment in agriculture also contribute to the pressure for
cities.

The foundation of cities was established in the colonial period.
These cities are remarkable for their village or folk characteristics. Coexisting within their boundaries one usually finds both
modern and indigenous areas of contiguous villages. Cities are
overurbanized with low productivity and living standards, inadequate housing, inadequate sanitation, high morbidity and mortality rates and high illiteracy. Vulnerability to epidemics and
droughts, a rapidly expanding birth rate, inadequate food production, rapid and uncontrolled movements of peasants to overcrowded urban cities and failure to develop decentralized
industrial programs further add to the urban problem. Many
countries are encouraging return to the rural areas, through

agricultural programs, rural credit, cooperative methods, village and cottage industries, the decentralization of new industrial development, resettlement and land tenure programs. New jobs and work relationships also create tensions in the urban area. The shift from ascriptive to achievement criteria brings together co-workers from different backgrounds. Personal and tribal ties lose their economic significance but become sources of friction if preferences are shown to majority groups.

The absence of community organizations reduces opportunities for progress. The lack of common languages and ties, conflicting backgrounds, the loss of traditional leaders and the impersonal relationship of the work situation generate insecurities and low morale.

The most striking aspect of urbanization in the developing countries is the growth of the shanty towns, impoverished areas built of scrap materials by squatters without tenure rights on the fringes of cities or on land unsuitable for building. These settlements grew rapidly during the forties and fifties in almost every large city of Latin America and, since the Second World War, in Africa and Asia. The shanty towns have absorbed the greater part of the population growth of many of the cities in the developing world and constitute huge peripheral areas of land covered by small one-family houses whose inhabitants rarely participate in the life of the city. Many aspects of traditional rural culture persist in the urban enclaves or shanty towns. Many slum dwellers lead integrated consistent lives which can be understood in terms of specific values and patterns which differ sharply in kind rather than degree with the values of the larger society. Slum dwellers have not necessarily failed to meet the goals and expectations of the larger society but have often positively adapted them in terms of their own assumptive world. The case studies of Oscar Lewis are particularly relevant in this connection.

THE CULTURE OF POVERTY

The culture of poverty, according to Lewis, does not refer to backward, isolated, integrated, self-sufficient primitive people— the peasantry, the working class or the proletariat. Rather, it refers to people at the bottom of the socioeconomic scale, "the poorest peasants, plantation laborers, and that large heterogenous mass of small artisans and tradesmen usually referred to as the lumpen proletariat." These people are marginal, illiterate, uninvolved in political labor, social welfare or cultural activities, unemployed or underemployed, without savings or food reserves and often in debt.

According to Lewis, the social and psychological characteristics of the culture of poverty include crowded quarters, inadequate privacy, gregariousness, alcoholism, violence, physical abuse in child training, wife beating, early initiation into sex, free unions or consensual marriages, high incidence of abandonment of mothers and children, mother-centered families, a predominant nuclear family and authoritarianism. Also characteristic are present time orientation, inability to defer gratification and plan for the future, a sense of resignation and fatalism, a belief in male superiority, a martyr complex among women, high tolerance of psychological pathology and alienation from the values and institutions of the larger society.

Slum children are neglected, inadequately socialized, untrained in frustration tolerance and postponement of immediate gratification. The limited restraint on the expression of sexual and aggressive drives which develops is rationalized in terms of the values placed on male dominance, female submissiveness and a preference for violent rather than rational solutions of conflict.

The unskilled slum dwellers of the developing world suffer from unemployment, low wages, minimal social political and economic organization, discrimination and a negative stereotype of personal inadequacy or inferiority. They are often viewed with apathy, suspicion and fear and come in contact with few social institutions save for the jails, the army and the public relief systems.

Oscar Lewis has noted that the poor constitute a special subculture at the lower end of the social system who differ from the middle and upper classes in quantitative not qualitative terms. While he has suggested there is something positive in the "culture of poverty," it seems that these people have simply not acquired the necessary skills for adapting to the labor society, in part because of psychopathological problems.

These poor know the middle class values but do not live by them. They do not marry, although they recognize marriage and the church. There is no economic reason to do so. They have fewer resources to maintain the stability of the family. There is a minimum of organization beyond the level of the nuclear and extended family at the community level. The low level of organization of the poor contributes to their marginality in complex, specialized, organized societies. They have little knowledge of the ways to acquire the skills or courage to participate in the community. Childhood is not a protected period because of economic hardship. Children are early initiated into sex and violence.

To some a diagnosis of immature or psychopathic personality explains the whole range of traits. The slum may very well breed psychopathic personalities which in turn account for their low involvement with the social system and the kind of culture and patterns of living which evolve in a situation where psychopathic personalities interact at high frequencies.

The family is weakened in the city by occupational social and geographical separation of kinsmen, intergenerational conflicts, the reduced impact of traditional authority and the breakup of extended families. The primary family becomes the focus of security and must cope with numerous ambiguities in the norms governing relationships. It cannot control the marriage choice and courtship of the more independent young people. Women gain authority through economic independence, responsibility for the household and the unavailability of the male parent who loses authority by virtue of his reduction of status within the social system.

The pattern of urban slums that has developed is clearly an obstacle to modernization. These slums breed psychopathy, low morale and crime and create a large class of dependent people who drain the limited social services available and are also so alienated from the system as not to be able to contribute to productivity, growth and development.

It should be noted that the assumption that the traditional family was free of tension and conflict was not always the case. Conformity to tradition may have been due to apathy and resignation. Tensions are rife in many pre-industrial societies and are channeled into witchcraft, ritual rebellion and various institutionalized activities. Furthermore, changes in the urban family and even high rates of divorce and marital instability are not always indicative of a change for the worse but may represent changes in the nature of interpersonal relationships brought about by the different social and economic requirements of urban living. The urban situation permits greater freedom in interpersonal choices which has undoubtedly contributed to a reduction in family size and the relationship between men and women.

INDUSTRIALIZATION

The developing societies are pre-industrial, tradition-bound and economically inefficient. Life focuses around the preservation of tradition. Change and innovation are resisted. These societies are nevertheless highly complex. Unlike Western societies where specific tasks are associated with specific goals, social acts in pre-industrial societies have multiple purposes. Economic activity not only may produce money, goods or food but may also have social and religious significance in terms of establishing and defining relationships between people and between man and God. When new forms of economic, social or medical activities are introduced without meeting the less obvious needs of the people to the same extent as old forms of behavior, tension, conflicts and resistance ensue. Participation in a meaningful relationship with a native healer who behaves in a predictable and characteristic way not only serves the cause of health but serves to reduce anxieties. Symbolically meaningful native healing rituals are often more effective in promoting mental health and group integration than impersonal scientific procedures.

Modern industrial societies value achievement, individual initiative and responsibility. Traditional societies place greater weight on fixed, predetermined roles, determined at birth. Traditional societies value the soil, the home, the ancestral ways, the family and the community. Individualism and the urban situations (Redfield) are suspected. Knowing one's place in traditional society and the rules and sanctions regarding behavior and relationships makes for a certain security. The stress on personal achievement in the urban areas is by contrast less well defined and therefore more conducive to anxiety. Tribal and voluntary associations, founded on ascriptive criteria stabilize the world for some. Old loyalties conflict with new demands. Tribal and kin patterns oppose self-interest and create conflict for those unsure of their individual aims. Personal modesty and a proper sense of *hiya* or place is important to Philippinos (Sechrest). "He thinks he is too good for the rest of us" is a major form of scorn. Conflict between a desire for status and recognition and group emphasis on humility is common to Philippinos. Accomplishments arouse envy and hostility in others, whereas mediocre performance brings acceptance.

According to Barbara Ward, the developing countries have not benefitted from the "intellectual revolution of materialism and this-worldliness, the political revolution of equality, and above all scientific and technological revolution which comes from the application of technology and the sciences to the whole business of daily life."

The failure to develop a work ethic has been due to traditionalism which supports existing strata, is inimical to equality and is opposed to change for its own sake. Rigid social systems discourage both personal and social progress.

Because of the relatively young age of the populations in the developing societies both the state and the family must assume a large burden for their care. This is particularly true if an adequate number of individuals are to receive technical training and education to meet the needs of a modernizing society. In general these young people cannot enter into the labor market as rapidly as is necessary, which puts an excessive strain and burden on a smaller number of people. Because of the age distribution of the population a great number of children reach school age each year, there are always a lot of young people looking for jobs and always many families seeking homes.

To keep pace with these increasing population pressures means that the number of places in schools, the number of jobs and the number of dwelling units must rise considerably each year. Such needs coupled with consumption needs interfere with economic advancement by increasing expenditures which might otherwise be utilized for long-term investment in education, equipment and capital needs. To maintain economic growth, industrialization must expand beyond present rates.

The population explosion is an obstacle to capital accumulation and expansion. While industrial societies can absorb population increases in new industries, the developing societies cannot. Industrialization does not absorb enough of the urban labor force. Surplus labor filters into service occupations of low productivity. These people cannot afford to live anywhere but in the ever expanding shanty towns. While low cost housing projects have, in some areas, alleviated overcrowding among the lower middle classes and the better paid workers, they have done very little for the populations of the shanty towns whose housing is extraordinarily substandard. Migration to urban areas has simultaneously reduced the rural work force.

Almost everywhere one finds a middle class of white-collar workers, government employees, merchants and the military. This middle class group has continued to grow, particularly in the urban areas and its increasing size is seen in the increase in the demands for consumer goods, expansion of housing in the middle income brackets and the rapid development of services of all kinds from middle income groups in the large cities of the developing world.

Most of the middle class expect a higher standard of living than they can actually afford. The middle class family is also very subject to change. Socioeconomic changes have altered the status of women. In many places they can vote, obtain divorce and own property and are actively participating in the economic life. Furthermore in some countries the state is beginning to assume family functions as in public education and social insurance which further alters the traditional role of the family. In addition the nature of urban life is not conducive to the extended family of more traditional societies.

The disruptive effects of change are thus not confined to the urban slum dweller. By attempting to take advantage of certain social benefits and educational experience, the original sense of identity of the middle income groups may also be challenged not by failure to accommodate and succeed within the new system but by succeeding which also disrupts the individual's sense of confidence in his traditional ways of believing and behaving and at the same time makes him increasingly uncertain about the future, particularly if he can never be sure what factors were responsible for the success.

HEALTH CONDITIONS

The crude annual death rate and the infant mortality rate (number of deaths of infants under one year of age per thousand live births) declined between 1950 and 1960. The decline in the death rate between four weeks and twelve months was the most dramatic evidence of better health care, for this is an age where environmental factors can be manipulated. Little impact was made on the first four weeks of life. Inadequate medical facilities and personnel, inadequate food supplies, poor housing, inadequate sanitation, malnutrition and ignorance contribute to the poor health of the population in developing countries. Trachoma, intestinal parasites, bowel infections, TB, respiratory tract infections and venereal diseases are especially prevalent in crowded urban slums. From a public health viewpoint, poor sanitation is a major cause of poor health. The effects of poverty, urban slums and large-scale disruptive social movements are not restricted to physical disorders only.

As Eisenberg points out, the broad designation of deprivation syndrome "requires of us that we specify what it is that the child has been denied: food, protection, stimulation, consistent and predictable interpersonal contact, ordering of the environment and so on. Maternal ill health that impairs normal pregnancy, inadequate spacing of births, and poor pre-natal care

are all precursors of the deprivation syndrome. These may produce physical as well as psychological consequences."

Abnormalities associated with pregnancy and parturition include epilepsy, behavior disorder, reading defect, mental retardation and cerebral palsy. To the extent that pregnancy complications are clearly related to social and economic deprivation, preventive efforts can have a positive result in reducing these conditions.

Abnormalities associated with pregnancy and parturition in preventive efforts can have a positive result in reducing these conditions.

Severe malnutrition, accidents and infections which affect the central nervous system are also preventable. Intellectual understimulation can be reduced by improving crowded home and school conditions. Efforts to diminish parental mortality and desertion will also reduce the psychological consequences of early loss. Family planning, good health care, decent housing, unemployment compensation, case work service to minimize family breakdown, substitute care for homeless children, school programs and recreational, vocational and other social services must be developed. The application of these will go far in contributing to beneficial effects in the developing countries.

Although health conditions are far from satisfactory, they have been improving throughout the Third World. Campaigns against cholera, malaria, tuberculosis, smallpox, yellow fever and plague have been successful. The distribution of insecticides and antibiotics and vaccination programs had a considerable effect in reducing the incidence of infectious diseases.

The health problems in the developing world results from a combination of factors. Cardiovascular diseases, cancer and the degenerative diseases of old age are rarely reported because of the relatively young age of the population. Numerous parasitic and contagious diseases were partially controlled by public health measures.

Immunization programs against childhood illnesses, such as measles, whooping cough, diphtheria and tetanus, are rare and the prevalence of these is still high. There are only sporadic programs for the control of the zoonoses: rabies, brucellosis, hydatidosis, anthrax and hoof and mouth disease. Diarrheal diseases still account for the death each year of a large number of children under one year of age.

While many of these diseases are preventable with available and proven techniques most developing countries lack the means and techniques to develop such programs on a national basis. The mortality and morbidity problems of children relate to customs, beliefs, ignorance, agriculture, nutrition and water supply, the study of which is most important if one is to introduce programs to the developing societies.

New programs in agriculture, selective breeding and animal husbandry should greatly reduce the food problem facing the world. The synthesis of low cost protein substitutes, iodized salts and enriched foods will help considerably to relieve problems of malnutrition, vitamin deficiency, goiter and the like.

The problems of children include high infant and neonatal mortality, illegitimate birth, insufficient moral and material support, undernutrition, malnutrition, juvenile delinquency, lack of primary education for the handicapped and a high incidence of accidents in urban areas.

In addition, vagrancy, illegitimate and abandoned children, exploited child labor, child prostitution and child drug addiction are inextricably interwoven with some of the same environmental factors that relate to the infectious and nutritional diseases.

OBSTACLES TO DEVELOPMENT OF MODERN AND MEDICAL PSYCHIATRIC PROGRAMS

There are numerous obstacles and general resistances to introducing modern psychiatric programs let alone medical programs and social change to the developing countries. Oftentimes this is difficult for Westerners to see, so committed are they to the view that change is a positive value. In Africa, for example, tribalism threatens the stability of new forms of political and social organization which require cooperation across tribal boundaries. Economic shortages due to the payment of heavy foreign debts incurred at the outset of political independence usually leaves little for much needed programs in health, education and welfare.

The introduction of modern medical practice is difficult in societies where illness is viewed as affecting the whole group. Such groups generally expect to participate in the decision to seek help and to remain with the patient undergoing treatment. The integration of the group into the treatment program has been successfully demonstrated by Lambo. However, when the Western-trained physician does not recognize the implications of illness for the group and does not seek to integrate them into the treatment, he may encounter difficulty. Group rituals are important for maintaining the harmony and protection of the group, and it is therefore crucial to allow individuals to adhere to their customs.

Health is not positively valued in many cultures, where short life expectancies and high rates of endemic illnesses foster fatalism. Food, water supplies and roads are often given higher priority by the people, and attention to them first may be strategic for introducing medical programs.

Certain values impede the development process. Traditionalism leads to fatalism. Life is seen as part of an infinite experience which continues after life. This creates a secure feeling but the here and now is ignored and efforts to change the world cannot emerge. Initiative, decision-making and activism are threatening adherence to ancestral, parental and community customs, where age, sex, family and kinship are well differentiated. In traditional societies the elderly are venerated and youth conform in the knowledge that they will gain this same respect in the future. The change from a traditional ancestor-oriented culture to a modern industrial society in Japan was followed by social unrest and a decline in morality and the traditional authority of the family. According to Doi, the emphasis on filial obligation regulated the desire of *amae* before the war. The postwar deemphasis of traditional homage to the emperor and parents fostered a resurgence of the potentially disruptive and narcissistic desire of *amaeru* which contributed to the increase in neurotic disorders.

Contemplation, withdrawal and meditation as in Yoga and Zen rituals or transcendence through spirit possession are valued as opportunities to withdraw from social interaction in order to preserve a private "space" or individual dignity. Such valued activities are antithetical to development, support the status quo and obstruct social change.

Views of man and the supernatural may also impede development. Mexican Americans view the world as subject to the will of God who must be supplicated if things are to go well. Disease and disaster are punishments which can be prevented by prayer. The Navajo see man in a balance with nature. Disequilibrium leads to illness, which must be corrected by retaining the balance rather than by active mastery. Dubos's view that the control of one TB bacillus simply led to a resurgence of stronger forms is a view based more on the notion of harmonious equilibrium than on the mechanistic view of man overcoming nature through efforts.

Emphasis on the past retards development, especially where there is great concern with malevolence, ancestral spirits, ghosts, death and illness. In Africa, the belief that spirits of the dead provide continuity through the generations relates to the view that events are controlled forces. In Latin America this relates to the Manana attitude that things can be postponed.

FAILURE OF EXISTING PROGRAMS: A SUMMARY

To the extent that existing medical and psychiatric care does not meet the needs of the population, it does not contribute to a redirection in the problems of the developing society. Sources of failure and discordance are: insufficient resources; inappropriate allocation and distribution; incorrect models; failure to focus on highest risk groups or to recognize poor utilization of strengths; education systems which are too academic and too Western in their emphasis on the one-doctor–one-patient model; professionals who are too jealous of their prerogatives and unwilling to use paraprofessionals; and insufficient community contact and resulting failure to understand needs, provide community education and learn new models, for example, folk healers for medical and psychiatric care.

SOCIAL PSYCHIATRY'S CONTRIBUTION TO CONCORDANCE

The introduction of health programs and other development programs require behavioral changes, which means focusing on life styles and values at the community level and not simply the imposition of an inappropriate model of medical and psychiatric care.

The social psychiatrist can identify sources of stress and obstacles to the development process. Psychiatric insight provides perspective on such matters as the deprivation of the urban slum child, the consequences of mass migration along with control programs, the role of sexual identification in the machismo complex, the psychological significance of tradition and other factors which must be considered in any scheme to reduce human distress and improve the quality of life.

Social psychiatry can also contribute technical and administrative competence in the establishment of specific health, education and welfare programs in the developing societies on the basis of practical experience as well as on the basis of a special self-examining process inherent in the field and a particular knowledgeability in the area of assisting people to enter into self-renewing or self-actualizing processes, the kind of educational orientation most relevant to societies in flux.

SPECIFIC PROGRAMS

In Haiti, in 1959, Drs. Nathan S. Kline and Louis Mars, with the assistance of several American pharmaceutical companies, the National Institute of Mental Health and the Haitian Government, established a small twenty-bed psychiatric clinic. Prior to that time, an abandoned Marine barracks, Pont Beudet, had provided custodial care for some 250 patients of whom five died, five escaped and five improved each month. In the first five years, only eleven of some 1,200 patients who were seen at the psychiatric clinic had to be referred to Pont Beudet.

In Haiti, Liberia, Iran and Indonesia where trained personnel and financial resources were—and still are—minimal, psychopharmaceuticals increased the psychiatrist's ability to handle in a rapid, effective, inexpensive way, larger numbers of patients than were possible ever before. The experience of the International Committee in Indonesia points to another kind of approach to the problem of handling vast numbers of people. In Djakarta, seventeen general practitioners were trained over a brief period of time in the use of these medicines and the rudiments of psychiatric diagnosis. This project proved that it was possible for them to see a large number of people in the course of a year and to treat them quite effectively, thereby avoiding the poor care given in the existing custodial institutions.

Another approach in developing countries is to use existing medical facilities. At the University de Valle in Cali, Colombia, the International Committee, in collaboration with Dr. Carlos Leon, initiated a program in the three existing medical clinics in the *barrios* (slum) areas. These clinics have been working on birth control, tuberculosis control and on nutrition programs, but they had had no psychiatrists. With our support, they have arranged for a psychiatrist to work in these clinics in immediate contact with the population and with the other doctors. In such medical clinics patients can be seen in the early stages of their illness. The crucial point is that facilities exist but they are not always being used in the best way. They may not be used all day and are frequently not used in the late afternoons. It is possible to save a tremendous amount of money for architectural expenses by putting psychiatrists into the medical clinics and conceivably other facilities such as police stations to establish direct contact with the population at the earliest stages of difficulty.

Another approach—and here we are a little more radical—is to utilize the skills of the folk healers, as did Dr. Lambo in Abeokuta, Nigeria, and Dr. Tigani El Mahi in the Sudan. In parts of Africa where these healers are banded together in a guild or an organization, there are controls on their behavior, traditional standards and, sometimes, designated training periods. Certainly, for the less severe disorders—neurotic depressions and psycho-physiological cases—these people are often far more effective than Western-trained psychiatrists, particularly in that they know the culture, its stresses and the kinds of problems that the patients have encountered.

Another approach which would maximize and multiply the effect of the psychiatrist is to set up a closed-circuit television referral network. The idea is to put a small satellite clinic into a village area which currently receives no psychiatric or medical treatment. The village facility would be hooked up with a center closer to the main urban areas. People from the villages would be trained to take crude medical or psychiatric histories. Examination would be monitored by the psychiatrist at the central facility and those people requiring emergency care would be flown in.

We are currently involved in an investigation of the technological problems of such a system in Colombia. The government is especially interested in introducing closed circuit television referral hospital networks into areas receiving no care. Everybody talks about the rural areas being in greatest need of care, but virtually all the available funds go into the urban areas—partly because the problems also exist in the urban areas and are much more dramatic and partly because the people in the rural areas have no political leverage. Another possibility is to use television networks for educational purposes. With today's technology, this is certainly possible.

Other kinds of programs that may be applicable in the developing countries include the use of such medicines as fluphenazine enanthate on which Dr. Wintrob carried out clinical trials before it became commercially available. This is an intramuscular tranquilizer that stays within the system for two or three weeks and facilitates the management of disturbed patients much more effectively than oral medicine which patients may not take as prescribed. At least for two or three weeks they may be kept under control and one can space out the visits. Many people may not have to be hospitalized if they are treated in this way.

Other programs need to be investigated for the prevention of the less severe disorders, most likely to be affected by environmental factors—that is, alcoholism, delinquency and drug addiction which are reportedly on the increase in most of the developing countries.

The African, in a tribal setting, grows up with numerous parental surrogates, rather than one parent with whom he can identify. During adolescence pressure is placed on the individual to become involved in peer group activities so that they do not develop the kind of individuality of the person in the Western World. When these people move into urban areas and encounter the numerous pressures of unemployment and overcrowded housing, they experience difficulties compounded by the fact that they do not have the group support upon which they relied at home for maintaining their psychic integrity. Much more must be learned about the psychodynamic issues involved in such transition situations.

Another problem worth considering is how to take advantage of the existing educational institutions and developing industries. The best place to put a psychiatrist may not be in a psychiatric hospital, but in a school or factory where there is a tight network and he can get in touch with the people, thus not relying on their spontaneous need for help. Where there is no money for building or for adequate personnel, one has to try to get to the patients during the very earliest stages of illness.

While these are fascinating issues and most important for an understanding of the basic problems of psychiatry, the real and more pragmatic issue in the developing countries is, how do we deliver services to these people? How do we get people to accept modern psychiatric care when the native medicines are really ineffective? These are crucial issues which, in a broad sense, demand first priority.

Chapter 16

Group Dynamics in Contemporary Africa:
Concordance and Discordance

ELLIOTT P. SKINNER

A MAJOR PROBLEM in human affairs is that the formation of groups is often a result of conflict with other groups. Thus there is a constant dialectic of concordance and discordance among social groups. This process is so nearly ubiquitous that men often despair of humanity ever reaching a stage of unity that precludes discordance and conflict. Nevertheless, one must also note that not all human groups come into existence for the same reason, and the structure, function and conflicts of groups evolve over time. What often looks like a pendulamic movement in which groups form and disintegrate with accompanying patterns of concordance and discordance is really an helixical movement in that the same groups never reappear after their demise. Instead, the formation and later disintegration of groups reflect ever-changing biosocial and cultural factors. Failure to understand the helixical nature of socioculture change and the nature of the resulting discordance may in fact delay the emergence of a new concordance.

One of the major results of European domination of the world was that other peoples and their cultures were viewed as belonging to different and inferior stages of evolution.[1] Thus instead of a situation in which nothing human was viewed as strange, anything non-European was relegated to the realm of the bizarre and the primitive. Like Shakespeare's Shylock, the non-Europeans were viewed as alien to the normal patterns of human development and their problems consigned to another realm. Other people did not eat, they fed; they did not smile, they grinned; they did not procreate, they bred. Similarly, the conflicts which arose in many non-European societies were not viewed

240

as common to all men but were attributed to "primitivity" and "barbarism."

For example, "tribalism" is most often blamed for the many economic, social and especially political problems of contemporary Africa.[2] The troubles in Congo Kinshasa in 1960 were attributed to "tribalism" and so was the subsequent and terrible civil war in Nigeria. Ironically, even Africans, exhibiting that interesting psychological state in which the oppressed eventually view themselves through the eyes of their oppressors, concur that "tribalism" is the basic cause of all their difficulties. Thus at the meeting of the first all-African Peoples Conference in Accra in 1958, the African leaders denounced "tribalism" as an evil practice and a "serious obstacle" to the unity, political evolution and rapid liberation of Africa.[3] Later, during the troubles in Congo-Kinshasa, Mr. Alphonso Massamaba-Debat, President of the neighboring Congo-Brazzaville, complained that "tribalism is the trap which the Congolese people most easily fall into." He warned that "the way of tribalism is the road to perdition." [5]

Given the alleged power of "tribalism" to create difficulties in African societies, it is surprising to note that there is no clear-cut understanding of this phenomenon. Fried pointed out that the concept, tribe (with which tribalism is associated), lacked sociological rigor from its inception.[5] Most scholars have recognized the difficulty of delimiting the entity called tribes. Nevertheless both scholars and laymen use the concepts tribe and tribalism as though they were readily definable and understandable. Thus, while the late Professor Herskovits admitted that the concept, tribe, was "difficult to define," had "little utility, whether for scientific or practical purposes" [6] and vowed to avoid its use in his book, *The Human Factor in Changing Africa*, he continued to use the concept "tribalism." In the same book, he wrote that in the Congo

Tribal loyalties and ancient hostilities generated fears that erupted as colonial controls were relaxed, so that actual warfare, often with weapons that antedated the introduction of firearms, broke out between the Baluba and Benelulua in the Kasai even before independence.

Thus, even Herskovits while attempting to eschew the concept "tribe" saw in "tribalism" a device for explaining much of the political problems in contemporary Africa.

But what is "tribalism?" As far as can be ascertained, most people view "tribalism" as an atavistic sentiment of "primitive" peoples. These people live in anarchistic kin-organized groups and have either been unable to build complex societies or resisted incorporation into larger sociocultural entities. It follows, therefore, that the contemporary "tribalists" are conservative traditionalists who hanker over the past and want nothing to do with modern ideas and new forms of government. In other words the "tribalist" is "atavistic." Note how Herskovits unconsciously juxtaposed "tribal loyalties," "ancient hostilities" and warfare with "antique weapons," in the quotation above. The same view is expressed in the following quotation:

> *Nigeria* was only a collection of tribes for centuries. Britain took over for 100 years. . . . A new breed of *Nigerians* [appeared and] took over a new nation in 1962. . . . *But the veneer was thin.* Tribal rivalries broke through in bloody change in January [1966].[7]

The assertion here is that the primordial ties and suspicions that had always separated the peoples in Nigeria reemerged and that the "Nigerians" returned to their old "tribal" ties.

Several problems arise when the conflict, competition and cooperation between social groups in contemporary African societies are attributed to "tribalism." First, this belief supports the distorted view that precolonial Africa was inhabited primarily by antagonistic "tribal" groups. Second, it ignores the many drastic changes that occurred in Africa during the colonial epoch. Third, it masks and oversimplifies the nature of the struggles now taking place on that continent.

The belief (often spelled out in great detail) that precolonial Africans lived in mutually hostile small groups is largely incorrect. In fact, Professor Evans-Pritchard holds the opposite view. He advised scholars that "it is particularly in Africa that relatively large-scale [indigenous] political societies can be studied." [8] He also said that the Azande of the northern Congo and southern Sudan were an amalgam of about "twenty assimilated foreign peoples." These exhibited all stages of integration "ranging from political absorption but cultural autonomy to total assimilation, both political and cultural."

Scholars can make the same statement about most of the larger and more complex societies in Africa.[9] The Ashanti, Baganda, Bakongo, Hausa, Mossi, Ngoni, Songhay, Yoruba and similiar societies represented the end product of political and other sociocultural processes by which different ethnic groups had been welded together. All of these societies were internally differentiated with social classes and associations even though class and associational ties were often expressed in kinship terms. The larger and more complex the societies were, the greater the number of cross-cutting loyalties, allegiances and identities among their people. Conversely, in the smaller-scale societies of Africa, allegiances and identities were more constricted. Like all other human beings, African peoples were also subjected to crises of identity when conquered, dispersed, enslaved or driven into marginal areas for fear of their powerful neighbors.

Historically, group identity for Africans served the same purpose as it did for other groups and appears to have been as relative. People have either been welded into larger societies by wars of conquests or have organized themselves into social, cultural or political entities so as to be able to compete against others for whatever goods and services were valuable in their society. The nature of the society and the nature of the goods often conditioned what types of groups formed, the manner of their formation and the duration of their cohesion. African societies developed or were transmuted as a result of trade, new technologies and ideologies introduced by migrants, merchants or conquerors.

European conquest and colonization was the latest and probably the most dramatic in the history of African societies. The Moslem Arabs had an impact on large areas of the Sudan and East Africa, but European conquest brought all African societies into radically new and larger imperial frameworks.[10] The Europeans often marked off political boundaries on the map without taking into consideration the ethnic, linguistic and political groupings affected, but they also fostered or facilitated the coalescence of erstwhile disparate groupings. Again, while the Europeans often followed a policy of divide and rule, thus frequently disrupting the political systems of African societies,[9] they also "manufactured" chiefs and provinces for peoples who had no such political institutions.[11] All of these changes profoundly affected African societies.

Africans found new, if often contradictory, identities during the colonial period. The most pervasive of these new identities was that of "native" or "indigene" or "indigenas"—a label which lumped all colonized people into a group, distinct and inferior to their white colonizers. Africans also acquired new identities either as a result of Europeans imposing new group identities upon them or as a result of novel types of contact with other Africans. Thus, peoples whose major loyalties had been to kings and chiefs saw these allegiances eroded and subordinated to those based on language or culture—that is, Ashanti, Mossi, Hausa, Yoruba and Bakongo. Peoples who had lived in small village communities with more restricted allegiances, similarly, found themselves members of larger linguistic and cultural groups— that is, Chiga, Ibo, Kikuyu, Ngombe, Tonga and so on.[12]

Africans who migrated to the developing towns also took on radically new identities. Thus the "Ibos" (from such communities as Onitsha and Owerri) and the "Yoruba" (from such kingdoms as Oyo and Ibadan), who went to the northern Nigerian emirates, became known to the Hausa-Fulani as "southerners." Similarly, in the Western African towns the Fons, Popos and Bariba peoples from "Dahomey" became known collectively as "Dahomeans."[13] In contrast, the ethnic Xhosa in Durban, South Africa divided into the urban-born "x-cuse me" class and the rural-derived migrant "red-people."[14] Some urban people who hailed from the same or contiguous rural areas often formed *unions* and *associations* for urban self-help and rural development. Other urbanites from diverse ethnic backgrounds but having similar interests or occupations formed associations of clubs. Still other Africans with better education and with European value orientations became identified as *élites, assimilados* and *evolués* and, depending upon the territory, were considered or considered themselves French, Portuguese or black Englishmen.[15]

There were some Africans who found identity in universalistic sects such as the Jehovah Witnesses (Kitawala in Swahili) which believed in the apocalypse and new non-European heavens on earth.[6] More secular-minded Africans not only discovered their "Africanness" and *négritude* but sought to unite with all the colored and white workers of the world—the wretched of the earth. The important fact is that during the colonial period many Africans developed new identities, had multiple loyalties and diverse allegiances. The more urbanized and acculturated the Africans were, the more complex and diffuse these identities and allegiances. Conversely, the more rural and traditional, the more uniplex the identities and allegiances.

Despite the growth of many new loyalties and allegiances in colonial Africa, very few African colonies developed into true societies.[1] At best they could be considered plural societies. The dominant white groups faced outward with allegiance to and identity with Europe. Foreign middlemen groups (either of African, Asian or Mediterranean origin) had all the attributes of marginal "strangers." The indigenous peoples held loyalties of various strengths to local rulers, regions, linguistic and cultural groups, incipient or actual social classes, religious sects and other types of associations. In none of the African colonies did the major institutions of the dominant Europeans penetrate all social strata in the population. In fact, the Europeans often left the African peoples to their own devices, especially in the areas of religion, local government and social life. Even the assimilationist French often believed that metropolitan institutions were too revolutionary for their territories. In time the inevitable reaction arose among colored Africans and they formed anti-European associations. In the process they took on the new and revolutionary identity of "nationalists." The "Kikuyu" of Kenya formed several types of nationalist associations "to prevent [European] government actions inimical to Kikuyu."[16] Later these same Kikuyu would revolt and many would be identified as "Mau-Mau" terrorists. Thus, as the need arose, Africans formed groups and adopted new identities.

One of the first consequences of the African independence movement was that the incipient leaders needed political constituencies. The black world and the vision called *Africa* could not provide a real base for their activities and they were forced to retreat to their homelands. Thus it was that after the Fifth Pan-African Conference in Manchester in 1945, such men as Nkrumah and Kenyatta went back to the Gold Coast and Kenya respectively, thus leaving behind their larger identity with all "black men" and close collaboration with "New World Negroes." Ironically, the Africa to which these men returned had also changed. The stay-at-homes now had new types of identities, belonged to different types of groups and had also started to struggle for power. A Marxist-oriented Nkrumah met with suspicion and hostility from the Ashanti-based conservative lawyer, Dr. Danquah, who was seeking power in the name of the "chiefs and people." Nkrumah was forced to retreat to his home area at Salt Pond to gather political strength from his Nzima people and their neighbors. Kenyatta too had to seek support and strength among the Kikuyu people when colonial whites prevented him from playing a meaningful political role in Kenya. He was later to be imprisoned as the presumed leader of the so-called "atavistic" but really revolutionary Mau-Mau. Thus both Nkrumah and Kenyatta, who had left their kinsmen for many years, returned to them to obtain the necessary political support for a struggle on colony-wide levels.

The situation in Nigeria was similar. Nnamdi Azikiwe, who had preached the liberation of all of Africa while living in America, Liberia and the Gold Coast, found to his chagrin that his political organization, the NCNC, was labeled "Ibo controlled" and attacked as such by "Yoruba" law students studying in England. It is perhaps significant in this context to note that the organization which led this attack was a newly created *Egbe Omo Oduduwa* (the sons of Oduduwa), the mythical ancestor of all the "Yoruba" people. When later the Egbe gave rise to the Action Group, the AG was considered a "Yoruba" political party. The rise of political parties in Southern Nigeria stimulated the Northern Fulani emirs and their Hausa subjects to create a Northern Peoples Party.[17]

A similar pattern developed in French Africa. Politicans like Lamine Gueye of Sénégal, who is 1945 was a hero to all of French Africa for his civil rights victories, found his power and appeal limited to Sénégal when France permitted Africans to vote for local Assemblies. The then radical and well-known Houphouet-Boigny was refused political support from the Mossi kings who saw in the elections an opportunity to detach their kingdoms from the Houphouet's Ivory Coast and recreate the Upper Volta colony which had been created and later suppressed by the French. Had it not been for the strength of the reactionary colonialist bloc in Paris, French Africans led by a victorious Houphouet may not have united across territorial lines to form such organizations as the *Rassemblement Démocratique Africain.* Interestingly enough, the RDA broke up into its constituent parts when in 1956, France promised more local self-government in her territories.[18]

The need of African politicians to secure political constituencies during the decolonization period often led to a further trans-mutation of group identities than had developed under European rule. A young Frenchman studying in the French Congo told Dr. Carter: "We anthropologists thought that tribes were small in this area. . . . But the rise of local political organization seems to have stimulated the *re-emergence of larger tribal associations than we had ever identified*" [18] [italics added]. Political rivalry appeared to have been severest between two "tribes," the Bakongo and M'Bochi, who in the words of Carter "clashed in barbaric savagery within the Brazzaville suburb of Poto-Poto, where the two groups had long lived together in harmony." Dr. Carter, believed that "it was a struggle for political power, rather than any specific issue which precipitated trouble." She added

. . . in Brazzaville, political organization and the stimulus of elections may, in fact, revive old and half-forgotten tribal connections and make them again significant. As the fierce riots in Poto-Poto revealed, political tensions with such a tribalized base may create *divisions which were not there before* [italics added].[18]

In other words as the politicians sought political constituencies, the process created new group identities necessary for a radically different type of power struggle. However, this process is not new. At other times and in other places, "racial" antipathy, religious animosity or even cultural chauvinism have been built up and similarly exploited by men and groups seeking power. Carter characterized the "tribal" struggle as "barbaric savagery." Were they of a different order from the antiseptic "final solution" attempted by "civilized" Nazi Germany?

Bakongo "tribalism" or *"L'Abakism"* was held to have played an equally disruptive role in the political development of the neighboring Belgian Congo. Lemarchand declared

> This movement, or sentiment, had as its ultimate political objective . . . the erection of an autonomous Bakongo state coterminous with the boundaries of the old Kongo Kingdom which meant that the Bakongo peoples—presently divided among Angola, the Congo and the former French Moyen Congo—would eventually become re-integrated within a single territorial unit.[19]

But when faced with the strong opposition of the colonial powers and with political competition in the Belgian Congo itself, the leaders of the Abako decided to secure their own territorial base and proposed that the

> province of Leopoldville was to be organized into an autonomous 'democratic and social republic.' Its 'national' territory was to be divided into five provinces, roughly coinciding with the existing districts, and each province was to be divided into territories and communes. Executive authority was to be vested in the hands of a popularly elected president who would be assisted by a bicameral legislature elected by universal suffrage. In other words, 'Kongolese nation' was here envisaged as a sovereign state, operating under its own constitution and according to its own laws.[19]

It is quite clear that in an helixical motion Bakongo "nationalism" and not "tribalism" was to be used to group people into a *modern nation-state replete with new institutions unknown to the ancient kings of Congo and their people.*

Ironically, the fact that there were ethnic Bakongo on both

sides of the Congo River now acted as a source of conflict between Joseph Kasavubu and Abbé Youlou, both Bakongo, but both Presidents of distinct nation-states. At one time or another, each of these men tried to extend his power over Bakongo in the other's nation-state. Youlou even tried to weaken Kasavubu by aiding the latter's enemies. He sheltered both the Lumumbists, who were struggling for a centralized Congo relatively free from ethnic divisions, and the Tshombists, bent on Katangese secession. Youlou's concern for the aggrandizement of his nation-state took precedence over any feelings of Bakongo "tribalism" he may have had. Later when he fell from power, Kasavubu did give him shelter, but in contrast to erstwhile European feudal lords, he did not use the sentiments of either "brotherhood" or "tribalism" to attack Congo-Brazzaville—an adventure which would have jeopardized the security of his frail nation-state.

It is unfortunate that "tribalism" is judged the cause for the irredentism among groups in contemporary African nation-states, when modern power politics or even attempts at *anschluss* are better explanations. Thus, after the traditionally leaderless Somali had formed a modern nation-state out of areas formerly controlled by Italy and Britain, they sought to incorporate the Ogaden area in Ethiopia and the northeast province of Kenya both inhabited by some ethnic Somali. As to be expected, both Ethiopia and Kenya rejected the claims of the Greater Somali republic to their *territories* and *citizens*. The Kenyans declared the following:

> The Kenya Government wishes to reiterate and confirm that it will show no mercy toward the *shifta* (Somali nomads), who are described as nationalists by the Mogadisciou government, or toward *shifta* sympathizers. The Kenya Government wishes to make clear to all Somalis and their friends that the Kenya Government will not allow the Northeastern Province to join the Somali Republic.[20]

The Kenya Government expressed dismay that this request could be made:

> How does the Mogadisciou Government expect the Kenyan Government to hand over part of its territory: The Somalis are not the only ones to be divided in east Africa. The Masai are divided between Kenya and Tanzania. The Galla and Boran . . . [peoples] live in

both Kenya and Ethiopia. There are whites, Indians and other races who have families in both Kenya and their home countries, but none of these peoples claimed the lands on which they are settled. They never said that 'this land belongs to us.' They settled there and worked to improve their conditions and prospered.[18]

The current pressures against the Indians would suggest that not all of the groups living in Kenya are equally happy. Nevertheless, the point being made by the Kenyans is clear: ethnic affiliation, whether "Somali," "Indian" or "white," will not be permitted to challenge the integrity of the Kenya nation-state.

Somali irredentism created a problem for Somaliland when the inhabitants there were asked to devise a new relationship with France. On January 25, 1967, a reporter of *Agence France Presse* wrote the following:

In Djibouti, the gap grows between the Afars and Somalis . . . In less than two months before the referendum in French Somali, we witness from day to day a growing 'crystalization' among the two ethnic groups in the area. Observers in Djibouti note that Afars and Somali are today forming two hostile groups between whom the gap widens. Until now Afars and Somalis had collaborated, particularly in the Government Council, where four Somalis belonging to the 'moderate or Center Party' sat with three members of the 'Afar Democratic Union.' The collaboration was also found within the 'Organization Committee' where the ADU representatives sided with the leaders of the Popular Movement Party (PMP) representing irrendentist Somalis and with them organized demonstrations demanding Home Rule at the time General de Gaulle visited Djibouti.

There is no doubt [the report continued] that in the face of growing Somali unity, the Afar political leaders, pushed by public opinion marked by tribalism, will hurry to renew their own unity.[22]

Other reports from the region contradicted the view that it was "public opinion marked by tribalism" that pushed the politicians toward greater partisanship. The fact is that the political leaders in this geopolitically strategic area were under intense pressure from Ethiopia, France and the Somali Republic to vote one way or another. One Ahmad F. Kahin speaking in Mogadisciou, Somalia declared the following:

The Somali Government has made it clear on several occasions that it supports independence for the Somali Coast. . . . However, the people there must realize that the road to independence is not carpeted. There must be patience and a readiness to deal with the major difficulties which face any nation seeking independence. The present struggle there for independence must be regarded as a jihad.[22]

Another Somali spokesman spoke on January 25, 1967:

The people of the Somali Coast will soon be given the chance to decide their future. We appeal in advance to the Arab residents in the Somali Coast to support the Somali demand during the referendum. We assure them of the falsity of the colonialist propaganda that Arabs would be robbed of their rights and property when the Somali Coast became independent. We believe that they will live a better life after the local people have attained their indpendence. Both Somalis and Arabs must keep in mind God's holy commandments in the Koran that all Moslems must unite and allow nothing to separate them.[22]

The Somali spokesman was unduly sanguine about the Somali not expelling the Arabs when and if they got independence. Unfortunately, history tends to support the "colonialist propaganda" that strangers were often expelled when African countries did indeed achieve independence. This explusion, attributed to "tribalism" took place in the Congo (B), Congo (K), Gabon, Ghana, Ivory Coast, Nigeria and Niger. People of the emerging nation-states (and in regions within states) did expel those foreign groups whether African or non-African which functioned as economic, political, sociological and psychological buffers between rulers and ruled, during the colonial period. What is still not clear is whether such middlemen groups must be extruded if the ex-colonial territory desires to create an integrated modern society.

The expulsion of strangers is still a continuing problem in Africa and as usual is blamed on tribalism. On January 23, 1967, all foreigners living in the Cameroon Republic were requested to deposit a repatriation fee of ten pounds. The purpose of the deposit was allegedly to check illegal entry into the republic of persons on dubious missions. It was also designed to defray the cost of sending home foreign nationals whose repatriation had become inevitable for "personal or other reasons." [23] The Cameroon was obviously striving to protect the interest of its nationals and use the criterion of "citizenship," a new group identity, to get rid of competitors. Thus it is often only coincidental that many of these outsiders are identified by ethnic affiliation. In many cases the basis of expulsion is citizenship such as Dahomean or Voltan. One of the many events that precipitated the civil-war in Nigeria was the expulsion of "Southerners," especially the "Ibos" from the Northern region. Subsequently, "Easterners" were also expelled from the "Western" region.

The belief that "tribalism" is an impediment to African unity, both regionally and continentally, permits many people, Africans included, to evade the real issues facing that continent and its peoples. The experience of the Mali Federation is a case in point. When the formation of the federation was announced, Leopold Senghor, the President of Sénégal declared

> We have made a good start in Mali by uniting populations whose natural characteristics—climate, soil and blood, language and customs, art and literature—are similar. Sénégal and the Soudan constitute, moreover, a rather homogeneous and relatively rich economic ensemble.[24]

In contrast, when the Federation broke up Senghor lamented

> We underestimated the present strength of territorialism, of micronationalism [a euphemism for 'tribalism'?] in Africa. We forgot to analyze and understand the sociological differences among the territories of what used to be French West Africa, differences that the colonial administration had reinforced.[25]

It is doubtful that micronationalism was an important issue in the dissolution of the Mali Federation. Indeed, Modibo Keita, President of the Soudan believed that "there was a contradiction between the economic, political and social systems to which the leaders of Mali (Soudan) and Sénégal belonged." [26] Some disinterested scholars felt that "basic opposition lay in the fact that in the terminology of the *Union Soudanaise,* the UPS (*Union Progressiste Sénégalaise*) was essentially a 'bourgeois' party, whereas the Union Soudanaise was a 'socialist' party." [26] In other words, not "tribalism" but differing ideologies of leaders was held to have been the cause for the dissolution of Africa's first precolonial federation.

Differing ideologies, different colonial experiences, and membership in different and often competing postcolonial or neocolonial economic systems are serious impediments to African unity which have so far defeated dedicated Pan-Africanists. Thus it is the height of ignorance or mischievous malice to state that "tribal rivalries keep black nations apart even in the Organization of African States, where 'allies' often see one another as *tribal enemies.*" [27] "Tribalism" or ethnicity is not strong enough to hinder African unity, nor does it appear that the simple disappearance of local identities will bring it about.

The emerging nation-states of Africa will be plagued by many tensions and conflicts growing out of their colonial past and their desire to create modern societies. During this process different groups will emerge, will take on different identities and compete on the basis of different interests and ideologies. African groups will also claim continuity with earlier groups if only to profit from any legitimacy those pristine groups may have possessed. Nevertheless, any analysis of either the structure or function of these groups will show them to be different entities from those of the past.

To believe, as most Europeans and even some misguided Africans are wont to do, that "tribalism" is rooted in the African psyche is racism or paternalism. That this notion is racist is seen from the conscious or unconscious juxtaposition of "tribalism" with savagery and barbarism instead of with ideals judged noble by European standards. Attributing many of Africa's contemporary problems to "tribalism" is paternalism at its worst because it precludes an examination of and attempt to deal with the more basic causes of "discordance." The result is that the necessary steps towards the creation of concordance are frustrated.

There are no sure formulas for the formation of large sociopolitical entities among men. Wars of conquest whether waged for economic, political or ideological purposes have historically been the means of creating chiefdoms, kingdoms, empires and nation-states. In a few cases, visionaries and brilliant men, given the right situation and a strong faith in "union," could bring this about without warfare. But neither common descent, race, language, religion, economy, nor any other such factor has ever appeared to have been sufficient in and of itself to bring unity between peoples. In fact, peoples with many of these features in common have more often than not been disunited and at war with each other. People unite when they are forced to or when their unity gives them advantage in the overall struggle for better life. Perhaps the growth of a more efficient technology and radically new communication devices will bring about the unity of African societies and perhaps all societies. The problem for the African, and by extension for all men, would be to ensure that the resulting concordance permits freedom and is not a function of complete dictatorial control.

REFERENCES

1. Balandier, G.: The colonial situation: A theoretical approach. In *Social Change: The Colonial Situation*, edited by I. Wallerstein. New York, John Wiley & Sons, 1951, pp. 34–61.
2. Skinner, Elliott P.: *Group Dynamics in the Politics of Changing Societies: The Problem of 'Tribal' Politics in Africa. American Ethnological Society. Proceedings of 1967 Annual Spring Meeting.* Seattle, University of Washington Press, 1967, pp. 170–185.
3. Sklar, Richard L.: The contribution of tribalism to nationalism in Western Nigeria. *J Human Relations, 8 (3/4 Spring-Summer):*407–418, 1960.
4. Massamba-Debat, Alphonse: *Bulletin de l'Afrique Noire*, No. 442, November 23, 1966.
5. Fried, Morton H.: On the concept of tribe and tribal society. *Transactions of the New York Academy of Sciences, 28 (Series II, No. 4):*527–540, 1966.
6. Herskovits, Melville J.: *The Human Factor in Changing Africa.* New York, Alfred Knopf, 1962, pp. 67–70.
7. *U.S. News and World Report, LXI (No. 7):*54, 1966.
8. Evans-Pritchard, E. E.: The Azande State. (The Huxley Memorial Lecture). *J R Anthropological Institute, 93:*134–154, 1963.
9. Skinner, Elliott P.: *The Mossi of the Upper Volta.* Stanford, Stanford University Press, 1964.
10. Wilson, Godfrey, and Monica H.: *The Analysis of Social Change.* Cambridge, Cambridge University Press, 1945.
11. Colson, Elizabeth: The Plateau Tonga of Northern Rhodesia. In *Seven Tribes of British Central Africa*, edited by Elizabeth Colson and Max Gluckman. London, Oxford University Press, 1951, pp. 94–103.
12. Edel, May, and Abraham: African tribalism: Some reflections of Uganda. *Pol Sci Q, 80 (A3):*357–72, 1965.

13. Skinner, Elliott P.: Strangers in West African societies. *Africa, 33 (No. 4):* 308–309, 1963.
14. Mayer, Philip: *Townsmen or Tribesmen.* Cape Town, Oxford University Press, 1961.
15. Wallerstein, I.: Voluntary associations. In *Political Parties and National Integration in Tropical Africa,* edited by J. Coleman and C. Rosberg. Berkeley, University of California Press, 1964, pp. 318–339.
16. Rotberg, Robert I.: The rise of African nationalism: The case of East and Central Africa. *World Politics, 15:*75–90, 1962.
17. Sklar, Richard, and Whitaker, Jr., C. S.: Nigeria. In *Political Parties and National Integration in Tropical Africa,* edited by Coleman and Rosberg. Berkeley, University of California Press, 1964, pp. 597–654.
18. Carter, Gwendolyn: *Independence for Africa.* New York, Praeger Paperbacks, 1961, p. 90.
19. Lemarchand, Réné: Congo Leopoldville. In *Political Parties and National Integration in Tropical Africa,* edited by James S. Coleman and Carl G. Rosberg, Jr. Berkeley, University of California Press, 1964, pp. 573.
20. Nairobi Kenya Domestic Service in English, 1967, 1745 GMT 23 January 1967–K/L.
21. Castagno, Alphonso Anthony: Somali Republic. In *Political Parties and National Integration in Tropical Africa,* edited by James S. Coleman and Carl G. Rosberg. Berkeley, University of California Press, 1964, p. 512.
22. Mogadiscio Somalia Domestic Service in Somali, 1967, 1125 GMT 25 January 1967–K/L.
23. Lagos Nigeria Domestic Service in English, 1967, 1500 GMT 23 January 1967–N.
24. Senghor, L. S.: *Nationhood and the African Road to Socialism.* Translated by M. Cook. Paris, Presence Africaine, 1962, pp. 22–31.
25. Senghor, L. S.: *On African Socialism.* Translated and with an introduction by M. Cook. New York, Praeger, 1964, pp. 4–5.
26. Hodgkin, Thomas, and Morgenthau, Ruth S.: Mali. In *Political Parties and National Integration in Tropical Africa,* edited by James S. Coleman and Carl G. Rosberg, Jr. Berkeley, University of California Press, 1964, pp. 216–258.
27. *U.S. News and World Report, op. cit.,* p. 54.

Chapter 17

Deterrence and Peace: Toward a Social Psychiatry of Arab-Israeli Concordance

JOSEPH W. EATON

THE LIST OF chronic and seemingly unsolvable current international controversies is long. There have been deaths and injuries above the 100,000 level in India and Pakistan, in Korea, in the Biafra-Nigeria conflict and in the Sudanese Civil War. The opposing sides were unable to agree on a peaceful solution of their differences. They were willing to kill and be killed and to endure "scorched earth" destruction of their limited resources. Even when one side has "won" and seems in control, open hostility can break out at any moment. By comparison, the Arab-Israeli struggle seems subdued. There has been a fifty-year pattern of alternation between absolute irreconciliability at verbal levels and "let us live together" accommodations in reality.[1] The facts strongly support Professor Bernard Lewis' testimony before a U.S. Senate Committee hearing that "the Arab-Israeli dispute is not one of the main world issues. It is basically a local issue."[2]

What social variables account for the fact that so much international attention is given to the Arab-Israeli confrontation? The level of ferocity compared to other ethnic conflicts, as in Cyprus or Ireland, is not unusual. Could the attention be a function of the drama inherent in the location, the land holy to three major religions? While Israelis were always outnumbered and the Arab nationalists continue to take a most belligerent stance, each successive episode of combat left the Israelis stronger. In spite of being a pariah group in much of the world, terribly decimated during the Second World War in Europe, the Jews have built a vital modern democracy in the midst of a highly traditionalist Arab world. Israel has been experimenting

256

with many utopian ideas that appeal to social change oriented people. Arab nationalists in Palestine have consistently objected to the resurgence of national sovereignty of the Jewish people in their homeland after a hiatus of nearly two thousand years. Publicly, their spokesmen rarely deviate from verbal commitment to a "next round," in the hope that it would bring them "ultimate" victory. Privately, they have recognized that concordance could bring great benefits to all parties concerned.

Whenever direct negotiations seemed possible between the parties, great powers intervened as self-appointed and partisan "umpires," siding with one or the other opposing national movements to attain their own national objectives. Sides have been switched dramatically for seemingly minor gains. On two occasions, during the Suez War in 1956 and the Six Day War of 1967, the confused mosaic of big power intervention raised the possibility of a third world war being precipitated. Before such a calamity occurred, their governments decided to evade a direct military confrontation. Instead, they pressured both sides to agree to a temporary cease-fire.

Each such stalemate action, and there have been many such imposed "agreements" since 1919, was carefully calculated to enable Arabs and Israelis to coexist, but without direct negotiation, recognition or peace. In such a "cold war" situation, the big powers have continued a cynical pursuit of their diverse national interests, taking calculated risks with the welfare of the contending parties.

News reporters find conflict more dramatic than accommodation. Coffee house declarations of YIHAD (holy war) by Moslems against Jews make a better headline than of the existence of a network of cooperative endeavors. Even during periods of active diplomatic hostility, Jewish refugees from Arab countries were allowed to migrate to Israel. Over half a million were allowed to depart, under conditions often more thoughtful than those currently imposed by Russian authorities on the trickle of Jews allowed to leave the Soviet Union. The Jordanian Army gave humane treatment to most of its Israeli prisoners. Some Arab nationalists have accused it of much less generous treatment of Palestinian fighters during the current civil war.

In Israel the Arab minorities have prospered economically. They vote and have elected representatives in the Knesseth (Parliament). What is perhaps the most independent Arab newspaper in the world *El Kuds* is published in Jerusalem. It has advocated an end to Israeli rule over the territories occupied since 1967. More than 100,000 Arabs from all over the world peacably visited the West Bank in the summer of 1971. While the area is under Israeli occupation, none need fear persecution. No death penalty is imposed on terrorists, no matter how heinous their actions may have been.

Political compromises have been repeatedly explored by Arab leaders who had publicly vowed to fight for "1000 years" against the Zionists. The Mufti of Jerusalem, Abdul Nasser, the King of Jordan and the current ruler of Egypt have at one time or another shown a readiness to replace open conflict with accommodation in order to save their own power. In view of such evidence of concordance, the question arises, What are the social forces that provide a basis for considering the prospect that such negotiations could succeed? Can the common human needs of the antagonists overcome their deeply rooted difference? Can Israel and the Arabs live together just as France and its traditional enemy—Germany—are in a common European Union or as the United States has become closely associated with Japan?

Moslems, Christians and Jews share common religious traditions. Many Jewish Israelis enjoy Arab food, music and literature. There are probably more Jews in Israel today who speak Arabic than Yiddish. Not so long ago in Arab lands, Jews were viewed as tolerated but lower caste persons. Arabs have now acquired a healthy respect for Jews. The two sides watch each other's television programs. In the face of individual tragedy or medical emergency, responsible leaders on both sides have shown a capacity to respond pragmatically. Arabs from Jordan have been allowed to cross into enemy territory to get medical care at Hadassah Hospital. The hijacked airline passengers, Jewish and non-Jewish, even those with Israeli passports, were protected by Jordanian authorities at the risk of their own lives.

No one can anticipate all the relevant rational and personal factors that help shape the future. Prophecy is a risky function. Still there are several social factors that are favorable to a concordance. They provide a basis for an Arab-Israeli accommodation. Let me first list them and then elaborate briefly.

1. *The ambivalence factor.* The avowed Arab viewpoint of wishing to defeat the Zionists and force them to leave their country is counteracted by "ambivalence." There are strong social forces in the Arab world that would be threatened by such a total victory, if it could indeed be achieved.

2. *The self-interest factor.* The great powers who act as self-appointed umpires in the Arab-Israeli confrontation would lose much of their capability to maneuver in pursuit of their national interest, should there be a real settlement, either through peace or total victory of one side over the other.

3. *The reaction-formation factor.* The self-destructive Arab nationalist strategy of the last fifty years is beginning to show signs of modification. The motto "no negotiation, no recognition and no peace" which always governed the public behavior of the Palestinian Arab nationalist is questioned on the basis of evidence that it has actually served to strengthen the Israeli social system. It forced Jewish leaders to adopt maximum security positions, after each conflict, which in time became the new status quo and left Israel stronger than before.

4. *The "Auschwitz-Masada" factor.* There is a demonstrated readiness of the Israeli population to resist direct threats even at the risk of total destruction. From cabdriver to banker, among "doves" and "hawks" there is a determination to avoid what happened to Jews in concentration camps in Europe who died, unable to defend themselves. This fact provides a powerful deterrent force against full-fledged war. The technological capacity of man to engage in mutual and near total destruction is everywhere forcing otherwise deeply opposed forces to seek an accommodation. Many current international conflicts are being contained by a negotiated stalemate.

5. *The concordance factor.* Accommodation or peace requires that antagonists have common ground, sufficient in priority to overcome their differences. There are such common interests among Arabs and Jews.

THE AMBIVALENCE FACTOR

Should the Arab nationalist forces ever succeed in occupying Tel Aviv, Jerusalem and the rest of the country, victory could suddenly create a domestic crisis in several adjoining countries. The finely balanced negotiated accommodations between conflicting ethnic groups in Lebanon and Jordan could break down. A civil war in 1958 between Moslems and the Christian minority in Lebanon was stunted by the landing of United States Marines. In the same year, British troops stopped such a civil war in Jordan. Fighting broke out again in Jordan in 1970. Some of the battles between the Bedouin tribes of the East Bank who support King Hussein's rule and the Palestinian nationalists were merciless and bloody.

The Arab-Israeli conflict dissipates scarce resources of Arab governments confronting domestic difficulties. With a few noteworthy exceptions, such as oil-rich Kuwait and Libya, Arab lands, even with modest outlays in military expenditures, lack the economic and political means to close, with rapidity, the gap between popular aspirations for the "good life" and their government's capacity to solve domestic problems. The excuse that resources are needed for the "struggle against Zionism" provides a convenient rationalization for continued dominance of military over developmental priorities. Army officers can continue to command control over a high proportion of the national income. The accusation of pro-Zionism is being used to silence domestic opposition.

If the Palestinian leaders were to become politically powerful, they would represent a new force in the Middle East. Arab leaders now in power are uncertain if this would be good for them. Syrian, Iraqui and Lebanese politicians who publicly avowed a hard "line" against Israel, repeatedly held back support of Palestinian leaders during fateful moments of decision. There seems to be—now and before—widespread ambivalence among Arab politicans about support of Arab Palestinians. In several occasions they have attacked established Arab governments in place of the much more risky battle against Israel.

THE SELF-INTEREST FACTOR

The reading of the history of the independence war of 1948 shows that the British Government pursued very narrowly defined national interests while publicly avowing being only concerned with the issues of international justice. Britain tried to prevent the implementation of the United Nations partition plan. Risks were taken with the very survival of the outnumbered Jewish population for what now are known to be temporary tactical considerations. The United States Government vacillated in its policy. A general arms embargo was imposed on Israel, while the Arab Legion, which fought it, was armed and commanded by British officers. Israel was able to save itself at the cost of heavy casualties and Czechoslovakian arms, supplied with the active encouragement of the Soviet Union where Zionists were and still are hounded as subversive! France was closely allied with Israel from 1955 to 1967. Then there was a dramatic switch. Esteemed allies suddenly were called "aggressors."

Direct negotiations between Israel and Egypt were undermined by the big powers, after Egypt's total defeat in the Suez War in 1956. The governments of the United States and of the Soviet Union imposed a stalemate, leaving basic issues deliberately unresolved. The United States was concerned with being even-handed, keeping Arab goodwill by restoring occupied territory to them. The Russians were supported in the opposition to a negotiated peace, which the Israelis demanded.

The great powers act as if a status quo of political instability is of benefit to them. If there were peace, would the Arabs continue to invite a Russian military presence in the area? Similarly, if Israel were to be destroyed, the big powers could not play one local nationalism against the other. What labor-management conflict could be settled if the arbitrators were self-interested umpires, more concerned with serving their own

priorities than with the need to achieve the publicly avowed goal
of genuine peace for the people directly concerned? In 1948 and
in 1956, Israel had leverage to demand peace negotiations. They
conquered Arab territories. In 1948, the British threatened intervention to get the Israelis to give up their gains unconditionally prior to negotiation. In 1957 the same policy was imposed
by the United States and Soviet Union. Today, Israel has successfully rejected similar pressures for a third unconditional withdrawal demanded by the Arabs and many countries with interests
in the Arab world. Reestablishment of the status quo appears
much less likely than in the past. The United Nations Security
Council finally agreed on a resolution that there needs to be
a more stable accommodation than the previous stalemate.

THE REACTION-FORMATION FACTOR

For the first time in fifty years, Egypt and Jordan publicly
advocate a peaceful solution of the Arab-Israeli confrontation.
There is painful awareness of the reasonableness of the pun that
Abdul Nasser will go down in history as a great Zionist leader.
Why?

Only 55 percent of Palestine was allocated to the Jews when
Israel agreed to a partition plan. Egyptian leaders, including
Abdul Nasser, led regular troops and penetrated deep into
Israel, twenty-five miles from Tel Aviv. They were then surrounded and allowed to withdraw honorably. Subsequently, Israel's sovereignty was extended to 77 percent of the country's
territory. In 1956, Nasser tried to destroy Israel with guerrilla
warfare that brought sabotage and death to the heartland of
the Jews. When Israel struck back, its troops came within ten miles
of the Suez Canal. In 1967, after mobilizing the Egyptian Army
once more to throw the Jews into the sea, Nasser gave them an
opening to reach the canal itself, to occupy the entire Sinai
Desert and the strategic Golan Heights of Syria. The Suez Canal
that had been closed to Israeli shipping became an anti-tank
ditch, useless as a source of revenue.

Uncompromising hostility by the Arab nationalist movement
has led to Israeli expansion. They justify the need for new

borders by strategic necessity. In the absence of an early accommodation, responsible Arab leaders fear that the present cease-fire lines might become the permanent boundary. Certainly no significant Israeli withdrawal seems likely without an agreed-upon peace, under conditions which will make it unprofitable for the Arabs to violate it.

Arab hostility has not prevented a high rate of social-economic development in Israel, but it has undermined the strong Israeli political faction that once favored binationalism. The Israeli strategy has been to combine their own security needs with social economic benefits for the affected Arab population in the occupied areas with minimum interference in their day-to-day community life. There is more respect for civil liberties and more hope for economic progress than when Arab rulers occupied parts of the territory of Palestine. The Israeli troops are not welcome, but their policies have helped undermine Palestinian Arab support for their self-selected nationalist spokesmen who preach war in Beirut coffee houses but lack a program for practical social economic development.

The Arab spokesmen, divided by petty power rivalries, have been able to agree only on what approaches a policy of "unconditional surrender." Such a strategy boomerangs even in a country which is militarily strong because it leaves the opponent with a maximum incentive to resist. "Unconditional surrender" demands become a recipe for disaster when advocated by technologically underdeveloped Arab countries confronting a highly developed population.

The extremism of the publicly avowed Arab position has constrained full-fledged support from otherwise friendly powers. Few wish to risk a defeat of Israel, with the possible repetition of Nazi concentration camps, of the massive casualties following the Chinese invasion of Tibet or the recent policy of near-genocide of the defeated Bengali nation by primitive West Pakistani troops.

THE "AUSCHWITZ-MASADA" FACTOR

Terror can discourage an already weak and demoralized population. But during the 1948 independence war, when many

Jewish settlements were isolated, few were evacuated. None fell without a bitter battle. Terror has had a steeling effect on the Israelis. When on occasion, Jews were captured by Palestinian guerillas, mutilations and torture were common. Negotiation is more likely to wrest concessions from Israel than military threats.

Israel is populated by survivors of the Nazi holocaust. For them, the epic of *Masada* has become a vivid symbol. Most soldiers have been to this desert fortress where Jews made one of their last military stands against the Romans in 73 A.D. After seven years of resistance, when the Romans fought their way into Masada, they found that all but three of the defenders had taken their own lives and killed their families in preference to becoming slaves. This epic event is often contrasted to the defenselessness of Jews in Germany's concentration camps where over six millions died with less compassion than given to animals.

In the spirit of Masada, the Israelis preferred to rebel against the British, forcing them to make the decision to evacuate Palestine. The British had over 100,000 soldiers and the British Navy, pitted against less than 650,000 Jews. In 1967 Russian leaders made thinly veiled threats of open military intervention when the battle turned against the Arabs. Planes with Russian pilots appeared before the 1970 cease-fire went into effect. Israelis downed them in dogfights. Unlike the Czechoslovak people, Israelis have shown a capacity to fight, even against seemingly hopeless odds.

The odds seem less hopeless today than in the past. The Israelis are now well armed. If the Arabs or the Russians tried to invade, there would be a vehement resistance. Few observers doubt that it would take a heavy toll in the principal Arab cities, that are very vulnerable. If war broke out again, it might only last a few hours—not even six days—with severe losses on all sides.

This current balance of potential terror favors the alternative of political accommodation. Some of the great powers have begun to show signs of doubt that instability in the area continues to contribute enough to their national interest to take the risk of direct involvement. A negotiated stalemate promises more to the Arabs than renewed active military confrontation.

THE CONCORDANCE FACTOR

After fifty years of seemingly uncompromising confrontation between two rejuvenated nationalist movements laying claim to the same area, Arab leaders are quietly considering peaceful alternatives. They know that their past puristically uncompromising strategy has not worked. They have been forced to experience that there are positive benefits to be derived from Arab-Israeli concordance.

Arab leaders are under pressure to deliver more of the "good life" to their populations. Modernization and urbanization are raising the level of aspiration in all developing countries. This cannot be done when resources are siphoned off by a military elite, limiting those left to build schools, highways, factories and to combat the many endemic diseases that shorten the lifespan.

Since 1967, over a million Arabs in the occupied areas are co-existing with the Jewish state. Health, education and welfare benefits not available in Jordan, Syria or Egypt are increasingly available from Jewish authorities. Arab nationalist leaders offered only slogans and terror. Its most numerous victims are local Arabs. Nationalist guerrilla cells throw most of their bombs into busses driven from Gaza by Arabs for Arab workers who have jobs across the old border in Israel. Since the 1967 war, more Arabs than Jews have been killed and maimed by these Arab nationalists. Reduced by internal rivalry, they can now do little to harm Israel. They have lost much standing in all Arab countries.

The Israelis have unilaterally decided to compensate their Arab citizens, who lost property as a result of the 1948 independence war. Similar payments to Arab refugees in Jordan, Egypt, Lebanon and elsewhere could be negotiated, if there were to be peace and if Israeli economy could be devoted more fully to the production of developmental and consumer goods. Arabs' rights in Israel are strong even under the limitations imposed by security regulations. Due process of law is highly developed. There is no death penalty. In contrast, the concept of civil liberty is still weak in the Arab world.

Many young Arabs are dissatisfied with their traditional leadership. They oppose Zionism, but they also lack confidence in their self-appointed leaders. More women are questioning Arab customs which still deprive many of them of the vote and of other key rights. Some are not free to control their own person. Traditionalist parents and male relatives continue to marry off girls, sometimes against their will.

There is a good deal of mutual interest and respect between the elites of the two contending forces. The study of Arab language and literature are encouraged in Israeli high schools and universities. Arabs have come to admire many Israeli accomplishments. The unemployment problem among the refugees in the occupied territory is nearly solved due to the availability of well-paid work in Israel.

Borders lose their sting when there is peace. Today there are more Germans in France than even during the period when the Nazis occupied the area. Similarly in Israel, there are open borders allowing for trade and visits by Arabs from formerly hostile countries. Hundreds of thousands from all over the Middle East have personally been in Israel since 1967. They continue to come in ever larger numbers. They have been able to correct some of the incredibly crude progaganda lies which Arab leaders and communication media used to broadcast with impunity. Barriers are being breached each day with human and economic facts of coexistence, including intermarriage.

CONCLUSION

Predictions of the future are risky. It is never possible to collect all relevant data needed for rational decision-making. There also are other than rational factors that influence individuals as well as nations. They could lead to further war in the area. But there are positive points of contact between Arabs and Israelis. There is considerable evidence of a "reality therapy" in the Arab-Israeli confrontation.

The significance of the social forces that favor accommodation and peace cannot be estimated easily. It certainly cannot be determined on the basis of public political pronouncement by Arab leaders. Like all such statements, they reflect tactical objectives much more than actual sentiments.

The capacity of the great powers to intervene as self-interested parties has been greatly reduced. They have had to show their hand openly and thus undermined their creditability as "umpires." In 1948 and 1956, Israel was too weak to pursue an independent policy. Its leaders agreed to unconditional withdrawal without peace from all Arab territories. Not so in 1967. The Israelis have successfully resisted all political pressures, even by a majority of the United Nations, that would have made them withdraw unconditionally for the third time.

The last four years have been put to good use to establish direct lines of communication with Arab Palestinians, a majority of which are now under Israeli occupation. The barbed wire curtain that had existed for decades has been removed except around the Gaza Strip. The Arabs in Nablus can drive freely to the Israeli beaches. They do something their soldiers could only dream of doing. They can sit in a coffeehouse in Tel Aviv and be served by Jews!

There is attendance of Arabs in Israeli universities, especially in Haifa. There is joint action to prevent epidemics like cholera. While the two nationalities have engaged in open confrontation for more than half a century and their differences are exploited by big powers, many individual Arabs and Jews experience the normal consequences of life in the same community. Their differences are likely to be fought out in a court of law than with a gun.

Even in the midst of open Arab-Israeli battles, destructive forces have been balanced by awareness that there will have to be coexistence when the battle is over. In July 1971 nearly one hundred Palestinian nationalist fighters asked for refuge in Israel. They entered the land they had vowed to destroy "at any cost," not with bombs but with white flags! They believed that a more humane reception would await them there than surrender to the Jordanian Army with which they had engaged in a political and jurisdictional dispute.

These realities are easily missed in the smokescreen of rhetoric through which so few newsmen penetrate. At its worst, the level of hostility between many of the Arabs and Jews never attained the depth of irrational rejection of humane values of the so-called class struggle in the Soviet Union during the Stalin era or in what is now occurring in East Pakistan.

The prophets of doom, who speculate that a third world war might begin in the Middle East, need to consider weighty contrary evidence. In the land, holy to three religions, many residents are demonstrating by how they think and act that concordance and coexistence are possible. There has been much politics in the Middle East, if this process is defined as the "art of the possible." What has been lacking is statesmanship—"the art of the impossible."

Many geopolitical conflicts never get settled; men learn to live with its contradictions. In this reality lies hope for a sort of peace—good enough to live with, even if not secure enough to satisfy.

REFERENCES

1. Kurzman, Dan: *Genesis 1948: The First Arab-Israeli War*. New York, The World Publishing Company, 1970.

   Also Shapira, Avraham (Ed.): *The Seventh Day: Soldiers Talk About the Seventh Day*. New York, Charles Scribner's Sons, 1970.
2. Lewis, Bernard: Statement Before the Subcommittee on National Security and International Operations. U.S. Senate, Committee on Government Operations, 92nd Congress, First Session, March 17, 1971, Part 4, p. 92.

PART IV
CLINICAL AND CULTURAL APPLICATIONS

Chapter 18

The Role of Family Medicine in Social Psychiatry

LeRoy P. Levitt

TWENTY-FOUR YEARS AGO, the great medical historian, Henry E. Sigerist [1] said the following:

> It is important to know that the medical ideal has changed a great deal in the course of time and is evolving constantly. As a result, medical education can never reach definite forms but is obliged to adapt itself to changing conditions. Every society requires of its physician that he have knowledge, skill, devotion to his patients and similar qualities. But the position of the physician in society, the task assigned to him, and the rules of conduct imposed upon him by that society, change in every period. The physician was a priest in Babylonia, a craftsman in ancient Greece, a cleric and scholar in the early Middle Ages. He became a scientist with the rise of natural sciences, and it is perfectly obvious that the requirements put upon the physician and the task of medical education were different in all these periods. We must keep in mind that the picture a society has of its ideal doctor—the goal of medical education—is determined primarily by two factors: the social and economic structure of that society and the technical means available to medical science at that time.

It will be my attempt in this brief time to go a bit beyond the immediacies of the times and comment on the vicissitudes of the family doctor from the standpoint of his personal identity and some of the reasons why it has become so battered. The family physician is the new Cinderella of medicine, replacing the psychiatrist in this role. Having been gradually and inexorably rejected in the past thirty years, family medicine has gained recognition; she has been fitted with the glass slipper and achieved queenly status. Whether the fit will continue and the crowned head will become secure or remain uneasy occupies the concerns of many of us. Much will depend on our being sure of

271

our historial and personal identities and particularly the less visible components.

Many of the opponents of family medicine concepts state that historical fate spells the doom of these concepts. They rely on the anterograde method of viewing history. It is a human, almost compulsive, need to consider first things first, and everyone in every discipline is caught up with the "present" with its tensions, distresses, outraged feelings, and emergency needs.[2] The "now" sabotages attention to anything but the current period.

In human behavior and thought, however, the "now" does not stand alone. It is compounded of and infiltrated with centuries of "nows" reverberating and re-echoing in obscure ways in our thoughts, inner feelings and reflex or automatic behavior. Just as our physical structures contain palpable reminders of our biologic heritage, so do our psychic functions and institutions carry rational and irrational elements, the possession of those who preceded us. The core of experience which gives an individual his characteristic integrity as a personality relates him to his own ancestors as it does to the entire race. The exaltations and the defeats of the human spirit are reflected in difficulties now, as in the past, bearing witness to the sameness of human experience.[2] Dr. Sigerist may be right that every physician is a product of his time, but it is my contention that the healer and the wish to heal, as well as the forces involved in that healing, are no different now than they were in the past, no matter what garb, no matter what magic, no matter what therapies.

From Sushruta in the fifth century B.C. saying, "A physician should protect his patient as his own begotten child,"[3] to John Shaw Billings saying in 1892, "He who aspires to be his brothers' keeper must know how his brother lives," the message is clear. It is the personal and then the professional identity of the physician that must prevail.

The medical Cassandras that have attempted to demolish family medicine have denied the awareness of the new expanding role of this family physician identity, this at a time when the human condition cries out for a broader understanding, a keener concern and a more effective management of our medical affairs.[5]

Einstein once wrote, "Creating a new theory is not like destroying an old barn and erecting a skyscraper in its place. It is rather like climbing a mountain, gaining new and wider views, discovering unexpected connections. But the point from which we started still exists, although it appears smaller and forms a tiny part of our broad view." [6]

A number of societal, cultural, academic and economic factors have conspired to bring about visible changes in the previous identity structure of family practice as well as to imply its future disintegration. Since the medical student stands at the nexus of choices, I wish to focus on a few of these factors that affect him and in turn produce considerable impact upon family practice. These factors are (a) his original identifications, (b) his social milieu, (c) the educational process and (d) the medical educational environment.

HIS ORIGINAL IDENTIFICATIONS

Ordinarily identification is considered to be a means of maintaining a close relationship to an object. In fact, Freud [7] ventured the opinion that identification was perhaps the earliest expression of an emotional tie to another person. It is the process by which one places oneself in the situation of another person and assumes the characteristics of that person. It is a psychological phenomenon central to emotional development and undergoes many changes throughout life. It is the task of every society to provide children with worthwhile figures for this purpose. Identification is linked closely to empathy which is a form of communication on a nonverbal level. Sullivan [8] believed that this can be traced back to the relationship of the infant to its mother. It is a direct and immediate apprehension of feelings in another person. It is not intense in the infant, tending to decline with subsequent growth. It is here that the memory traces and imprints are laid down that form the basis for the later capacities for compassion, altruism and help-giving. One might say that it is here that future doctors are born. These capacities can be impaired or damaged by a host of factors within the family including inadequate mothering, poor nutrition, physical disability, absence or remoteness of father and large families.

In spite of an enormous amount of investigation of the genus medical student, these unconscious identifications have not yet been fully explored. It is my impression that the medical student interested in family practice, like the student interested in psychiatry, have strong fundamental identification ties to the significant maternal figure. Evaluation of this area would perhaps aid us in our selection process.

HIS SOCIAL MILIEU

It would be presumptuous of me to attempt any overview of this, except to say that original identifications that have a solid core of empathic gifts get sorely buffeted as our potential family physician enters the world. Our current society with its turmoil, wars, rapid and distorted communications, economic savagery, atomic threats, racial stresses, environmental hazards, just to name a few, seem to undermine these finer ego strengths so that the moral and religious ethic of caring for another is forced into a penumbra. The rise in student social and personal consciousness promises to be one of the most hopeful signs of the future, since it represents a return to consideration of human dignity and worth.

THE EDUCATION PROCESS

If the medical student-to-be has been able to integrate and crystallize his primary identification, preserving the character derivatives that relate to motivation, grace, tenderness and humaneness and he also is able to search and find some islands of personal stability and beliefs in the horrendous social confusions, he then must enter the process called the educational course. In the main, extending from kindergarten through college, it consists of a sequence designed to "turn off" one's natural learning avidity and to enforce an intellectualism that is a series of obsessional fact-gathering. Success is via the examination route which tests the retention of general irrelevancies and the speed of their regurgitation into the mouths of computers. The student, still intent on the study of medicine, "plays the game" by a heavy program in the sciences at the expense of a truly liberal education. It is a source of constant amazement that so many young men and women still are pursuing their wishes to become physicians. However there remains the gnawing sense of concern that many, many thousands of others have been deflected because of the so-called social, economic and academic screening which serves to eliminate many who are poor, uninformed, less obsessional, more human, black and not masochistic and who could well be physicians of excellence.

THE MEDICAL EDUCATIONAL ENVIRONMENT

At the bottleneck of medical school admissions, where about 50 percent of applicants are selected, another serious flaw develops, especially in regard to the potential family physician. Primarily, admissions are in the hands of about eight hundred faculty members in our nation's medical schools. These good people, using the discrete data of academic records, Medical College Admission Test scores, and committee or individual recommendations or both, hedged in by various state requirements, age, financial capacity and other factors and lacking often any assessment or evaluation of the candidate's emotional set, tend to select an intellectualized, scientist-type applicant.

But then, regardless of selection method, the practice of medicine demands the achievement of a professional identity wherein the student evolves those personal attitudes that will aid him in his responsibilities. This professional identity, when it is fully blossomed, is compounded of sympathy, understanding, respect and tolerance for the ills of others. There is little question that the pressures of scientific advance, the demands upon the student to master enormous data and the overriding emphasis upon research brought about by large-scale financing have tended to perpetuate a trend away from the acquisition of a personal and professional identity.

It is beginning to change now, but up to recently, the medical student had a limited number of faculty with which to identify himself, primarily specialists in areas often remote from the concrete experiences of human interrelationships and stresses. We need again to get outside the walls of the medical centers and into the community homes and hospitals as an equal part of training programs and offer opportunities for perceptions and emotional responses that will foster and revive the compassionate awareness of the inequity in human lives, the vast range of deprivations, which are suffered by a sizeable proportion of the population. The academic medical curriculum must become humanized and related to the needs of people in a closer manner.

The technocrats of biology and medicine—Leach [9] calls them the biocrats—have almost taken charge of our lives. There is certainly the good chance that with the changes inevitably to come in our social, educational and medical philosophies, the biocrats must yield to the obvious priority—compassionate and personalized attention to health needs, not episodic, but a continuum; not impersonal, but human; not haphazard, but comprehensive; not mechanical, but contactual; not judgmental, but wise.

To this end, the family physician will rise to a new level on his old territory to provide the synthesis imperative in preventing further erosion of services to people. In the long-run, the people will speak, not the medical profession. They will say, "Serve me as a human, and understand me in my illness, and treat me with grace."

To my knowledge, the family of physicians, cognizant of their role as social psychiatrists, have always done that.

REFERENCES

1. Sigerest, H. E.: *University and the Crossroads: Addresses and Essays.* New York, Abelard-Schuman Lt., 1946.
2. Bromberg, W.: *Man Above Humanity.* Philadelphia, J. B. Lippincott Co., 1954.
3. Sushruta: *Sushruta Samhita,* Chap. 25. (Fifth century b.c.)
4. Billings, J. S.: *Medical News,* 60:230, 1892.
5. Bryan, J.: *The Role of the Family Physician.* St. Louis, Warren H. Green Inc., 1968.
6. Einstein (quoted by Rabken, R.) : The Szasz review. *Psychiat Soc Sci Rev,* 4:5, 1970.
7. Freud, S.: *Group Psychology and the Analysis of the Ego.* London, The Hogarth Press, 1923.

8. Sullivan, H. S.: *Interpersonal Theory of Psychiatry*. New York, W. W. Norton, 1953.
9. Leach, A.: *The Biocrats*. London, Jonathan Cape, 1970.

Chapter 19

The Evolution of Attitudes in Social Psychiatry

JOHN L. CARLETON

UNTIL THE LATE 1940's, there prevailed a worldwide attitude of pessimism about the effectiveness of treatment measures for those suffering from significant and severe emotional illness. This attitude existed in the lay community as well as in the treatment professions. Sometimes expressed overtly, sometimes implied, it greatly influenced the kind of mode and outcome of therapeutic intervention. It is, of course, easier at times to maintain a nihilistic attitude than to suffer repeated disappointment and disillusionment from failures. Scientific information was lacking or poorly disseminated. Examples of successful treatment and recovery from severe illness were not sufficiently influential.

Nevertheless, there were other striking examples of unusual success in the treatment of emotional problems. The recovery of Clifford Beers is a case in point. Doctor Leo Bartemier * once cited the results obtained at a hospital which treated psychiatric patients as if they were ordinary people, members of a family group. The attention was focused upon emotional support and caring in addition to the physical and social needs of the patients, who thus did surprisingly better than those treated in the conventional institutions of that time and this. Doctor Isaac Ray† is an excellent example of a psychiatrist who had not only the courage of his convictions but much more optimism than was generally possessed at that time.

---

* A talk to the 8–0–10 Neuropsychiatric Course at Brook Army Medical Center, Fort Sam Houston, Texas, during the Winter of 1953.

† Ray, Isaac: *Medical Jurisprudence of Insanity.* Boston, Little, Brown Company, 1838.

My own involvement in formal psychiatric experience began in 1945 under the tutelage of Dr. S. Spafford Ackerly, Professor of Psychiatry at the University of Louisville School of Medicine. It was Dr. Ackerly's custom to hold small group seminars with students in their first or second year of medical school. These seminars were held in a conference room on the psychiatric ward of the Louisville General Hospital and lasted from two to four hours. In retrospect, Dr. Ackerly was optimistic about the treatment of the emotionally ill and conveyed his conviction in these seminars. I began to think of "crazy" people as having problems rather than being strange, unfathomable, frightening creatures, totally foreign and different from myself in all regards. In August of 1970 a group of eminent psychiatrists, including Dr. Jules H. Masserman, presented papers in honor of the seventh-fifth birthday of Dr. Leo Bartemier. These papers have been collected in a book which is titled *Hope: Psychiatry's Commitment** and emphasized Dr. Bartemier's unalterable attitude of hope which has continued to motivate him in his most exemplary involvement with the emotionally ill.

In recent years optimism prevails as to treatment based upon the principles of dynamic psychiatry applied with tenacious persistency and coupled with ever-present emotional support, caring and love † for the patient as a human being. Dr. Vladimir Hudolin,‡ Chairman of the Department of Psychiatry at the University of Zagreb, Yugoslavia, has demonstrated that modern scientific treatment combined with adequate active support from volunteer groups and the community as a whole can achieve spectacular results in the treatment of alcoholics.

My particular area of concentration has been the schizophrenic patient. It is my contention that an attitude of confident

---

* Sipe, A. W. R. (Ed.) : *Hope: Psychiatry's Commitment*. New York, Bruner/Mazel, 1970.

† Seguin, Carlos Alberto: *Love in Psychotherapy*. New York, Libra Publishers, Inc., 1965. In this book Dr. Seguin elaborates the kind of "love," (the "psychotherapeutic eros") which he feels the therapist must have for his patient if therapy is to be successful.

‡ Lecture at Camarillo State Hospital, Camarillo, California, Monday, May 17, 1971, and personal communications.

optimism is justified in the treatment of these patients also. I offer a brief report of a recent experience we had in Santa Barbara which I feel supports this attitude.

In the Summer of 1970 Doctor Joshua Bierer, Chairman of the International Association for Social Psychiatry, suggested that a social psychiatry workshop be held in Santa Barbara. I asked the Psychiatric Foundation of Santa Barbara if they would put on such a workshop and they responded with great enthusiasm. From start to finish the workshop has been (for it continues to exist in a motivational sense) an excellent example of social psychiatry in operation. It was international, multidisciplinary, stressed audience participation, had interactional lunches in the homes of friends of the Foundation and was put on by patients and their relatives.

The Psychiatric Foundation of Santa Barbara was formed in the Spring of 1970 by patients, their relatives and some professionals. It has legal status as a nonprofit foundation and its purpose is research and education for mental health. The first task of the Foundation was the establishment of a halfway house. The Foundation is motivated and directed by the nonprofessional members. This is particularly important because it means that the benefits of the existence of the organization are most directly experienced by the patients, their family members and friends. The Foundation is a healthy manifestation of people on their way to developing healthy egos.

Members who participate actively in an organization benefit most. Many mental health organizations do not include enough patients among their membership. "Patients" and "mental health" can occupy positions of poor seconds on the benefit scale. "Charitable" organizations can increase rather than decrease—the unhealthy dependency of patients and low self-esteem. Perhaps more than with any other medical and social entity, the emotionally ill person needs to be provided the opportunity to be a participant member of a team involved in his own therapy.

At our workshop the patients handled the registration desk, ran errands for the participants, took care of members of the audience who were in need or who had lost something, taped the speeches, controlled the microphones, heating and lighting, hosted the dinner and cocktail parties, and attended the sessions. One hospitalized patient, a teacher suffering from anorexia nervosa, attended all the sessions. Although I saw her as only a part of the audience during that time, she was much better after than before the workshop started. None of the Foundation members had emergency psychiatric needs during the workshop. None of them related to me other than as a social acquaintance, Foundation member, friend or program chairman during the entire workshop. It was their workshop and they supported me throughout.

The Foundation members proudly held an open house at their halfway house and invited all who wished to attend. About forty people took advantage of this opportunity. They were shown around the house and various patient-directed activities: clay therapy, wood carving, furniture refinishing and so forth were explained in detail. They were served refreshments and had a social evening.

Healthy identification occurs mainly only when people are actually involved in doing something with an organization, other individuals or groups. The more intense the involvement, the more important the identification. The more they love it, the more concordance there is. If we want to help patients, we must get them involved in activities that will help them help themselves. That must be the objective of the organization. If we want to have man for humanity, concordance instead of discord (even if concordance must arise from discord) at an international level, we must have the international involvement of as great a number of people as possible. When people have a common involvement, they develop a common identity and that is the goal. One part of the answer to the mental health problem is to get patients involved in those activities which promote and develop their own mental health. If we are to have international concordance, we must have international people involved in organizations and activities which promote and develop concordance

by virtue of the internal interaction and the interpersonal relationships inherently stimulated and promoted by the functional
operations of the organizations.

Chapter 20

The Adjunctive Role of Therapeutic Social Clubs

STANLEY R. DEAN

IT IS CONSISTENT with the democratic ideal that help for the mentally afflicted should be available to every individual rather than the privileged few. To achieve that goal we professionals must envision a system of outreach that literally permeates every level of society. We must speed the day when preventive and therapeutic first aid will be immediately available, not only for full-blown syndromes but also for the everyday crises that may be their forerunners. Only then will psychiatry, itself, attain maturity.

The Expert Committee of the World Health Organization in 1958 stated that "the dignity and the right to security of every disabled person is no less than that of a normal individual and that everything possible must be done to rehabilitate the disabled in order to restore them to as normal a life as possible in the society in which they live." [13] This includes the mentally disabled as well as the physically disabled.

It is no exaggeration to say that current demand for psychiatric service is greater than ever and its prestige is at an all-time high. In a relatively few years psychiatry has undergone a transition from the status of an isolated specialty to that of a major branch of medicine; the reasons being more affluent middle and lower income groups; popularization of psychiatry by mass media and government; accelerated physiochemical therapy, making it more akin to medicine as a whole; closer sociopsychiatric rapprochement due to escalating pressures at home and abroad; and increasing eclecticism within the ranks.

All these and other factors peculiar to our complex times have

---

Note: The author wishes to acknowledge the invaluable assistance of Miss Valerie J. Anders in collating and editing this chapter.

283

combined to create a veritable psychiatric explosion. To cope with it, the new psychiatric task force will have to expand its horizons. It will have to recruit sergeants and corporals as well as commanding officers. It will have to concern itself not only with theory and etiology but also with the necessity of tiding a patient over his immediate hangups. It will have to combine forces with adjunctive disciplines of all kinds in a cross-fertilizing atmosphere of concerted effort. In short, we envision a psychiatry that is versatile rather than static, pluralistic rather than insular, liberal rather than conservative, protean rather than stereotyped. Despite resistance from the parochial old guard, the innovative shift from institutional and office-based therapy to domiciliary and community involvement continues to make stubborn headway.

Already various paraprofessional psychiatric aides have validated their roles in modern treatment, especially psychiatric social workers, clinical psychologists, occupational therapists and psychiatric nurses.[16] But in addition, there are also many informal self-conducted "therapeutic clubs" within the community*—for example, Alcoholics Anonymous, Synanon, Weight Watchers, Recovery, Inc.—whose potential resources have been largely unexplored by professionals, although they have withstood the test of time and bid fair to become a permanent feature of the sociopsychiatric scene.

Self-directed therapeutic groups have characteristics that are particularly adaptive to patients afflicted with stigmatizing problems, since they aim to offset the isolation and estrangement imposed on such patients by family and friends at home or by the geographical dislocation of an institution remote from home. We might say that they provide an aura of community acceptance.

Self-directed groups do not provide "deep" psychotherapy, but their emphasis on faith, willpower, self-control and day-to-day victories do achieve constructive treatment goals. After all, who knows better how a mental patient, alcoholic or drug addict

---

* I have borrowed the phrase "therapeutic social clubs" from Joshua Bierer, famed pioneer of social psychiatry and Founder of both the British and International Associations of Social Psychiatry.

thinks or feels than other victims of the same malady? It is this unique feature that is so conducive to the effectiveness of self-directed groups.

The following list will serve to define self-help group therapy vis-à-vis orthodox psychotherapy. It is intended merely as an objective comparison and does not infer any superiority of one over the other.

APPROXIMATE COMPARISONS •

Orthodox Psychotherapy	*Self-Help Group Therapy*
1. Professional, authoritative therapist.	Nonprofessional leaders, group parity.
2. Fee.	Free.
3. Appointments & records.	None.
4. Therapy-oriented milieu (psychiatrist's office, clinic, etc.)	Nontherapy-oriented milieu (church rooms, community centers, etc.)
5. No family confrontation.	Family encouraged.
6. Psychiatrist is presumed normal, does not identify with patient.	Peers are similarly afflicted, identify with each other.
7. Therapist is not a role model, does not set personal examples.	Peers are role models, must set examples for each other.
8. Therapist is noncritical, nonjudgmental, neutral, listens.	Peers are active, judgmental, supportive, critical, talk.
9. Patients unilaterally divulge to therapist, disclosures are secret.	Peers divulge to each other, disclosures are shared.
10. Patients expect only to *receive* support.	Patients must also *give* support.
11. Concerned about symptom substitution if underlying causes are not removed.	Urges appropriate behavior, not concerned about symptom substitution.
12. Accepts disruptive behavior and sick role, absolves patient, blames cause.	Rejects disruptive behavior and sick role, holds member responsible.
13. Therapist does not aim to reach patient at "gut level."	Peers aim to reach each other at "gut level."
14. Emphasis on etiology, insight.	Emphasis on faith, willpower, self-control.
15. Patient's improvement is randomly achieved.	Patient's behavior is planfully achieved.
16. Therapist-patient relationship has little direct community impact.	Peers' intersocial involvement has considerable community impact.

• Condensed in part from Hurvitz, N.: Similarities and Differences Between Peer Self-Help Psychotherapy Groups and Professional Psychotherapy. 75th Annual Convention of the American Psychological Association, Sept. 1, 1968. Unpublished manuscript.

17. Everyday problems subordinated to long-range cure.	Primary emphasis on day-to-day victories: another day without liquor or drugs, another day without panic, etc.
18. Extracurricular contact and socialization with psychiatrist discouraged.	Continuing support and socialization available.
19. Lower cumulative dropout percentage.	Higher dropout percentage.
20. Patient cannot achieve parity with psychiatrist.	Members may themselves become active therapist.

The group that this report is especially interested in is known as Recovery, Inc. It is a structured self-help program based on willpower. It was founded in 1937 by a Chicago psychiatrist, the late Dr. Abraham A. Low, who was convinced that even the mentally ill could develop their willpower. The present author was the first psychiatrist to promulgate it thereafter.[15] Recovery, Inc., now has 725 groups in the United States and 35 in Canada, with more than 12,000 in weekly attendance. Recovery maintains an ongoing program of cooperation with formal psychiatry. Hundreds of actual panel demonstrations are given each year for the professional staffs of psychiatric hospitals and clinics.[17,18] A panel demonstration was presented at the annual meeting of the American Psychiatric Association in May, 1969.[19]

Dr. Low's book, *Mental Health Through Will Training,* is the handbook of Recovery's members.[14] It has been criticized by some psychiatrists as being unorthodox and authoritarian. However, it was intended for patients who do not understand the jargon of psychiatry. Low devised a simple vocabulary of key phrases in order to provide a uniform basis among his groups for understanding, communication and procedure.

This vocabulary stresses such down-to-earth concepts as "willpower," "muscle control," "endorsement," "spotting nervous symptoms" and "sabotage." To some psychiatrists that might seem rather naive and archaic; however, such simple homilies have proved effective in a lay setting and I have never found them to interfere with our more recondite pontifications.[6]

Members learn to spot and analyze the emotional nature of a disturbing symptom when it occurs. They also learn how to deal with it through "muscle control," forcing one's self to behave or react in an approved way. Having the member recount before others how he spotted a disturbing situation enables him to obtain cathartic relief in a setting in which he also gains enthusiastic group approval (endorsement) .[2,10]

Each session centers about a topic selected in advance from Dr. Low's book, *Mental Health Through Will Training,* or a prerecorded comment by Dr. Low on the topic. Examples and discussions by four or five panel members follow for approximately one hour, then a free-will offering is collected. Next comes a brief mutual aid period which is usually accompanied by simple refreshments. During this half-hour group members have an opportunity to become better acquainted and to discuss Recovery techniques informally.

Organized large-scale social activity is kept to a minimum with the possible exceptions of a Christmas party and a midsummer picnic. While the members are encouraged to associate during meetings on an informal and friendly basis, they are often known to each other only by first names and last initials.

DISCUSSION

Recovery, Inc., stresses that the organization does not diagnose or treat or supplant the doctor. Each member is at all times expected to follow the authority of his own physician or other professional. Recovery, Inc., is not intended to be a substitute for psychiatry but rather a self-directed program that may be used either to supplement psychiatry or alone in certain situations where psychiatric treatment is not available or mandatory. The ideal referral to Recovery should come from a physician or psychiatrist, with the patient remaining under his doctor's care, for the latter is best qualified to know the needs of the patient and to supervise his progress.

However, the fact of the matter is that such ideals are not enforceable and are often ignored, with the result that patients are accepted from many sources—lay and professional—and some are even self-referred. Therefore it follows that Recovery, although often serving an important need, is not an unmixed blessing. Its many advantages should be carefully weighed against the following disadvantages [9,10]:

1. There are no members under the age of eighteen.

2. No disruptive patients are admitted.

3. No records are kept; there is no adequate follow-up.

4. There is a high percentage of dropouts.

5. Leaders receive only a few days training plus short periodic refresher courses.

6. Members are accepted without adequate screening or referral.

7. Noninnovative, formulistic procedures are employed.

8. There is a tendency to downgrade other techniques.

9. There is frequent disregard of the admonition to follow the physician's authority.

10. There is a tendency to assume a "panacea complex."

11. There is risk of bungling by inept amateurs.

12. There is danger of delaying adequate professional care in serious cases.

13. The groups are not subject to professional, legal or other regulatory restraints, as are licensed professionals.

14. There is an antitherapeutic suppression of ambivalence and hostility.

15. The emphasis is only on social therapy (correction of environmental factors) rather than medical therapy (correction of organic and intrapsychic factors) .

In view of the above, it must be stressed that Recovery, Inc., is not a substitute for psychiatry, but a self-directed program that may be used to supplement psychiatry or alone in certain cases where psychiatric treatment is not available or mandatory. The ideal referral to Recovery should come from a physician or psychiatrist qualified to know what best fills the needs of the patient; but it is also important that *all* behavioral professions should become acquainted with the unique and valuable services that Recovery has to offer.

In addition to its value as an adjunct to psychiatry, Recovery can serve an important "caretaker" function in those cases where psychiatric treatment is not available for one reason or another, such as lack of funds or resistance on the part of a patient or his family to psychiatric treatment.[4]

Although group psychotherapy does not go as "deep" as individual psychotherapy, it provides some unique advantages that only group therapy can offer. There is a certain contagiousness about group attitudes that is transmitted to the individual. The collective mind and the collective will are stronger than that of the individual. A person who cannot utilize his own will to get better finds that he can surrender more readily to the will of the group. This group contagiousness explains to a large extent the cohesiveness of thought in political parties, religious denominations and other organizational activities.

The emotional climate of a group is an effective instrument for countering the feelings of isolation and withdrawal of the patient. Mass suggestion and mass identification help to extrovert a patient's emotions and "draw him out of his shell." People who are themselves afflicted are more sympathetic and understanding to fellow sufferers. Most people feel better when they learn to share their troubles with kindred spirits. In Recovery each patient is encouraged to confront his problems, to air his symptoms and to examine the validity and appropriateness of his emotions. At home this might meet with arguments, objections, indifference or even pampering. In the group it meets with understanding and support.

It would appear that as patients confess their fears and eccentricities and observe no reactions of dismay on the faces of others, they feel accepted. They feel safe in the group because the shared secret evokes no condemnation. They are all in the same boat, so to speak. They reinforce each other by their mutual acceptance.

Still another advantage of Recovery is the competitive element that it provides. Patients consciously or unconsciously compete with one another to see who can improve most completely and quickly and thereby win the approval of the rest of the group. In turn, the actual demonstration of objective improvement from week to week is a source of great encouragement and inspiration to the others. Part of the program for each is the support and reclamation of other patients. This spirit of working together toward a common goal cannot be overemphasized. In union there is strength. Helping others is one of the surest ways to help one's self. These truths have been known through the ages. In Recovery they are brought into sharp focus where patients can actually observe them in practice.

A major advantage of Recovery, which is rare in the orthodox type of individual or group therapy, is a provision for family participation. The family is thereby able to obtain greater insight into the problems of the patients. The family members realize that behavior problems are universal and not a unique and personal affliction. As a consequence, they learn not to feel so sorry for themselves. At the same time they acquire a new dimension in sympathy, tolerance and understanding. More important, since disturbed individuals often come from disturbed families, the latter may learn through Recovery to spot and correct their own abnormal reactions. It is a psychological truism that "we treat situations rather than individuals." Recovery provides an excellent opportunity to bring the entire situation into focus.

Finally, in patients just released from an institution, Recovery helps to smooth the transition from hospital to society. Without such a medium the patient may find it difficult to cope with the sudden immersion back into an environment that presumably contributed to his breakdown in the first place. The Recovery group is a sort of miniature society that can serve as an important buffer between the patient and his environment. If he is accepted by Recovery, it lessens his fear about being accepted by society.[9]

Although Recovery, Inc., prefers professional referrals, if the need arises it will accept members who, for economic or other reasons, are not currently under psychiatric care. Does that pose a threat to private practice? Not at all. The present author can affirm that a physician who refers selected patients to Recovery will find that it is like bread cast upon the water—in terms of cross-referrals, therapeutic progress, prestige and self-esteem.[7,8]

What results may be expected from the Recovery program? As yet the answer to that question can be given only on an empirical level. Practically all the articles that have appeared so far were

written by psychologists, sociologists and feature writers.[1,3,5,20]
A thorough search of the literature reveals only one statistical
study, conducted by Donald T. Lee, Chief of the Social Service
Department at the Camarillo State Hospital in California. It is
an ongoing study, as yet incomplete, but Lee's clinical impression is that the Recovery program tends to create a "well role"
model in the important area of interpersonal relationships for
the participating patient.[11,12] A favorable clinical impression has
also been briefly noted by Shoichet.[21]

The present author agrees with those impressions. Over a period of twenty years I have referred some two hundred patients to
Recovery, Inc. Most of them continued simultaneously under my
care. In my opinion this concurrent group, as a whole, showed
better progress than nonparticipants. There was more rapid
symptomatic improvement; less self-consciousness and embarrass-
ment; a greater sense of pride, accomplishment and degree of
commitment; better coping behavior; accelerated social rehabilitation; and less tendency to decompensate under stress.

Any fears I may have had about dependency and secondary
gain were soon allayed by the observation that any element of
dependency upon the group was more than compensated for by
responsibility to the group and ultimately a social obligation to
get well and become a productive member of society.

REFERENCES

*1. Alexander, J.: They "doctor" one another. *Saturday Evening Post*,
    Dec. 6, 1952.

*2. Berland, T.: How the mentally ill are helping themselves. *Family
    Weekly*, Feb. 2, 1969.

3. Berzon, B., and Sonomon, L. N.: The self-directed therapeutic group:
    Three studies. *J Counsel Psychol, 13:*491–497, 1966. Also several
    mimeographed papers available at the Western Behavioral Science
    Institute, La Jolla, California.

4. Carner, C.: Now: Clubs for mutual mental help. *Today's Health,* publ.
    by American Medical Association, March 1968.

*5. Crane, P.: Self-help in emotional illness. *The Liguorian*, Dec. 1968.

*6. Dean, S. R.: Recovery, Inc. *Am J Psychiatry*, Correspondence Section,
    125, May 1969.

Editor's Note: An asterisk identifies a direct reference to Recovery, Inc.

*7. Dean, S. R.: Recovery, Inc.: Giving psychiatry an assist. *Medical Economics,* Sept. 2, 1969.

*8. Dean, S. R.: Self-directed group psychotherapy: Focus on Recovery, Inc. *Medical Tribune* (Current Opinion Section), June 23, 1969.

*9. Dean, S. R.: *The Role of Self-Help Group Psychotherapy in Mental Rehabilitation.* Proceedings of the 4th Pan Pacific Rehabilitation Conference. Hong Kong, Sept. 1968.

*9a. Dean, S. R.: The role of self-conducted group therapy in psychorehabilitation: A look at Recovery, Inc. *Am J Psychiatry, 127:*7, Jan. 1971.

*10. Harris, E.: Recovery, Inc. *Am Weekly J,* Jan. 15, 1961.

*11. Lee, D. T.: *Aid in the Transition from Hospital to Community: Recovery, Inc.* Presented at Southern California Psychiatry Society Convention, 1968. Unpublished manuscript.

*12. Lee, D. T.: Recovery, Inc.: A well role model. *Q Camarillo, 2:*35–36, Aug. 1966.

13. Leigh, Denis: Quoted in *Psychiatric Hospital Care and Rehabilitation: Report on a Travelling Seminar.* Copenhagen, World Health Organization, 1968.

*14. Low, A. A.: *Mental Health Through Will Training.* Boston, Christopher Publishing House, 1950 (11th ed., 1967).

*15. Low, A. A.: Personal communication to the author, June 1, 1947.

16. Mendel, W. M.: Maladjusted psychiatry. *Med Opinion Rev,* March 1969.

*17. Bessent, T., and Sandron, L.: *What is Recovery, Inc.* Recovery Panel Demonstration. Annual Convention of California State Psychology Association, Jan. 31, 1968.

*18. Cozens, W. R., Palmer, J. D., and Sandron, L.: *Recovery, Inc. as an Innovative Self-Help Psychotherapy Group.* Annual Convention of California State Psychology Association. Recovery Panel Demonstration. Jan. 31, 1968.

*19. Grosz, H. J.: *Recovery, Inc. in Action.* Annual Meeting American Psychiatry Association, Miami, Fla., May 1969.

*20. Recovery Reporter, published by Recovery, Inc., National Headquarters, Chicago, Illinois, Jan.–Feb. 1969, vol. 32.

*21. Shoichet, R.: Recovery, Inc., *Canadian Family Physician,* Nov. 1968.

Chapter 21

Sociopsychiatric Contribution to Human Concordance

Vladimir Hudolin

O N REFLECTING UPON THE theme here, I have had to face a number of terminological problems. However, apart from difficulties in the sphere of terminology, there appear also numerous difficulties, psychologic and philosophic in nature.

The query to be raised is, What do we actually understand by peaceful, positive relationships? It is most likely that disordered interhuman relations reflect among other things certain social structures, which, in turn, are the reflection of a certain time or period and not solely of a possible psychologic normality or abnormality. I shall assume that certain social structures have actually been formed on the basis of definite types of interhuman relations, mutually causally interwoven. Every society has endeavored to create social structures that are the most positive for the conception of a given society. On the other hand, humans have always been inclined to interrelations that will make possible a full and free development of individual personality, so that most likely a given social climate has been formed in accordance with existing wishes and aspirations in interhuman relations.

If that indeed be so—namely, that social structure had been that frame which had delineated the interhuman relations of a given period, conferring upon them a special quality and moral significance—then in such a social structure and given form of interhuman relations, there must have been created also the role played by psychiatry, provided that it was possessed of a clear social place and if it contributed to such social structure. Psychiatry and psychiatrists would have to actively participate in creating mutual understanding in a given society; however, to achieve this aim, psychiatrists ought in this sense to be educated and trained, while psychiatry would have to be organized correspondingly. A special problem is that relationships among humans should be harmonized also on a world plane, in which domain both the psychiatrist and social psychiatry could contribute not a little. However, what does harmonizing of interrelations on a world plane spell, and what is the role of the psychiatrist here?

Historically, the organization of psychiatry has always corresponded to the structure of a given society. To be more precise, psychiatry has a function in a given social structure in a given time period. On the basis of the role psychiatry has played in society we are able to categorize the whole historical development of psychiatry into several phases. Thus, for example, we are entitled to speak about a phase in which psychiatry represented a social service aimed at protecting society, in the majority of cases to the detriment of the patient himself. Although it cannot be denied that also in this phase psychiatry was concerned with the balancing of interhuman relations, it is obvious that such a role of psychiatry would not satisfy the majority of contemporary psychiatrists. In the phase in question psychiatry would eliminate a certain number of human beings from interhuman relations.

Further we may speak of a phase of psychiatry when, besides protecting society, it commenced being concerned to a certain extent with the patient himself, after which a patient constituted its focus. On considering such essential differences in the approach to psychiatry, it becomes evident that also the following terminological and essential queries ought to be answered: What is psychiatry? What is social psychiatry? Some think that social psychiatry is an attempt at improving relations within a psychiatric hospital, that in a general way the atmosphere within a psychiatric hospital should be altered. Such a viewpoint is not sufficient, both formally and from the aspect of the contents. Others again are of the opinion that social psychiatry stands for the introduction of new relationships between the therapist and the patient in a psychiatric hospital, taking advantage of possible special therapeutic procedures. The majority of such people belong to the group of psychiatrists engaged in a therapeutic community. However, such conceptions of the functions of psychiatry does not contribute either to the solution of tasks we have set ourselves to solve.

Then there is the most recent integrative phase of psychiatry, which protects society, true, but also protects the individual—namely, it tries to integrate the individual into society, endeavoring to find a place for the individual in society.

However, the query should be raised, Is for such psychiatry the classical psychiatric education the most suitable? Further, is the classically educated and trained psychiatrist the person most competent to concern himself with this problem? Still today there exist forms of psychiatry that are characteristic of all the aforementioned historical phases, not only in world proportions but very frequently also in one and the same country.

The modern social psychiatrist must understand the development and problems of the social structure in which he lives and must integrate his therapeutic and rehabilitative procedures with the tissue of the social structure. Thus there arises a problem of ethical-moral character—namely, whether the psychiatrist is to accept also the conceptions typical of the social structure in which he lives and works, without trying to impose his dominance.

Social psychiatry can achieve these ends in cooperation with all other forces that are present in society. In this, the most important role is played by the patient. Social psychiatry would be unthinkable if the patient were to remain but the object of the therapeutic procedure.

The patient must become a subjective factor on an equal footing in the sociopsychiatric process. Social psychiatry cannot extricate itself from society by teaching it from an academic rostrum; it has to be integrated into society and should try to alter this same society with the aim to create such interhuman relations that will ensure a full, free development of the personality. The social psychiatrist cannot be a judge of his own society but a dedicated social worker aiming at contributing to the development of social relations. This, however, is not to imply that the psychiatrist should assume the role of a passive onlooker of social processes; as an active sociopolitical worker he should endeavor to influence these processes in order that they be directed towards a positive, progressive goal.

Socialism facilitates this activity of social psychiatry but does not automatically solve all existing problems. Furthermore, the socialistic structure itself is possessed of characteristics of its own, which contribute to the appearance of social conflicts and problems and call for a meticulous assessment by the social psychiatrist and for his utmost activity. Hence the socialistic social structure will not by itself shape social psychiatry, so that even in a socialistic social structure it is possible to find the most conservative psychiatric attitudes. The attitude towards war and peace in individual countries and in socialistic and capitalistic social structures speak eloquently of these ubiquitous variations.

The physical, mental and economic well-being of every individual should constitute a right safeguarded by the fundamental principles of society. The creation of positive interhuman relations in society is a function of the psychiatrist.

As I work in the sociopsychiatric field in a socialistic land, the problems of social psychiatry in a socialistic society are familiar to me. Since I am particularly engaged in problems of alcoholism, I will endeavor to illustrate on the example of alcoholism the procedure we have introduced in Croatia, one of the Republics of the Yugoslav Federation.

We began with epidemiologic investigations and studies of attitudes on the part of health services, social protection and society in general towards psychical disorders, notably in regard to alcoholism. Our investigations were initiated by having organized a Republican Register of alcoholics being institutionalized in psychiatric hospitals in Croatia. We further carried out a number of investigations in the general population and studies of representative samples among the populations of individual industrial branches. We also made a careful study of all cases that in Croatia present themselves because of working disability before first-degree disability commissions. All these studies and investigations have shown that among the adult male population in Croatia, one should expect about 15 percent of them to

Figure 21–1. Map of Yugoslavia with borders of the six republics.

Figure 21–2. Psychiatric centers in Croatia which provide institutional treatment for alcoholics. Black triangles are clinics; white triangles, day centers; circles, hospital facilities.

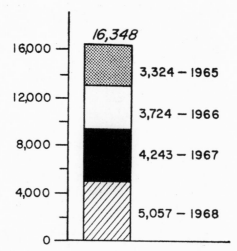

Figure 21–3. Alcoholics under institutionalized therapy in psychiatric institutions in the S.R. of Croatia in the period 1965–1968.

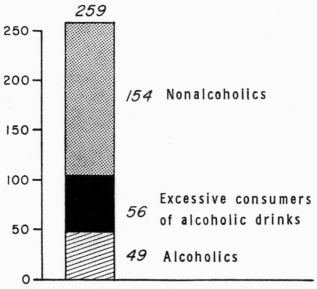

Figure 21–4. Alcoholics in a sample of 259 respondents of a male population of a commune in the S.R. of Croatia.

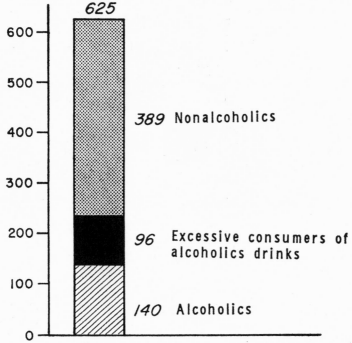

Figure 21–5. Alcoholism in a population totaling 625 respondents in a catering business enterprise.

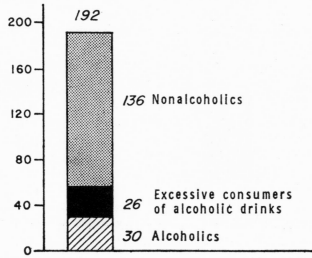

Figure 21–6. Alcoholism in a sample of 192 respondents which are direct producers, aged 20 to 50, in a metal-processing enterprise.

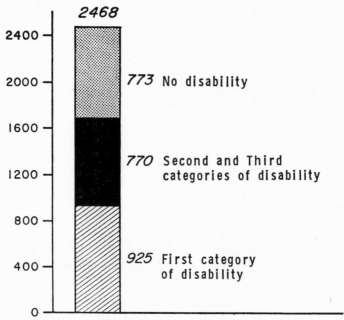

Figure 21–7. Total number of examined alcoholics by first-degree disability commissions in relation to categories of disability.

be alcoholic and another 15 percent to indulge in alcohol to a sufficient extent to cause personal and family trouble.

On the basis of these investigations it has been possible to establish that it is impossible either to plan or implement treatment of such immense numbers of alcoholics by using the classical medical individual procedures. I had likewise become aware that it would be impossible for psychiatrists alone to perform such an immense task, but that we would have also to engage general practitioners, social workers and medical nurses. However, even taking for granted that all the enumerated professions were to take a part, it would be impossible to cope with it if we were not to enroll the patients themselves and their families in an active manner as a subjective factor in this work. In order to achieve this, we asked of every alcoholic and all members of his family to study the problem of alcoholism and then to pass an examination on alcoholism. In order to achieve this, we assembled the alcoholics, the members of their

Figure 21–8. Clubs of treated alcoholics on the territory of the S.R. of Croatia.

families and the experts working with them in a widely organized network of Clubs of Treated Alcoholics.

Concurrent studies have shown that no major results can be scored unless we contrive to change the attitudes of society and of the health services towards alcoholism. For this purpose numerous technical, professional and educational meetings are arranged. Once a month we convene plenary meetings (400 to 800 delegates), which are organized in one of the seats of Clubs in the Republic. Once a year the clubs convene a congress; last year's congress was attended by three thousand participants. The clubs propose their candidate, who is elected to the Croatian Parliament and who deals with the problem of alcoholism on a parliamentary level. Thus Parliament is in a position to pass laws and give recommendations, bearing in mind the problems of alcoholism. Parliament also invites representatives of alcoholics, who thus are in a position to participate directly in discussions dealing with their specific problems. Alcoholism is also on the agenda in discussions of political organizations, trade unions, communal assemblies, etcetera. In this manner it is possible to form regulations that prescribe that every commune should elaborate its own program in the field control of alcoholism.

In a similar way we have commenced solving the problems of registry, mental retardation in children and so forth.

This brief report is best illustrative of how it is possible that social psychiatry introduce a new quality into interhuman relations, solving simultaneously on a broader social plane also the prevention, treatment and rehabilitation. Such a process ought to be initiated also on a world plane and efforts on the part of the International Association of Social Psychiatry are being directed accordingly.

Although the role of social psychiatry is not to reform society, it is obvious that no significant results will be attained unless interhuman cooperation is raised into a higher, more progressive level. In such work also the activity of the social psychiatrist weighs heavily. The activity of the social psychiatrist and of social psychiatry has been very fruitful so far, both in individual countries and on an international level.

Chapter 22

Man for Humanity

ARTHUR M. SACKLER

IN ITS CONSTITUTION, the World Health Organization has declared certain principles as basic to the happiness and harmony of all peoples: First among these, "Health is a state of complete physical, mental and social well-being and not merely the absence of disease or infirmity." Second, health is a fundamental right "of every human being without distinction of race, religion, political belief, economic or social condition." Third, "The heath of all peoples is fundamental to the attainment of peace and security."

It is unfortunately clear that the actual health of the world mirrors the discordance, the gross and unacceptable inequalities, among men of different races, economic and social conditions and reflects the failure of both national and world societies to fulfill the "fundamental rights" of their citizens and fellowmen.

We live in a world in which the transistor has condensed time, and as instantaneous dissemination of news by satellite communication has replaced the millennia it previously took for diffusion of man's cultural and technologic attainments. The jet engine has collapsed space and is homogenizing cultures. In such a world, human concordance is not possible in the face of the discordance in man's longevity, infant mortality and gross national product.

Life expectancy is seventy-seven years in one society (Sweden) and thirty-one years in another (Chad). *Infant mortality* is 12.8 per thousand live births in Norway and 259 in Zambia—a twentyfold difference. *Gross national product* is approaching $4,000 per capita in the United States and as little as $50 per annum in several African states—an eightyfold difference.

Exactly thirty years ago, the great medical historian, Henry

E. Sigerist, wrote "There is an iron rule which is valid everywhere, namely, that no individual and no family can lead a decent and healthy life unless they have a certain minimum income. . . . If this is not done, people will of necessity become anti-social, may develop illness or break the law, and in such cases society must pay a far greater bill by erecting and operating hospitals and jails." [1]

We live in a world which must choose between concordance, which is possible only with economic and social equality, and discord, in which, to paraphrase Sigerist, "society must pay a far greater bill" for military installations, ICBM silos, bombers and tanks. The choice is between rockets and food, between bombs and antibiotics.

We live in a world in which the discriminatory differences in gross national product, infant mortality and longevity are paralleled by the inequities of available health care. The difference in physician-patient ratios between one country and another are almost one hundred to one. The differentials in regard to psychiatrists are even greater. There are twelve countries *without* psychiatrists. In twenty-seven countries the ratio of psychiatrists to population is an incredible one psychiatrist to almost three million people. Who will care for the 189 million people in twenty-six countries who have available to them a total of sixty-five psychiatrists, and for the countless millions like them elsewhere?

For decades our group sought the physiologic mechanisms whereby man has spontaneously recovered from psychic disasters. Fortunately, the new psychotropic drugs have reduced mental hospital populations and have given a new impetus to social psychiatry. Unhappily, some psychotherapists are now challenging biochemotherapy, contending that drug abuse epidemics are iatrogenically induced. Can this be reconciled with the epidemic abuse of marijuana in Zambia and India, of the poppy in the Middle East, or with the chewing of cocoa leaves in the Andes? Has psychopharmacologic prescribing led to the thousands of years of man's psychotropic abuse of alcoholic beverages and marijuana or his resort to peyote and the "sacred mushroom"?

Can we or should we restrict our efforts to allay the internal conflict of man to one modality? If that modality be psychotherapy, can we or should we proclaim the unproved primacy of a therapeutic approach which is by force of circumstance denied to the hundred of millions of economically disadvantaged and, in effect, unavailable to the vast majority of the world's population?

We live in a world in which medicine must be more than a profession, an art and a biological science.

For all medicine is, ultimately, social medicine. The *raison d'etre* of medicine is man—not a political system and not an economic structure.

All medicine is world medicine as all physicians are bound to their forebears in science: to Hippocrates, Vesalius and Galen; to Virchow and Ehrlich; to Claude Bernard, Pasteur and the Curies; to Lister and Flemming and to Pavlov and Freud.

Yet, despite the central role of medicine and its potentials for man's security and peace, the world faces an increasing shortage of physicians in all categories of health manpower. Even if one thousand new medical schools were to spring from the earth *today*, we would be short in medical manpower *tomorrow*.

We live in a world in which man's economic, social and political behavior tends to reflect a cross between the all-too-real fantasies of Lewis Carroll's *Alice in Wonderland* and the doomsday predictions of Orwell. In *Alice in Wonderland,* the Mad Hatter reflected the occupational mercury poisoning common among the unprotected felt hat workers. But in our modern, advanced, mass production society, mercury poisoning is shared by all as the world has become one, in its least pleasing aspect, environmental pollution. Pollution, environmental or otherwise, is not the exclusive prerogative of any one social or political system. Unhappily, there are no political distinctions in regard to physical or other forms of pollution, such as the semantic pollution of ideals and the poisoning of ideas in which words convey one meaning and reality another as the world is wrapped in the smog of hypocrisy.

We are concerned, and rightly so, about man's war on his

environment, but are we not unbalancing our concerns by permitting this focus on tomorrow to blur our obligations to those dying of starvation today because of their inability to cope with the environment as it is? Are we not engaging in an inexplicable and unforgivable neutrality in the war between man and hunger? Is not our neglect, in effect, embargoing their life essentials? In the face of rampant starvation and malnutrition, does not our immediate focus on ecology conjure the picture of individuals complaining that smoke stacks such as those of Auschwitz, Belsen and Buchenwald would contribute to air pollution?

We live in a world whose gross and *in*human inequities makes *dis*cordance not just an inevitability but a tragedy. To assure *all* men the right to health, "a state of complete physical, mental and social well-being" will require concordance among men of good will; a *unity* in understanding and action of physicians and scientists, of the young and the old, and of people of every color, of every religious or political belief. Without *dis*cordance there can be no change; without concordance there can be neither progress nor continuity.

REFERENCE

1. Sigerist, Henry E.: *Medicine and Human Welfare.* New Haven, Yale University Press, 1941.

Chapter 23

Mass Psychotherapy for Intergroup Conflict

BRYANT WEDGE

A DOZEN YEARS AGO, when I announced to my friends an interest in applying psychiatric approaches to the problems of conflict between nations, their kindest reaction was one of skepticism. It is true that there were a few methodological problems, summed up by a colleague who asked, "And pray, sir, how will you get a nation to lie on your couch?"

My friends were right, in a way. It has proved difficult to move from the consulting room into the arena of international affairs, and quite a few modifications in theory and technique have been forced upon me by the peculiar nature of the rather unwilling subjects, including their sturdy resistance to considering the possibility that they might sometimes entertain distorted images of the other fellow and a striking reluctance to employ any service that might suggest possibilities for adjusting conflicts different from those established by long custom.

Nevertheless, it has proved possible to enter into conversation with members of nations and groups in conflict with one another; Americans and Russians, Egyptians, Palestine Arabs and Israelis, revolutionaries and Establishment officials, bureaucracies and congresses. As the outlines of a coherent approach begin to emerge, my own experiences have been greatly extended and modified by the systematic field trials of some seventy graduate student colleagues* entering into a wide variety of communities in conflict; police forces and motorcycle gangs, military organizations and peace groups, mental hospitals and hippie groups among them.

---

* Graduate students of international communication at the Center for the Advancement of Communication at Fairfield University (Connecticut) and of Diplomacy at the Fletcher School of Law and Diplomacy as well as less complete trials by psychiatrists in training, Peace Corps Volunteers and Marine Corps Officers.

From the first, moreover, it was evident that while the conceptual framework and working methods of clinical psychiatry could provide a procedural basis for approaching the problems of intergroup conflict (after all, the professional function of the psychiatrist is to act as an intercessor between individuals alienated from one another and their reference groups), the professional discipline lacked experience with a wide range of factors operative in organized group life. It was therefore necessary to reach beyond the normal boundaries of the discipline for the tools of analysis; in fact, to construct multidisciplinary teams so that we could achieve a satisfactory understanding of the issues involved in any given case or, as we became able to generalize from the accumulation and comparison of cases, in all instances of intergroup conflict.

Among the resources that have proved indispensable in given cases and in general are the applied sciences of group psychology and sociology, which provide models for the formation, organization and behavior of human groups; experimental and social psychology which provides knowledge concerning the formation of images and ideas as these affect group behavior; anthropology as the source of models for the analysis of the influence of culture and its values in change and interaction among groups; political studies which identify the role of power and of authority processes in the organization of group behavior; economics that define the realistic probabilities for the survival and prospering of any group, the so-called rational factor; history that can identify the evolution of the memory of groups that so profoundly affects their outlook and perception of events; and communication science that provides the tools for identifying the channels, flow and consequences of information exchanges.

It is a matter of deep regret that neither I nor anyone else has been able to find the resources to sustain a multidisciplinary group committed to problem-solving and professional discipline-building approaches to intergroup conflict in the real world; practically, each case has been approached on an *ad hoc* basis with scientific participants taking time from their normal pursuits to contribute to understanding the case and to building the

basis for a professional applied science. Nevertheless, the basis
for a systematic psychotherapy of intergroup conflicts has
emerged. After some general remarks on groups and intergroup
conflict, I shall sketch out an elementary model of the mass
psychotherapy process.

ON GROUPS

So long as mankind evolves, groups of men will come together
to pursue new purposes. Each of these constantly arising groups
passes through a natural history of some duration, almost always
and inevitably perceiving itself as coming into competition and
conflict with other groups at various points in its history. Frequently intergroup conflict gets out of hand, the threshold between interaction that is stimulating and productive of human
satisfaction and progress, and conflict that produces violence and
increasing human cost is passed, and the conflict assumes a dynamic life of its own even when decoupled from its origins.
Knowing what we do about man's need for groups and group
tendencies toward conflict, it is impossible to visualize any future
state of human evolution when these processes will cease. So it
behooves us to grasp group processes as a prime element in the
human condition.

Three distinct levels of group life can be defined: the small
group of six to sixteen members, the large interest group or
organization, and the nation; there are qualitative differences
between these levels of organized group systems but there are
also fundamental regularities in the processes of group formation
and interaction. Experimental observations of small groups have
generated the basic descriptive models while methods of organizational study, opinion and image analysis, and historical-
political comparison have demonstrated the universality of basic
processes.

Men form themselves into groups whenever they come into
contact, however accidentally, in circumstances that provide them
with common purposes. Such groups evolve and define their
boundaries so that members and nonmembers can be distinguished and territory and interests defined. They develop in-

ternal social structure and distinctive functional roles for their members, their own customs, language, values and loyalties; in short, their own identifiable culture. As evolving groups pass through events that require common action and involve common tribulations, they establish increasingly definite identities and acquire new purposes, one of which often comes to be the survival and well-being of the group itself with all its cumulative values.

Soon or late, in the life of many or even most naturally occurring human groups some outside force is perceived as threatening group territory or values; very often that force is embodied in other established groups. Up to a point, such competition stimulates cooperation within the group, encourages cohesion and common action, tightens the definition of boundaries and hastens social invention and change. However, as frustration of value achievement mounts, competition tends to turn into conflict. The competitor is then seen more and more hostilely and becomes the object of group projections, eventually to be seen as the enemy. The conflict process arouses virtually identical responses in small groups, large interest groups and nations; the "enemy" is increasingly defined as evil, devious and ill-intentioned while one's own group is seen as moral, honest and peaceful in purpose. The substance of any given conflict tends to be perceived reciprocally so that conflicting groups develop "mirror-images" of the enemy. Some of us have argued and think we can eventually prove that much of the fuel for intergroup conflict is not from conflict of interest in any real sense but from conflict of understanding—that is, of culture.

The outcomes of intergroup conflict depend on a great many factors; the presence of supragroup third parties, the customary ways of conducting conflict at various levels (including, of course, war at the international level), the relative capabilities and will of the competitors, and so on. Intergroup conflicts may become institutionalized and carried on over decades and centuries; they may be resolved temporarily by the dominance of one group over another or broken off by formal or tacit agreement on boundary limits; most rarely by the mutual transformation of the groups toward a transactional mixture from which each may benefit. The most regular feature of conflict-level reduction is the occurrence of communication between the hostile groups, especially when some level of direct contact is involved and the discovery of some benefit to each of the parties by subscribing to a common, supraordinate goal, however partially such goals may involve the overall interests of the groups.

A regular feature of the human landscape then is that groups form, come into conflict and eventually reduce the levels of conflict to degrees sustainable by the group. The problem that our own group characteristics poses for humanity is, Can we find ways to keep intergroup conflicts from getting out of hand, to intervene so as to limit the level and type of conflict to minimal violence and human cost? Here, I want to be explicit, the aim of the mass psychotherapeutic approaches proposed is not to eliminate conflict nor to achieve general peace in the world between nations and groups but only to reduce the intensity, duration and human costs of out-of-hand intergroup conflict interactions.

A MASS PSYCHOTHERAPEUTIC MODEL

I have noted that communication and contact, together with the discovery of some common action that is seen as satisfying some need of all parties to intergroup conflict (even lessening the strain of maintaining the contest) tend to reduce the intensity of the conflict process. It is to these ends that the mass psychotherapeutic model that I will sketch out is directed. As you will see, the basic model is very simple, consisting of five principal stages and identical with the basic processes of most reality-oriented psychotherapies.

The place of such intercession is *not* in the structure of intergroup relations in the world as it is. I do not suggest a replacement for the role of authority and representation in group life, although I hope that an adequate development of such social inventions could make these functions more easy and might even change them somewhat in the long run. I do not advocate any substitute for the functions of diplomacy in negotiation between sovereign governments (whether of nations, universities or trade

unions) ; the long-developing and highly specialized arts of diplomacy are invaluable in codifying agreements and building a
body of world law, and they are already under pressure enough
from complex and changing times.

What I propose is technical mass psychotherapeutic approaches
to out-of-hand conflicts at largely subgovernmental levels for the
purpose of establishing communication linkages and even common institutions (intersystem systems) between parties at conflict. Such links and institutions, I am satisfied, can serve as
restraining forces in the intensity of conflict, just as threads were
useful in tying Gulliver down. In actual practice, as in the Soviet-
American cultural exchange agreement or establishing a university technical assistance program in the Dominican Republic,
there is evidence that even single links can provide channels of
communication that filter widely in the societies and reach and
are used by the highest levels of government.

The relevant steps are those of (a) establishing dialogue
separately with the groups at conflict, (b) of identifying their
self-perceived interests and mutual interests, (c) bringing the
parties into communication and/or contact with these interests
in mind, (d) encouraging programs of direct cooperation for
mutual interests and (e) terminating the intercession. First
though the psychotherapist of intergroup conflict must find some
sort of base for his efforts. The time may not be far away when
client groups or interested third groups will actively seek the
services of the mass psychotherapist, but it has not arrived.

The therapeutic intercessor in intergroup conflict is, so far,
somewhat in the position of Freud as the first psychoanalyst; he
is self-appointed to his task and has to offer his services and seek
his clients wherever they may be found. What is necessary is that
he set criteria of rigorous neutrality with respect to any quarrel
and insist on freedom of movement and such access as he may
arrange by his own merits. While he should undertake to exercise
precise ethical discretion with respect to confidences, he cannot
ever be bound by bureaucratic or administrative controls. In
other word, the intercessor is a volunteer but the role requirements are exacting in the extreme. The responsibility is solely his

or the group that he may represent; the Quakers and a few peace research or peace action groups have defined such group positions. Funding for his work can come from any source that accepts the criteria; from his own pocket or from visionary sponsors and foundations. The United States Government has sponsored some experiments meeting these conditions and the Scandinavian and West German governments have done so indirectly through support of peace research groups.

THERAPY MODEL

The intercession begins with the decision to undertake the mass psychotherapeutic effort in a given case and the recruitment of enough resources to support a professional effort. Sometimes this is quite modest, as when one student interceded between airport-political authorities and a local community up in arms over a runway extension, or when another maintained dialogue with the Cambridge police and MIT student groups during a confrontation; more often, costs involve compensation for time, travel and consultation, as well as secretarial and communication expenses. In any case, once the intercession is begun, the most rigorous technical requirement is the precise ordering of the stages of action; any prematurity of purpose-oriented behavior or even intension damages the process.

Establishing dialogue with the groups in conflict is accomplished separately and sequentially, usually by moving back and forth between the groups while spending some time between on neutral territory to summarize the last episode and prepare for the next. The dialogues are conducted entirely within the cultural requirements of the host group as it responds to the outside intercessor. The purpose is to understand the group's hopes and aspirations, concerns and fears, in its own terms while maintaining a position of benign neutrality. Absolute honesty with respect to the intercessor's contacts with the antagonist seems to provide stimulus and interest in expressing the group's outlook.

The requirements for entering a boundaried group as an outsider and conducting conversations cross-culturally are quite distinctive. I outlined my own efforts at systematic description in a fifteen-week course, much assisted by students who test the methods and rules of conduct in their own field trials. The basic process is identical to that of the psychiatric interview series; it involves successive approximations to comprehending the prevalent viewpoints in the group or society through the encouragement of verbal expression by inquiry, restatement and trial interpretation, as conducted in socially acceptable settings with groups and individual persons.

Here too the requirements of phasing are exacting; until sufficient knowledge of the communication preferences and social norms is gained by consultation, observational scouting and covert rehearsal, there is little point in engaging in direct contact and seeking access to representative group members. Until access has been gained and working credibility established, there is no possibility of exploring viewpoints in any depth and until a relatively extensive exploration of the mental landscape is completed, focus on the salient interests of the group is premature.

The question that the intercessor must constantly ask of himself in the dialogue process is, How do I appear to my hosts? The feedback input to this query provides for constant correction of one's own behavior and of one's interpretation of the aspirations of the group. It is the question that permits one to judge and strengthen the credibility essential to further steps. It is forever humbling. However well-intentioned one's motives, the intercessor is always seen as an outsider, a stranger, a possible danger. He finds himself being tested and retested, doubted and "misunderstood," accused and maligned. The same group or person may be seen as antisemitic in Israel and as a Zionist spy or spies in Egypt; as a "leading agent of cultural imperialism" by Latin American revolutionists and as a Communist dupe or secret sympathizer by the same nation's Establishment. It is well to know of these images, not to deny them but to correct for them.

Despite all these difficulties and problems in dialogue, a strict adherence to role, including steady answers to the three constant questions of an outsider—Who are you? What is your purpose here? How long are you going to stay?—almost never fails to establish a genuine circumstance of sympathetic dialogue (of my seventy student trials, only one failed to reach this stage, and his fellow students were able to diagnose his basic antipathy to the hippie communes he was approaching).

The second stage involves the identification of the principal interests of the parties, particularly the interests that may be mutual or complementary. Since the intercessor is already known to be in contact with the antagonistic group, entry into this stage is almost automatic, each group party to intergroup conflict is invariably fascinated by its adversaries and eager with proposals for changes in the adversary's behavior. In all of my experience the duration of the phase of exhilaration in combat is remarkably brief, especially when violence is involved and the desire to disengage from out-of-hand conflict is constant, while steps in that direction are impeded by the respective group's preoccupation with acceptable terms and in the absence of communication, by a kind of resigned wonder that the other side cannot seem to see that its behavior is what prolongs the conflict.

The technical problem of this stage is to sort over and identify interests, most often complementary, that could be satisfied by some mutual program—not a single action, since these sometimes help reduce conflict but do not lead to the continuity necessary to build an intersystem system of communication. Quite often, the interests to be gratified are asymmetrical—that is, the values gained by one side are quite different from those satisfied for the other. For example, the United States supported a technical assistance program in the Dominican Republic to contribute to stabilization, while the revolutionists who controlled the university sought a base to prepare for reforms; the Three Environment Test Ban Treaty represented a strategic advantage to the United States which was far ahead in its weapons tests and a political advantage to the Soviet Union that then sought limited detente. The problem is to find and encourage thinking about some measure that can be accepted by the parties as working to their interest as they see it; such measures must also be large enough to gain public and leadership attention and small enough to avoid inciting unmanageable opposition. In practice, it is best to offer a selected shopping list of such propositions as have the approval "in principle" of each of the groups.

It may be useful here to review some of the group phenomena that appear with great regularity in the stages of establishing dialogue and exploring the interests of groups in conflict. The first is that the boundaries of hostile groups are invariably patrolled by outgroup advisors who are both knowledgeable and zealous in their predictions of dire consequences from engaging the group. Students entering ghettos have regularly been warned that they will be mugged or knifed—none has been; those entering homosexual communities have been warned of rape, seduction and drugs in their drinks; those entering prisons have been told that convicts never talk—they do; and so on. I have been told innumerable times that I, as a Jew, cannot visit both Israel and Egypt with any but a hostile reception. The political officer of an American Embassy insisted, before I could stop him, that it was impossible to enter the local University—where I had been received with honors—without immediate arrest; and so on. This is not to assert that there is no line that cannot be crossed in perfect safety, but that a cautious assessment has to be made in each case and the channels of access and lines of withdrawal kept open until the dialogue is established.

A second experience is that the internal boundaries of each group are also guarded by gatekeepers; group members whose function is to assess and turn away unwelcome outsiders—in corporations they are called public relations representatives, in national states they are often experienced hosts to foreigners. Rarely do the gatekeepers open channels—that is not their function—nor do they have the capability of access themselves. The problem usually is to bypass them through channels of personal introduction to socially central group members.

Once a group has been engaged and the preliminary rounds of testing and declaration-making have been negotiated, the outlines of the group outlook begin to appear in the dialogue. These are frequently at considerable variance with the official stances and public declarations that are exposed in the press or even to data-oriented experts. They regularly have characteristic perceptions of themselves and of the adversary; although the local content varies, the themes are constant. Every group in conflict with others feels itself victimized and put upon; a certain amount of fear and anxiety for the outcome underlies the brave protestations and dire threats. Every group feels itself to be righteous in its cause in ways that should be self-evident to any fair-minded observer. It generally believes its motives are directed toward justice and peace and that the solidarity with its leadership is much greater than others imagine.

Groups in intergroup conflict perceive the adversary in terms of what professor Ralph White has described as "hostile enemy images"; the enemy is supposed to be diabolical in its purposes and methods toward the reference group and is imagined to concentrate its resources on the group's discomfiture to an intense degree—as the United States has tended to grossly overestimate the priority with which the Soviet Union seeks its downfall despite Russia's other close concerns. The enemy is seen to be wholly unscrupulous in the pursuit of hostile aims, to be forcing the group to its own defense. How many times have I heard a plaintive, Why do they hate us so? from blacks and Arabs and homosexuals, even from significant personages in national administrations. Yet this image is modified by a curious conviction that the main body of the enemy group does not really hate, they are only misled and misinformed by ruling circles—open or hidden in their action—that manipulate power and opinion, what White has termed the "black-top image" of the enemy.

Then also there is the peculiar reception of communications from or about the adversary. Words or phrases that can be taken as hostile are given great prominence, those that are generous or placatory are bypassed. Evidences of weakness or of dissent among "the people" of the enemy camp are played up beyond recognition—the most extreme case being the CIA's misjudgment of Cuban disaffection before the Bay of Pigs charade. The greater the gap in direct communication, the greater tends to be the distortion; national judgment of Chinese aggressiveness has varied in inverse proportion to the number of people actually moving across the Chinese boundary with any potential adversary nation.

It should be clear from this that the intercessor who attempts to modify these views by relating his own first-hand knowledge of the other side would only lose credibility, even when he is reporting to his own group, as every ambassador knows full well. It follows that efforts at mediation—getting agreement between parties by seeking to define acceptable points—have very narrow scope and are best handled by professional diplomats. What is left is the intercessor's unique capacity to provide occasions for direct communication and contact.

The third stage then involves steps to bring about communication and direct contact concerning issues of acknowledged common interests. Often it takes some time to shift from the second to the third stage; a certain amount of ripening of the circumstances and of the idea is necessary. For example, it took seven months after conducting dialogue with the U.S. Government and the Dominican reformists before the third stage could be initiated and two-and-a-half months more before principal representatives were brought into contact. For more than ten years, I have been pursuing the moment when parties concerned with the Palestine Arab people could open real communication, and this has yet to come, although conditions are ripening. Sometimes, however, the response is very rapid, as was the case in the Test-Ban negotiations when the conditions became right. Some of my students have experienced almost instant success when one group has asked them to introduce them to members of another; for example, when a motorcycle band wanted contact with the police to settle certain boundaries for their activities.

At the outset of this stage, the communicator usually acts as a private postbox, he simply conveys the willingness of one side to communicate with the other on a given subject. He does not negotiate, recommend or urge; he does not mediate or propose suggestions of his own; at the most he may express his estimate

of the seriousness of intent of the opposing groups. Here, however, he is certain to run into a very fundamental problem that
lies at the heart of the communication distortions mentioned
before—the differences in culture. Words in one group take on a
different meaning to the other, values as to what represent
worthy goals shift in their transmission, views of the very facts
at issue differ from one side to the other. Here the intercessor
must walk carefully; he is entitled, indeed required, to render
the meanings of each side to the understanding of the other with
maximum fidelity to *their* intentions. There can be no shading
of conditions or of message; the model is, "What they said was
literally this and what I think this means in your terms is thus
and so."

Usually, if the issue is truly complementary, it takes only one
exploration with each side before a concrete offer is made: the
form is cautious—"You can tell them that we might be willing
to discuss the matter"—and this leads to the first written
communication, for the response is a written invitation *to the
intercessor* to arrange such an action or meeting. This piece of
paper is very important for it specifies the subject while leaving
open the means. Now a round of consultation as to actual steps
is possible. Obviously, at this point, the intercessor is no longer
dealing with the whole range of the group's membership but with
a functional subgroup; little parties of advocates begin to
evolve on each side and it is their task, not the intercessor's, to
carry the communication flow within their larger community and,
moreover, to guard against steps that could set off substantial
opposition.

Quite often, the action chosen involves bringing more substantial third-party elements on to the scene; a technical assistance
program in touch with both sides, a small group of mutually
acceptable advisors who are expert in politically neutral matters.
In my experience, direct meetings have rarely been feasible until
these conditions are filled; a group of partisans from each side
with representation from leadership levels *and* the presence of
a tested and trusted third-party group. For example, in a dispute
between a college administration and a grouping of admitted

homosexuals, a number of nonhomosexual students satisfied the third-party requirement. In the Dominican Republic, a group of professors of undisputed competence enjoyed the confidence of both revolutionaries and the American Embassy.

Now, in order to make substantive progress with projects in which both sides have an interest, it is desirable to arrange for direct contact; while the conditions vary somewhat from case to case, it has usually been necessary to find a neutral meeting place, to have substantial buffering persons present (including the third-party group and sometimes prestigious neutrals) and rigorously to avoid formal agendas or even formal meeting arrangements. Food, drink and informal spaces with lots of nooks and corners seem ideal. The occasion is announced as an opportunity to meet, honor and socialize with the third-party visitor to the scene. (Here, I am aware that I am suggesting quite explicit rules and not all of them are equally critical; most of them have evolved from the analysis of failure in such experiments.)

The outcome of such meetings is apt to be a paradoxical reaction; the hostile stereotypes are affirmed while at the same time the participants conclude that it is possible to work with the adversary group on the issue at hand. Police do not fall in love with motorcycle gangs or ghetto residents with welfare workers, but they each discover that *their* lives can be eased by limited collaboration.

The stage is now set for the fourth phase, that of helping to institutionalize the working arrangement; here the intercessor must carefully retire to acting as a resource advisor. We have repeatedly found that continued active efforts to encourage any formulation of one's own is seen as interference, and the intercessor becomes the target of suspicion by both groups. Nevertheless, only the intercessor has enough knowledge of each group and of outside resources to carry out the necessary introductions and, to a degree, act as external advocate for the project. He will be asked if he waits and makes his availability known and should answer only what he is asked. As soon as self-sustaining communication linkages are formed, he should terminate his activity.

The stage of termination should have been very much in mind at every preceding stage; indeed, it is an essential question in establishing dialogue. It is most difficult from the "counter-transference" point of view, for one who has enjoyed a significant role finds he is no longer needed, indeed that he is surprisingly little thanked. A departure date is set and announced, personal goodbyes are made, and the groups, including the intergroup group, are given a chance to express their farewell in their own way. When one leaves group dialogue, leave-taking is a high moment, invariably marked by formality and declarations of esteem and affection, but the intergroup intercessor seems never to experience this; more likely, a few friends from both sides will provide a very quiet dinner, no speeches and a relatively routine farewell. It is likely, isn't it, that the affectionate ties between individual and group have been displaced by similar bonds between the groups?

THE FUTURE OF MASS PSYCHOTHERAPY

I have outlined what psychiatrists will recognize as a rather conventional process model for psychotherapeutic intervention, modified to accommodate the empirical requirements of intergroup alienation. The procedures have been specified as closely and concretely as possible at this stage of development in the hope that other psychotherapists may be encouraged to apply their approaches to intergroup conflicts and that we can begin to build a scientific art of mass psychotherapy.

Two other experiments in mass psychotherapy of intergroup conflict have been reported recently, and their main conclusions are identical with my own; communication and direct contact between groups in conflict can be facilitated by systematic third-party intercession and can significantly influence the hostile interaction. John Burton, an international relations specialist at the University of London, has succeeded in bringing together representatives of groups in violent interaction—including Greek and Turkish Cypriots—on neutral ground to engage in what

he terms "controlled communication." The third parties are
technical experts in politics, perception and group behavior,
who interpret and demonstrate the communication dynamics
of interchanges without getting into the substance of the
quarrels. In a second experiment, Richard Walton, a group dynamics expert from the Harvard Business School, has reported
on a "workshop" in which representatives of Ethiopia, Kenya
and Somalia met on neutral turf in Italy to discuss their bloody
border conflicts. Methods of group dynamic and sensitivity training were used by trained group leaders to facilitate interchange.
In each case, the participants underwent profound changes in
the hitherto prevailing hostile group attitudes which they had
shared.

These three experiments—Burton's, Walton's and Doob's,
and mine—demonstrate that we are approaching the "mass
therapy of destructive prejudices" that Harold Lasswell visual-
ized over thirty years ago and that President Franklin Roosevelt
called for when he wrote, just before he died, that "We are faced
with the pre-eminent fact that if civilization is to survive, we
must cultivate the science of human relationship—the ability
of peoples of all kinds to live together and work together in
the same world, at peace."

We have a vast distance yet to go before we can claim to have
developed a tested "science of human relationship" at the intergroup level. We shall have to develop multidisciplinary professional teams working full time at the theory and practice of
mass therapy; we have to learn for ourselves and train others. To
accomplish this, we shall have to mobilize substantial support,
both the moral support of professional and public confidence
and the financial support of practical visionaries.

I have no doubt that there *is* a future for mass therapies of
destructive intergroup conflict. People all over the world are
weary and sick of being victimized by the very group forces in
which they are embroiled; many of them have felt helpless and
hopeless to do anything about it. But the experiments of the
last decade have shown that something can be done, that therapy
is possible in at least some times and places. There is practical

hope in this and where there is hope there will be response. We can visualize a time when groups in conflict will request the professional services of the scientific mass psychotherapy team in their own interest. The question now is how fast we can press the development of a new and vitally important social invention.

REFERENCES

The writer's basic argument for psychiatric approaches appears in "Psychiatry and International Affairs." *Science, 157 (No. 3786):*281–285, July 21, 1967. A general description of his training program appears in "Training for Leadership in Cross-Cultural Dialogue," Institute for the Study of National Behavior, San Diego, California, 1968, and the theoretical model for intergroup system development is described by Edmund S. Glenn, Robert H. Johnson, Paul R. Kimmel, and Bryant Wedge in "A Cognitive Interaction Model to Analyze Culture Conflict in International Relations." *J Conflict Resolution, 14 (No. 1):*35–48, Spring, 1970.

While there is an extensive literature on group behavior, basic considerations are outlined in the classic study of Muzafer Sherif and his collaborators in *Intergroup Conflict and Cooperation: The Robbers Cave Experiment,* Institute of Group Relations, Norman, Oklahoma, 1961. Ralph K. White's *Nobody Wanted War: Misperception in Vietnam and Other Wars,* Doubleday, Garden City, 1961, outlines the development of hostile enemy images in polarized conflict. Hadley Cantril, to whom I owe profound gratitude for his inspiration and encouragement, has reviewed his experiences in applying psychological science to real world problems in *The Human Dimension: Experiences in Policy Research,* New Brunswick, Rutgers University Press, 1967.

John Burton's technique of controlled communication is outlined in *Conflict and Communication,* New York, The Free Press, 1969, and Richard Walton's report appears in "A Problem-Solving Workshop on Border Conflicts in Eastern Africa," *J Appl Behav Sci, 6 (No. 5):*453–496, 1970.

PART V

REVIEWS AND INTEGRATIONS

Chapter 24

The Cultural Image in Rebellious Conflict

Richard O. Fuller

FERGUS MANN AND I have been struggling for some time to understand the important factors in determining whether groups interact in a manner which is mutually facilitating or in ways which seem to be an unrealistic preoccupation with narrow self-interest. Two examples have most stimulated us: the groups of blacks in rebellion against the larger society and the rather similar uprisings among college and high school students. In this discussion I shall consider both groups to be involved in the same type of conflict situation, the down group in rebellion against the up group. I do see great differences between the black experience and that of students, but I wish to stress here an important element they have in common. It seems to me that in this particular type of conflict we can see vividly the importance of the cultural image of the situation within which group members operate. It is my thesis that uprisings now occur where previously there was no open conflict because while the ups and the downs once had complementary images of their joint situation, they no longer do. The image which the down group has of the situation has changed substantially while the up group's image of the situation has remained relatively static. How did such a shift occur? What is the significance of this disparity in images for the course of conflict between the two groups? How does conflict over images differ from conflict over priorities? To answer these questions we must begin with the concept of the cultural image of a group.

In the definition of image I follow Boulding[1] and Kelman.[2] Images exist in the minds of individuals, partly in the unconscious. They are an individual's internal representation of things and ideas. Thus an individual has images about himself, about the situation in which he finds himself and about groups of people in that situation. The images organize both information which the individual would call "facts" and attitudes about these facts. The distinction I wish to make here is between those aspects of a person's image which I will call personal, because they vary markedly from person to person within a given culture, and those aspects which I will call cultural, because they are fairly uniform from one member of the culture to the next. A person's image of policemen has personal and cultural components. The personal aspects of an image about policemen are influenced by the individual's general feelings about authority and by his personal history of learning about policemen, beginning at pre-school age with family talks and television shows. Because of these experiences, people differ widely in the personal aspects of their images of policemen. They may think of them as clever or dumb, as sensitive human beings or uncaring officials. However, much of a person's image about policemen is very similar to that of his neighbor and often quite different from the image of someone from another part of town. Common experiences with policemen and a shared cultural definition of the meaning of police activity work together to produce similar aspects of images in the minds of almost all members of a group.

Because the cultural aspect of an image is held in near unanimity, it has a power not held by the personal aspects of an image. The cultural image gets institutionalized into routine ways of doing things and into formal procedures. Where I work, lower level professional staff gets twice as much vacation time, per month worked, as salaried nonprofessional staff doing equally difficult work. This may have resulted from a cultural image among the policy-makers that the professional staff works harder. If there had been wide variation in the images of the policy-makers as to who worked harder, such a policy decision would not have been made, institutionalizing the image.

It is these cultural aspects of images, homogeneous within groups and differing markedly between groups, which play an explainable role in intergroup conflict. Interacting groups with differing images of their mutual situation are likely to be in conflict. That conflict will be harder to handle if the parties not only do not share images but also do not understand each other's images. Where this is the case, the others' actions, based on their image, will be misunderstood, resulting in an inappropriate response which may foster still more confusion. This seems to me part of the pattern in conflicts between ups and downs, and the disparity of images producing it follows understandably from the changing relationship of the two groups.

American blacks were once in circumstances where their lives depended on whites. Most plantation blacks had a relationship with the white race which in Dr. Manfred Halpern's classification scheme would be called *emanation*.[3,4] The down member in an emanation relationship is not seen as a complete person, by himself or by the up. In an emanation relationship, the up is felt to be endowed with a mysterious power upon which the down member depends, without which he could not survive. In these circumstances, common experience over an extended period of time leads individual downs to a self-image which is partially shared by all those in their culture. That cultural part of each down individual's self-image is, "We are not capable of sensing our rightful place in the world. Terrible things would happen to us if the ups did not support us." Every student too has in his history a relationship, childhood, which is based on emanation. For both students and blacks, circumstances have changed, allowing them somewhat greater autonomy. This has resulted in a change in the cultural image of what it means to be a down. The ups still have power over the downs, but it is no longer thought by the downs to be mysterious or desirable. Under these circumstances, the downs' cultural image of the down-up relationship is an image of what Dr. Halpern calls *subjection*. In subjection, the source of the ups' power is knowable and, theoretically, could be possessed by the downs as well. In a subjection relationship, ups' power may be tested. With rebellion, we have an attempt to break the relationship of subjection, but before turning to that, let us consider the ups' cultural images in an emanation relationship.

In the antebellum period, whites watched over blacks, directing their lives, and in all periods, adults similarly care for children. Just as an up-down relationship of emanation created an image of dependency in the downs, so it created a cultural image of competence and superiority for the ups. These are two sides of the same cultural coin, for the two parties to an emanation relationship must have overlapping cultural images, with shared definitions of what it means to be an up or a down. In discussing the ups' "inherent" superiority I wish to distinguish again between those aspects of images which are cultural—that is, similar throughout the culture and the personal aspects, which vary widely, according to the individual's personal history and genetic makeup. A school administrator may feel himself to be personally inadequate both in his marriage and with his fellow administrators, but this will not necessarily lead him to discard the general cultural belief that because he is an adult, he is competent to manage the lives of students. A slave owner preoccupied with his personal mismanagement of his plantation and with his poor performance in the county sporting circle need not have doubted his community's image that whites were the necessary trustees of blacks. Cultural images do change, but only with a change in the experience of most members of the culture. Thus it is possible to speak of individuals as prisoners of the cultural images of their time. Kuhn has documented this admirably in the evolution of scientific theory.[5]

The circumstances of the early up-down relationship forced the ups to make judgments crucially affecting the lives of the downs, and they found themselves competent to do it. It was soon part of the cultural image of both ups and downs that only the ups were competent to make such decisions. The down groups who are now in revolt in the schools, in the streets and in other areas of the American scene no longer hold this image. What must have happened is that the image of the relationship as one of subjection grew to be held by many downs because it was a better explanation of their changing situation than the old image of emanation. This new cultural image of the situation prepared many downs to support, or at least tolerate, challenges to the ups' control of things and to the old, formerly shared, image. It is because the challenges to the image are concerned with the self-definition of the downs and with the definition of what is going on between the downs and ups, that feelings among the downs can run high.

As the downs' views of themselves and of their circumstances change, their view of the ups alters correspondingly. The ups' actions are no longer seen as benevolent, but as oppressive. However, the ups' view of themselves does not change. Their cultural image of their relationship with the downs does not contain very much which can be summarized as "oppression." How can this be? Many whites have read the autobiography of Malcolm X; many school administrators have read Jerry Farber's *Student as Nigger*.[6] Why has there not been a similar change in the ups' image? As Kuhn showed so perceptively, for a group to accept a new cultural image of themselves or their world, the new image must explain important phenomena not comprehensible in terms of the old image. For most of the ups in our two examples, the world has not changed enough to require a substantial change of their image of it. The images which "explain" the changed life of the down group are not needed in the more static experience of the up group. The ups' old cultural image of their emanation relationship with the downs is workable, and most ups are preoccupied with other matters. Thus, even when an individual white comes to believe that Frantz Fanon tells it like it truly is, his personal perceptions are unlikely to receive support from his fellow ups, and thus redefinition of relevant images does not occur on a cultural level.

It would be untrue to suggest that there had not been a change in the ups' images of the situation in both of our examples, even before significant challenge from the downs occurred. Whites knew the blacks were not slaves; adults know that adolescents will soon be adults themselves. In its rational aspects the cultural image has changed considerably, but in the unconscious areas of individuals' cultural images and in the enduring customs and formal procedures which grew so naturally out of the old images, change is much slower, where it has occurred at all. Colored should have an equal chance in the world, but that did not mean they used the same toilet. The college kids will have families of their own soon, but that does not mean they are now trusted very far into the adult spheres of money, sex or prescription and nonprescription drugs.

It is with these conflicting images that the groups come into confrontation. The downs' most basic demand, often unformulated, is, "Recognize our image of the situation and treat us accordingly." The ups do not understand what is happening because the downs' image is not a sensible explanation of their world. The downs do not act according to the ups' scenario, and the ups are threatened. Any explanation the ups put on the situation is necessarily in the terms of their own cultural image of the situation, which may highlight the "childishness" of the downs' actions. The situation is necessarily further confused because it is seldom worth couching a demand for recognition in the abstract terms in which it has been stated here; demands are necessarily focused on changing symbols of the old dependent image, such as who controls the school curriculum, or they are focused on standard and widely appreciated grievances such as low wages. Sometimes down groups find an issue which is both understood by the broader society and which also symbolizes very well the down group's desire for a new recognition. This happened in the Memphis, Tennessee, garbage workers' strike during which Martin Luther King was assassinated. There one of the strongest demands of the striking garbage collectors was for recognition of their union by the city. Whatever the specific demands of the rebellious down group, it is often quite easy for the ups to interpret them within the ups' cultural image of the situation, not understanding that the group presenting the demands sees them with very different eyes. The ups naturally try to assume the conflict is based on differences in priorities within a shared frame of reference. It is only when this image of the situation fails repeatedly to "explain" the downs' reactions to the ups' attempts to fix things that the ups will begin to redefine their image of the situation.

The ups and the downs are a special case of the general problem which has been discussed at length during this conference, of conflict management between parties with different images. Dr. Wedge outlined five stages in what he calls the mass psychotherapy of social conflicts. They are rather intricate and extremely difficult to execute, but they have a primary goal which can be simply stated. It is to give the parties each an image of the other's view of the world comprehensive enough so that when they finally begin discussing their problems after their long history of noncommunication, they do not so misunderstand each other as to stop communicating again. The goal of the mass psychotherapist is not the actual resolution of conflict, that must be left the parties themselves. Dr. Wedge said specifically that the intercessor should withdraw as soon as firm communication links are formed. All the intercessor's efforts before that termination are devoted toward the end of trying to understand the image of each of the parties and transfer that image accurately into the image of the other group. If a group can understand the general cultural image of the other, then any action that other group might take is more likely to be understood. This is important because the clearer a group's understanding, even of hostile moves, the less it will falsely imagine slights, broken promises and general unreliability, the perception of which is so inimical to any sort of common endeavor.

Dr. Vassiliou was also speaking about cultural images: The Greek idea of how to help a friend's friend enjoy his stay in Athens is to direct that person's life while he is there. In the Greek image, such behavior is labeled as "friendly concern." In American culture, such behavior may be considered "an invasion of privacy."

Thus far I have discussed the differing cultural images of the ups and the downs and have tried to show how the discrepancy between images both increases conflict between the two groups and makes it more difficult to manage. We are now at the point of confrontation of the ups by the downs. Where will this all lead? Before hearing Dr. Halpern speak, I thought of the various results of confrontation as end states. Now it seems clear that they are relationships. I can imagine three general procedures leading to some sort of resolution following a confrontation episode: avoidance, unilateral action or a procedural resolution.

Avoidance of the issues posed by the downs in a confrontation may well be attempted by the ups. Should the downs be willing to avoid too, we would have Dr. Halpern's isolation. This solution has been proposed by the black separatists and by a few of the organizers of Free Universities. I do not know an up-down case where this has worked. An attempt at avoidance by one party only is a unilateral action and is likely to result in a unilateral action by the other. Such an action is taken by one without seeking the consent of the other. A unilateral action with unpleasant consequences for the other must rely on power. Power is a concept which has not been elaborated in this conference, yet it is of central importance in determining the outcome of any confrontation. Saul Alinsky, a veteran organizer of downs, maintains that nothing else matters. If your group gets strong enough, he argues, it will find the other group quite agreeable.[7] I am not prepared to discuss the topic of power, and I highlight the issue here only because I sense it has been slighted. In general, a power-based unilateral action will lead either to conquest or to a hostile truce. In a conflict between ups and downs, conquest is most likely to reestablish subjection of the downs by the ups. A hostile truce may either be a truce of mere exhaustion or it may occur when the parties are ready for a procedural resolution.

There are three types of procedural resolution, reconciliation, award and compromise. Reconciliation has connotations of transformation of the two parties, of a rising to superordinate goals which allow the parties to discover they are not really in conflict but brothers under the skin. I do not see it a likely resolution of confrontation between the ups and the downs. A much more likely resolution in this world of ours is award. Award requires a higher authority, in this country usually some level of the government. Either with or without the consent of the downs and the ups, the government, usually through the courts, may determine the outline of a new relationship between the downs and the ups.

If the ups and the downs agree that a procedural resolution is appropriate, but there is no third party to make an award, the former ups and the former downs will try to compromise. Compromise is not reconciliation, however. It is based on careful, if unspoken, considerations of power. It does not occur without the possibility of unilateral action on either side. It is also inextricably bound up with the parties' images, for the first clash in any attempt to compromise is based on images. What is negotiable? What is to be compromised on? In the Memphis garbage workers strike a number of picket signs read "I AM A MAN." [8] That is not a negotiable issue. The workers and the city of Memphis agreed that major issues on which they would attempt to compromise were wages and union recognition. Even then, whether compromise could be achieved was touch and go, requiring pressure from the Federal Government and a loan to the city from an anonymous benefactor.

In our discussion of conflict between the ups and the downs, we have come from the abstract theory of emanation and subjection relationships to a discussion of the wages and union recognition of garbage workers in Memphis, Tennessee. It must be so. The forming of a new relationship between the once ups and once downs is always based on the changing of a few specific things. However, in order to understand the amount of agony that goes into those particular changes, we must understand how those changes are linked to much larger issues of whose images of the situation will be institutionalized.

REFERENCES

1. Boulding, Kenneth E.: *The Image: Knowledge in Life and Society.* Ann Arbor, The University of Michigan Press, 1956.

2. Kelman, Herbert C.: Social-psychological approaches to the study of international relations: Definition of scope. In *International Behavior: A Social-Psychological Analysis,* edited by Herbert C. Kelman. New York, Holt, Rinehart & Winston, 1965.

3. Halpern, Manfred: A redefinition of the Revolutionary situation. *J Int. Affairs, 23(1):*1969. See also Dr. Halpern's paper presented earlier in this conference.

4. Elkins, Stanley M.: Slavery and personality. Chapter III in *Slavery,* edited by Stanley M. Elkins. Chicago, University of Chicago Press, 1959.

5. Kuhn, Thomas S.: *Structure of Scientific Revolutions,* 2nd ed. Chicago, University of Chicago Press, 1970.

6. Farber, Jerry: *Student as Nigger*. Hollywood (Calif.), Contact Books, 1969.
7. Lecture given March 17, 1971, in the Rackham Auditorium of The University of Michigan.
8. Marshall, F. Ray, and Van Adams, Arvil: Part 3 of *Racial Conflict and Negotiations: Perspectives and First Case Studies,* edited by Dr. W. Ellison Chalmers and Gerald W. Cormick. Ann Arbor, Institute of Labor and Industrial Relations, The University of Michigan-Wayne State University, 1971. This entire book has been particularly stimulating, especially Part 2: To negotiate or not to negotiate: Toward a definition of a black position, by Preston Wilcox.

Chapter 25

Psychosocial Perspectives:
A Summary

ARTHUR M. SACKLER

FROM TIME TO TIME, as in the evolutionary history of the species, the survival of societies requires new levels of equilibration. With quantum change in environment, the survival of societies may depend either on a sharp mutation or on a selection of those social characteristics which make a better fit with the new environmental milieu. With the advent of new political systems, survival may be best served by peaceful co-existence of differing political systems. In Manfred Halpern's concept (see Chap. 6), there is a time for transformation, a time for the fusion of collaboration *and* conflict, not apocalyptic disruption, a time for conscious deployment of man's creativity to assure both continuity *and* change, and a time for the attainment of the shared goal of justice.

Internationally, two contending political systems are locked in an awesome struggle. Twentieth-century man has spent literally trillions—thousands of billions—of dollars and can now attain utter destruction by blast and fire and radiation. How simple was the earlier cynicism of *aprés moi, les déluge.* As hundreds of millions of men, women and children needlessly starve; as scores of millions die of preventable and treatable diseases, the world's industrialized giants are engaged in a big power confrontation which is exhausting and can destroy all mankind. At a time of nuclear brinksmanship, one could expect modern man to create a sturdier, more effective and more dependable complex of signals so that the survival of all species does not hang on the slender and fragile thread of a "hot line." But are we really witnessing a discordance or conflict of [I dislike the term] ideologies? Or could it be, to extend Bryant

Wedges' comment (see Chap. 24), that this situation is not "a conflict of interests but a conflict of understanding or cultures" compounded by the "distorted images of the other fellows." George Vassilou strongly supported this view with data from diversified cross-cultural studies. In summary, he said, "The fact that attitudes, stereotypes, affective meaning system, categorization of concepts, roles, conceptions, etc., vary across milieux, results in misunderstanding which can have disastrous consequences." Vassilou stressed that the Hellenic Core culture's attitude which considers neutrality in human relations as hostility is highly relevant in a world where alienation prevails.

When stripped of propaganda and verbiage, are not many of the differences between the contending social structures being reduced? For better and for worse, are not certain of the political patterns trending towards each other under the impact of the technologic, scientific revolution of our day? Democracies and constitutional monarchies, socialist and communist states, all are capable of feeding, housing and providing health care to their populations *given* modern technology. Contrariwise, without such technology, other states with a similar range of political structures fail to provide such essentials. The truth is that a "commonality of interests" does exist.

How brief is the survival time of the memories of man's recent experience? For a short period after the Second World War, the export of bombs was replaced by an export of capital, of food and of expertise. Nations were rebuilt and children were born into a healthier world to better nourishment and greater freedom from disease. Then, with the rebuilding of both foes and friends, there seems to have been a change as the major items of our export became tanks and troop carriers, missiles and "Phantoms."

Man must seek a Great Plan for Peace *now*, a plan specifically programmed to assure that there be no new "World War Three," for man may not have an opportunity for a new "Marshall Plan" after the next world war.

We have previously referred to the big power confrontation. Size does not confer greatness. Greatness can only come when the big powers disengage from their destructive competition over lands and engage themselves in a new and better competition—a competition for life. In essence, the big power competition is neither different nor more civilized nor more advanced than the interethnic strife in Africa described for us by Elliott Skinner (see Chap. 20).

It has become imperative for all political leaders to pay more than lip service to the rights of man and the survival value of coexistence. Many different species can live in a common biotope without exhausting its resources. A wide range of effective patterns of behavior have evolved which have enabled fish, through color, birds through song, and many mammals through scent to share a given biotope with other members of their species on the basis of a space plan. Domestic cats normally share hunting grounds without conflict thanks to a scent-marked space and time plan. If fish can coexist successfully by using their eyes, birds by their ears and cats by their nose, what about man? One would hope that with the added advantage of a brain which is both quantitatively the largest and, as George Gaylord Simpson pointed out (see Chap. 2), qualitatively different, *Homo sapiens* should be able both to coexist and *enhance* and *not* destroy both his environment and his species. Behavioral research offers many other highly relevant social insights.

Konrad Lorenz [1] observed that violence in animals is commonly confined to *unusual* environmental conditions such as crowding, to territorial invasion and to social disorganization. Sol Kramer (see Chap. 1) beautifully elucidated the complex of signals whereby so many species confine aggression. The range of rituals and ceremonials and other, shall we say, "coexistence patterns" which contribute to concordance in animal societies is virtually infinite. Scott [2] has shown that aggressive behavior can be learned; that it is more easily elevated than reduced and is almost invariably stimulated by pain. We must add, hunger and disease are painful.

Matthews [3] notes that while in the animal kingdom fighting occurs widely, "aggressive behavior is common and apparently useful . . . only exceptionally does it become destructive or harmful." It is rare to find instances of "true overt fighting resulting in the death of a loser among mammals under normal conditions in the wild." How very civilized. Masserman [6] offers ethnologic and experimental evidence to the same effect.

It is remarkable that animals under normal environmental conditions *avoid* crowding, territorial invasion and social disorganization. Man not only engages in these abnormal provocations but adds to them the painful stimulation of discrimination and neglect.

Within the past generation intranational and international social disruption, territorial violations and the displacement of human populations have had massive and distressing social and psychic effects. Their impact has resulted in aggression and conflict. These developments may be more comprehensible in the light of recent behavioral studies. Southwick [4] reported a 50 percent greater incidence in aggression among rhesus monkeys trapped and established in a colony cage as compared to a free-ranging forest group. Recent population shifts from urban to rural centers, the overcrowding of ghettos and barrios may present a sad human equivalent.

Southwick demonstrated a tremendous increase in aggressive activity induced in animal groups by strangers; once again, one becomes concerned as to its relevance to man, to the ethnic and racial conflicts which may result from the planned or unwitting geographic displacement of minority groups as newcomers in closed or established communities. On the other hand, Southwick found a significant decrease in aggression after a five-day, 50 percent food shortage. One wonders if this explains the rationale of those who, throughout the centuries and even today, keep subject peoples in a genocidal state of starvation and famine.

The genius of man has revolutionized science and technology. The knowledge, the skills and industry which have brought virtually all species to the brink of nuclear extinction have contemporaneously illuminated the world so that the social and philosophical heritage of mankind has become the property of all men—black, white and yellow, young and old, poor and rich. For in this, our day, Juan Lopez-Ibor's statement (see chap. 7) has particular pertinence: "History itself has no meaning but acquires it through its relationship to man."

We live in a world which, as James G. Miller puts it, is in the "25th year of a revolution in information processing." We would agree that this revolution is closer to "the central nature of man."

Consciously or unconsciously, all men now live in a world forged in a series of struggles, a world molded by the political ideas of the British Magna Carta, the American Declaration of Independence, the French Revolution, Marx's *Communist Manifesto*, Lenin's *Russian Revolution* and China's *Thoughts of Mao*. These political branches have been grafted onto religious roots and a philosophic trunk which have embodied Confucian and Buddhistic concepts, Judaic commandments, the Islamic Koran and the Christian ideals of the Sermon on the Mount.

All now know that this is the day of moon voyages and space stations. Against such a galaxy of star-filled hopes, mankind—black and yellow and white, young and old, poor and rich—views the world as they are told it should be and see that it is not. Conditioned, in thought, to a wide range of theories of the good, man keeps bumping his head against the realities of the evils, the lies and the discrepancies which mark every society and political structure. The outcome is, of course, as real as it was predictable.

The laboratories of Pavlov, Gantt and Jules Masserman have documented and corroborated the consequence of a conditioning to one set of stimuli and the disruption caused by arbitrary changes; dogs and cats, monkey and man, all react in a common pattern to discordant stimuli and frustration; they evidence anxiety and other symptoms of neuroses. Normal neuroendocrine and behavioral patterns of concordance are disrupted. When isolated or subjected to painful or disruptive stimuli, animals and men react with withdrawal as well as aggression.

Withdrawal in man can be, and often is, self-defeating as a mechanism of defense. In James G. Miller's terminology, it is an abnormal "adjustment process" when it is "inappropriate" and "too costly." Such reactions lead to some of our major psychosocial problems. Reactive depressions confront the psychiatrist with an urgent, psychic emergency. Its toll is in the scores of thousands and is, unfortunately, heavily concentrated among young and highly productive sectors of society.

But by far the commonest withdrawal in every type of society, political structure or geographic region is addiction. The commonest form is alcoholism. There are few psychiatric states which even approximate alcoholism's devastating effects in terms of social and economic disruption, range of morbidity or extent of mortality. Over the millennia, few societies have been able to cope with this plague, and for those in which alcoholism was not a problem, other addictions "stood in," notably marijuana or the poppy. In regard to alcohol, the social reaction has been a schizophrenic type of behavior—it stigmatized alcoholism but tolerated alcohol. In fact, more than tolerated, alcoholic beverages have been made a central element in the social rituals in volving hospitality and in the ceremonials of our haute cuisine. As a result, psychiatry confronts a problem of such dimensions that most psychiatrists react to it by their own form of withdrawal. They either do not want to recognize it for what it is— probably the major psychosocial problem of man—or they would prefer not to see alcoholic patients and do very little work in the field of addiction. Psychiatric research has hardly begun to make a dent in this field.*

Even as alcohol is probably the major means of adult withdrawal, youth has experimented with a wide range of psychotropics. But youth has confronted, in states of every political complexion, a "righteous" indignation directed against *their* psychotropics. Yet they stop "dropping acid" when warned of chromosomal aberrations and psychoses with LSD. They will avoid marijuana and other drugs as toxicity is demonstrated. They have seen and know of the disastrous effects of their adults' psychotropics—alcohol and tobacco. They know that scotch, cognac, aquavit and vodka share a common addicting and toxic quality regardless of the social or economic system which produces them. They note that *no* state has seen its way clear to forego

---

* We were fortunate that among the social psychiatrists at this Colloquium were two of the most active and most outstanding experts in a field of addiction, Dr. Vladimir Hudolin and Dr. Alfred Freedman (see chaps. 16 and 10, respectively).

economic gain for the best interests either of its own people or their fellowmen.

At this time, when discordance and cultural shock seem to characterize the relationship between the generations, we must maintain historic perspective and philosophic continuity. We can face the future hopeful that its historians will not, in John Schwab's phrase (see Chap. 17), call this century "the unglorious 100 years"—thanks to the youth of all lands.

We must, as thinking and sensitive adults, as scientists and as doctors, not only acknowledge the truths of our perceptive youths but be in concordance with their discordance. We must understand and encourage their rejection of cant, of hypocracy, of lies. We must recognize that their discordance is with the falseness of so much of our lives; that they seek concordance in their lives between their ideals and their reality. In so doing, they seek a better world. We, in our time, have previously carried forward this function of youth. Our role as adults should be neither to repress, nor restrain, but to seek a constructive wedding of fundamentally valid knowledge, expertise and wisdom of the past to the vigor and innovation of the future. We can make a truly major sociopsychiatric contribution to human concordance by successfully lodging with everyone we can reach our deep conviction and our thankfulness that in all lands youth has eyes which are sharp, vision which is clear and ears that hear the cry of so much of humanity. They have the feeling to understand and the backbone and guts to respond. Paul Adams (see Chap. 4) has put it most succinctly when he said that "Life and intelligence are the cardinal corrupters of youth." We must establish a dialogue with youth using Bryant Wedge's model (see Chap. 24). "Who are we?" Social psychiatrists. "What is our purpose?" Concordance. "How long are you going to stay?" As long as is necessary, and then we will leave the scene to you.

There are a wide range of other psychosocial contributions to human concordance that we can make professionally as individuals and through our representative organizations. We must win support for the fundamental premises that

1. Man has the right to health, to complete physical, mental and social well-being.[5]

2. Man has the right to peace and security. In this respect we must consider Louis Miller's comment (see Chaps. 11 and 15) that "the absence of violence is not necessarily a state of peace." We must insist

3. That food adequate in protein as well as calories is basic to psychosocial as well as physical development and function,

4. That equality—social and economic—in jobs and compensation are essential for psychosocial balance.

5. That health care must be adequate in both preventive and curative medicine and toward that end adequate health manpower is a *sine qua non.*

The denial of food, jobs, housing and health are, in today's world, passive acts of violence. To use Paul Adams' phrase (see Chap. 4), they are "legitimization of murder." As to man's conflict with hunger and his war with disease, may I use the voice of George Vassiliou and say, "Neutrality is hostility" (see Chap. 22), not only to Greek eyes but in the eyes of all thinking men.

6. As social psychiatrists we must recognize that the most extreme discordance between need and available resources exists in our own specialty. We must, therefore, encourage the training of many more psychiatric professionals and paraprofessionals, foster research to multiply the productivity of psychotherapeutic procedures; explore, develop and introduce more preventive psychosocial measures; extend the use of effective and safe psychopharmacologic agents and devote more attention to the so-called simple stresses of everyday living which have loaded us with such a massive incidence of psychic dysfunction and somatic disorders.

We must conclude that the lessons of history are corroborated by the findings of behavioral science.

For concordance, we must apply the knowledge gained by modern behavioral studies of aggression to the conflicts of man.

For concordance, we must propose that international and national aggression be reduced by the avoidance of physical and psychic pain to others, by the respect for the territories, the children, the social structure, beliefs and traditions of others.

For concordance, modern mass communication media must be redirected to *eliminate* and *not* to *accentuate* the feeling of strangeness between different racial and ethnic groups and between different generations.

For concordance, we must utilize every valid modality to help our patients attain inner peace. We must be activists for peace at every level. In so doing, psychiatrists and behavioral scientists may best contribute to concordance—to peace for all patients and peace for all people.

REFERENCES

1. Lorenz, Konrad: *On Aggression.* New York, Harcourt, Brace & World, 1963.
2. Scott, J. P.: *American Zoologist, 6:*683–701, 1966.
3. Matthews, L. H.: *The Natural History of Aggression.* New York, Academic Press, 1964.
4. Southwick, Charles H.: *Animal Aggression.* New York, Van Nostrand Reinhold Co., 1970.
5. Constitution of the World Health Organization.
6. Masserman, Jules H.: *The Biodynamic Roots of Human Behavior.* Springfield, 1968.

Chapter 26

The Biodynamics of Concordance Versus Discord: A Review

JULES H. MASSERMAN

ANY ATTEMPT TO SUMMARIZE in a few pages the rich and protean contributions to this Colloquium on Man for Humanity would be analogous to condensing an encyclopedia on the subject. Permit me instead to subtend a supplementary approach to the historical, comparative and clinical vectors of our central themes of concordance versus discord and violence in human behavior. Herewith then are the three *leitmotifs* reconsidered:

Theme 1, Man's Ultimate (Ur-) Needs. In essence, this holds that man's basic necessities (ergo, his motivations, drives, wishes, fantasies, objectives, etcetera) are (a) a desire for physical health, skills and longevity, giving rise to the sciences and technologies with which we try to control our material milieu; (b) a seeking for human friendships and alliances through which we strive for culturally adaptive, sexual, familial and social securities; and (c) a yearning for various metapsychologic-theologic faiths that promise us the vicarious serenity of omniscience and immortality (Chapter 25)

Theme 2. When these physical, interpersonal and metapsychologic needs are satisfied sufficiently near *individual* expectations by mutual efforts within and among sociocultural groups, relative peace and concordance supervene (Chapter 17)

Theme 3. Conversely, when one or more of these Ur needs are actively or subjectively contravened, hostility against the frustrating person or group is evoked and may become irrationally generalized to spreading dissension, intensifying conflict and increasing violence (Chapter 7)

Admittedly, these statements are thus far only heuristic premises; to test their scientific validity they must be examined as to their accord with history, their compatibility with current knowledge of the dynamics of human behavior and their confirmation by inductive and experimental evidence. I shall here review the historical and comparative parameters only with utmost brevity, so that I may consider some additional experimental data in greater detail.

HISTORICAL VECTORS OF VIOLENCE

To cite only single examples of the Toynbeean times of troubles that resulted when any of the three essential human needs cited above were rendered seriously insecure, it will be recalled that the periods of greatest conflict in human history occurred during the following eras:

Physical challenges: When hunter-herder-nomadic hordes fought for land, water and material subsistence with the emerging agrarian-urban cultures of ancient Mesopotamia and Egypt (Chapter 9)

Sociopolitical stresses: When the disintegration of the Western Roman Empire disrupted the relative loyalties and securities of a putative world citizenship the Pax Romana had previously imposed (Chapter 8)

Religious conflicts: When the theocratic authority of the Catholic Church was challenged during the rise of Islam and again during the Renaissance and Reformation (Chapter 8).

So also in modern times when our sciences and technologies are rapidly making our fair earth uninhabitable for everyone, when our economic and political systems are almost everywhere in disarray, and when we have lost faith in our former theomythologies, many disillusioned and desperate human beings—when not resorting to nepenthic escapisms, wishful utopias or newer and ever more bizarre mysticisms—are increasingly prone to crime, violence and wars that may well, unless countered by greater wisdom and humanitarianism among the leaders we put in power, lead to a final world holocaust.

HISTORICAL VECTORS OF CONCORDANCE

These and other eras of discord may be compared with the centuries of *relative* social stability that supervened during the more providently agrarian, politically organized and theocratically hierarchic dynasties of Egypt; or the economically, juristically and morally enlightened rule of King Asoka in third-century India; or the commercially prosperous, culturally receptive and religiously liberal "heathen" Rome; or even the repressive but economically, socially and theologically stabilized feudal systems of medieval Europe. One may well contend that in the latter case impairment of human freedom and progress was a high price to pay, but the inference remains that men are relatively content and cooperative when their physical, social and credal needs are sufficiently met, but become restless, escapist or violent when they conceive these Ur-essentials to be threatened. The term "conceive" is used advisedly, since we must always add the codicil that man measures his happiness not by what he has, but what he has come to believe is his due.

THE CLINICAL APPROACH TO THE VECTORS OF VIOLENCE

Here we may invoke our knowledge of psychotherapy and reexamine the roots from which our basic anxieties and our derivative aversions, obsessions, regressions, escapisms and aggressions spring. In essence, these reach neurotic, sociopathic or even psychotic levels under the same three adverse contingencies, to wit: (a) when our physical existence or welfare seems in internal or external danger, (b) when our familial or social relationships seem alienated and (c) when our cherished faiths— be they "scientific," philosophic or religious—seem threatened.

Correspondingly, when patients so troubled come to us for therapy (Greek-*therapeien,* service), we respond in three coordinated ways.

First, as skillful physicians or other health experts, we alleviate their suffering and restore their physical well-being insofar as possible (Chapter 18)

Second, as humanitarians, we help them reconstruct acceptable and creative participation in their sociocultural milieu (Chapter 19.)

(Here both patient and physician have considerable latitude. In an illuminating recent review, Robert Edgerton   points out that within even "primitive" cultures the so-called implicit rules of conduct are ambiguous. Behavior remains individualistic (there are few "grey flannel loin-cloths [even in the most "primitive" cultures]) , and as in our society, major deviance is attributed to genetic or biologic defect, to deprivation, to subcultural differences or to inevitably perverse human nature—the last in accord with the Aristotelian dictum that "man is both angel and beast." Edgerton concludes [italics enthusiastically mine] that "man creates rules that *provide him with security and predictability* at the same time that he creates other rules *that permit him to express choice and to achieve personal advantage.*" So also, what Walter Goldschmidt calls the *arete* of a culture—its implicit ideal of individual conduct—has everywhere a broad range of inclusiveness. In essence then, guided social readaptation need never entail a stultifying loss of individuality or creativity.*)

Third, as implicitly assigned oracles and mentors, we guide our patients toward renewed confidence in some culturally compatible and thereby operationally effective system of beliefs. I venture to state that all forms of medicopsychiatric treatment—whether those employed by "witch doctors" as reported by Jerome Frank, Ari Kiev or E. Fuller Torrey or as practiced by Western-trained therapists as summarized by Morris Stein, Lewis Wolberg, myself and others—are successful only as they fulfill the physical, social and philosophic criteria outlined; insofar as they do not, they are correspondingly ineffective (Chapter 22) .

EVOLUTIONARY VECTORS

As to Chapter 1, the heuristic value of animal observations has recently been challenged from a new quarter by advocates of "systems theory" on the basis that so-called "zoomorphic" concepts of man fall into the errors of "anthropomorphising"

---

* Galdston, I.: *Interface Between Psychiatry and Anthropology.* New York, Brunner-Mazel, 1970, pp. 28–54.

animal behavior (Chapters 2 and 9) or "rattomorphising" (A. Koestler) human conduct. The former tautology is particularly whimsical in that, ever since Kant and Hegel, it has been difficult to conceive what "data," percepts, categories, premises or theories —including systems theory—can be other than processed by the categorical imperatives of human cerebration—ergo, necessarily "anthropomorphic." Aside from such semantic and philosophic strictures, however, there seems to be a current reversion, however subtle, to the fragmenting *taxonomic* Comtean stage of scientific thought (the first being *primitive-mystic* and the most advanced *dynamic-comprehensive*). For example, as deeply respected a scientist as Ludwig von Bertalanffy, in a recent summary of his views,* writes, "The theory of man as a 'mere' animal or 'naked ape' founders on the elementary fact that humans have 'culture,' articulate language, music and philosophy, machines and science, swords and atom bombs, cathedrals and department stores [whereas] animals—apes included—have nothing of the sort." The key qualification of such commentaries, of course, is what is meant by the phrase "nothing of the sort," since in my own writings and those of many others on ethology and comparative psychology, it has been repeatedly pointed out that animals *do* have a vast variety of rituals, conspecific relationships and relatively flexible social organizations ("culture") and that they construct material aids ("machines"), utilize specialized dwellings and storehouses ("cathedrals, department stores") and thereby seem to have life objectives ("philosophies"). So also, according to the fascinating recent work by Kathy Hayes, George Premak and others, primates can develop, despite the handicap of inadequate largyneal structures, vocal as well as manipulative communications and highly abstract symbolic concepts. Moreover, as the studies of Pavlov, Gantt, Liddell and those in our laboratory have shown, animals react to the stresses of adaptational conflicts and anticipatory uncertainties by developing aberrations of behavior disconcertingly similar to human neuroses and psychoses—admittedly short of constructing atom bombs or impressive churchly monuments to scarcely less homicidal religions. Were I to join in polemic

---

* System, symbol and the image of man. In I. Galdston. *loc cit.*

pejoratives such as dismissing all evolutionary-integrative approaches to human conduct as "merely zoomorphic," I might suggest that the current tendency to conceive man as remote by an unbridgeable quantum jump from all other living things be called the Old Testament Doctrine: after laboring over inferior matters such as producing the cosmos and engendering all things that creep and crawl, on the sixth day God created Adam (interestingly, still out of Cambrian clay) —and after this masterpiece, rested.

In effect, then, (Chapters 1 and 2) contrary to the common misinterpretation of the Darwinian phrase "survival of the fittest" to mean the triumph of the most strong and savage, Huxley, Montague, Simpson and other paleobiologists have pointed out that survival of *Homo sapiens* as well as of other species has in most instances been due to the emergence of interorganismic empathy and cooperation. Portmann, in *Animals as Social Beings* (Viking, 1960, p. 197) also writes: "The Darwinian doctrine of 'the survival of the fittest' has been so uncritically applied, even by scientists, that the combative and destructive aspects of evolution have been over-emphasized at the expense of those of mutual help . . . which limit or avoid destructive struggle." Indeed, many of the patterns of group behavior most important to social psychiatry can be traced almost to their Cambrian roots. As Bonner observed, even on the unicellular level the normally free and individualistic myxameba, when subjected to deprivation of food or water will dutifully congregate with its fellows to form a polycellular clone, many members of which then sacrifice themselves so that others may sporulate and live. Such relationships can be traced through the animate echelons to what may be regarded as operational altruism in many mammalian phyla. Burton, Katz and others have reported many examples: antelope sentinels voluntarily remain continually endangered as guards of the herd; wounded elephants are surrounded by their immediate neighbors and helped to escape to safety in the jungle; and otters will rescue a crippled comrade. Loveridge frequently witnessed male baboons defend threatened fellows from a predator, and females return in the face of lethal danger to protect a dead mate's body; similarly, Schalter observed that even the awesome mountain gorilla is "amiable and decent" to the weak and suffering of its own kind. In stark contrast are the effects of confinement and frustration: Zukerman noted that baboons kept in captivity act more like men in concentration camps; they attack the weak, the ill and the aged, manhandle the females after sexual satiation and otherwise act in a manner that would appear cruel and destructive to a human observer (Chapters 1 and 9)

There is corresponding ethologic evidence that if the young even of different species are raised together, peaceable relations can continue into adulthood. For example, Forel let baby ants of three ordinarily hostile varieties grow up in the same nest and observed that the adults coexisted amicably; similarly, Pattie observed that chicks raised in the company of mice later preferred them to fowl company. Kuo found that cats can be conditioned to kill a rat, to love it, to hate it, to fear it or to play with it, depending on their early experiences with each other. More bizarre friendships have been described by Burton between a goose and a goat, a goat and a llama, and a cat and ducklings; so also badgers, foxes and rabbits have grown up in mutual tolerance. At a private zoo in Moscow, I was privileged to witness a bear, a wolf, a fox, a raccoon, a parrot, a rabbit and a chicken act out a ten-minute playlet taught them with patience and kindness as they were being raised peaceably together.

So also, humans can be accepted by feral as well as "domesticated" friends. Jane Goodall, after spending months with a clan of chimpanzees in the wild, learned their language and customs so well that eventually she "was greeted almost as another chimpanzee—sometimes by a show of excitement and shaking of branches and sometimes by a complete lack of interest." Jerome Wooley (Masserman, 1967) reported that by similarly gentle overtures, he could convert supposedly savage adult wolves into canine companions. The Adamsons raised a lioness cub to be an affectionate friend and a lifelong mentor between them and her kind. Such observations call into further question Freud's postulate of a universal "aggressive" or "death" instinct; on the contrary, they indicate highly significant vectors in the dynamics of homogenous and heterogenous group concordance. Shall we, who have given ourselves the name *Homo sapiens,* ever employ this racially innate capacity for individual cooperation and race survival? (Chapter 10)

ANIMAL AGGRESSION

True, maneuvers to secure or defend individual perogatives are also common throughout the animal kingdom; however, the special studies of Lorenz, Eibl-Eibesfeldt and others show that in regrettable contrast to human combat, conspecific encounters in other species over food, territory or mates are mostly expository and almost never lethal. L. D. Clark, after extensive research into the fighting behavior even of "killer animals" such as *Onychomys leukogaster,* likewise concluded that "aggression is not an 'instinct.' Rage and attack are patterns of response, influenced by genetic factors but brought about by particular, threatening conditions; without the occurrence of these conditions, aggression need never occur." From a comprehensive review of ethologic evidence, Burton draws relevant analogies as follows: "Wild animals may throw their whole being into their hostile displays and sometimes go beyond the bounds of common animal decency, especially when two contestants are equally matched in prowess and determination; but really bloody fights are rare. . . . Fundamentally, loyalty is to the territory and only secondarily to the mate. The parallel is clear in business affairs. Wars are fought over territory, social revolutions arise from land-hungry masses; mere marital difficulties spring from having to share space . . . than from any other single cause." (Chapter 11)

PARASITISM VERSUS COLLABORATION

In our laboratory, cats or monkeys were taught to operate a switch mechanism that dropped a reward of food into a distant food box. When two conspecific animals so trained were placed together, in most pairs each would for a time alternate in working the switch while the other fed; soon, however, one would begin remaining near the food box and taking the food earned by its partner's labors. This usually resulted in the latter refusing for a time to work the switch in the absence of the pre-empted reward. Nevertheless a fairly stable worker-parasite "industrial" relationship would eventually be established in which the "worker" operated the feeder energetically and often enough to provide sufficient pellets so that he could hurry to the food box and secure a few before they were all eaten by the parasite partner. Moreover, two such workers among fourteen pairs proved to be sufficiently "intelligent" (that is, possessed of un-usually high perceptive-manipulation capacities) to jam the switch so that the feeder mechanism operated continuously, thus solving a social problem in a manner analogous to industrial "automation." Some monkeys continued to starve for several hours, though never more than half a day or so, rather than pull a lever to secure readily available food if they perceived that this also subjected another monkey to an electric shock. Such "altru-istic" behavior was, again significantly, less dependent upon the relative age, size or sex of the two animals than on whether or not they had been "well-adjusted" cagemates who had developed mutually predictable and favorable interaction. Again, human analogies are self-evident. (Chapters 4 and 12 to 17)

DOMINANCE VERSUS AGGRESSION

Even under constricted laboratory conditions, actual fighting between members of the same species to establish territorial, food, sexual or other privileges was minimal; primacy and dexterity manifested by only occasional gestures of preemption were nearly always sufficient to establish dominance. Indeed, physical combat appeared only under the following special circumstances, again whimsically reminiscent of human parallels:

1. When an animal that had attained a high position in its own group was transferred to one in which it came into direct conflict with new rivals themselves accustomed to primacy, and thereby had to adapt to renewed challenges.

2. Similarly, when an excessively repressive animal was finally provoked a conjoint rebellion by an alliance of subdominants.

3. When a female with borrowed power derived from mating with a protective male thereafter turned on members of her group that had previously oppressed her.

4. When a dominant animal, by being made experimentally neurotic, fell to a low position in its group and expressed its frustration by physical attacks both on animate and inanimate objects in its environment. (Chapters 1 and 9)

In effect, then, biodynamic data indicate that whereas violence may be evoked under conditions of traumatic frustration, interorganismic accord supervenes when modes of mutually beneficial conspecific or cross-specific collaboration can be developed. These findings are illustrated in films of experiments in our laboratory in which a feeding apparatus programmed to present unpredictably variable signals and inconstant rewards evoked destructive rages, stereotyped rituals, phobic retreats or catatonic immobility in three species of monkeys, whereas such reactions could be averted either by rendering the machine manageable or providing a monkey-like "therapist" automaton to furnish proper cues to restore order and certainty. (Chapters 10 to 23)

APPLICATION TO SOCIAL PSYCHIATRY

This then has been a tachistoscopic review of only a few of the historical, clinical and experimental data indicating that the roots of discord lie in physical, social and ideologic frustrations. Unfortunately, such insights are still of little practical value if we act only as office-bound theoreticians, since as individuals we cannot possibly counter the devastating effects on three billon human beings of a technologically, culturally and philosophically disordered world, currently manifest in spreading disease, crime and violence. Somewhat more effective, hopefully, may be our coordinated efforts in organizations such as the World Health Organization and our own International Association of Social Psychiatry, but here again only if we cooperate with our fellow humanitarians in economics, sociology, jurisprudence and other behavioral disciplines throughout the world in influencing, insofar as possible, the financiers, politicians and militarists who are still, under the banners of racist or nationlistic supremacy, trying to lead themselves and us on paths to disaster. (Chapters 3, 4 and 23)

L'envoi: But must we end our fugue with this atonal discord? As scientists we know how fallible our facile formulations have always been and may continue to be, and as cherishers of hope we cannot surrender to nihilism. Permit me then to paraphrase the coda to my Plenary Address to the Third World Psychiatric Congress four years ago, and in a final coda, reconsider in more sanguine terms the triune Ur-aspirations of man as follows:

Technical. Despite the advanced despoiling of our planet and the fact that we have at hand, with no known defense against them, enough nuclear explosives to kill everyone on earth twenty times over, I believe—I must believe—that with spreading worldwide indignation and concerted rational action, we shall reign in our Frankensteinian technology in time to save our species and, hopefully, others also.

Social. There is already an increasingly compelling worldwide outcry against the insanity of wars and an urgent recognition of the necessity to reeducate, rehabilitate and recivilise the thousands of predominantly decent young men we have plunged into mindless, dehumanizing armed conflicts which have driven many of them to profound misanthropy, nepenthic escapes and social vandalism. As to our current racist turmoil, since *Homo habilis* is a single, universally fecund species, differences of "race" or color will eventually become about as distinguishable as Lombard, Hittite or Estruscan strains are in their Mediterranean descendants. Men will become progressively more cognizant of the necessities of mutual respect, concordance and cooperation—and thereby move closer to a world community.

Philosophic-theologic. Finally, when we develop a deeper sense of cosmic identity that will transcend our current ideologic parochialisms and the animistic myths and rituals of our primitive religions, we shall become humbler, kinder, wiser, happier and perhaps more deserving of survival. Selah.

REFERENCES

Further discussion of the studies mentioned in the text and of several hundred others will be found in the following books and monographs written or edited by the author:

1. *Behavior and Neuroses.* Chicago, University of Chicago Press, 1943; reprinted by Hafner & Co. New York, 1964.

2. *Principles of Dynamic Psychiatry.* Philadelphia, W. B. Saunders, 1946.

3. *Practice of Dynamic Psychiatry.* Philadelphia, W. B. Saunders, 1955.

4. *Modern Therapy of Personality Disorders.* Dubuque (Iowa), Wm. C. Brown Co., 1966.

5. *The Biodynamic Roots of Human Behavior.* Springfield, Charles C Thomas, 1968.

6. *Psychiatry, East and West.* New York, Grune & Stratton, 1968.

7. *Youth, A Transcultural Approach.* New York, Grune & Stratton, 1969.

8. *A Psychiatric Odyssey.* New York, Science House, 1971.

NAME INDEX

SUBJECT INDEX

concern, 204
conflict, 309
dynamics, 309, 327
enmity, 310, 317
image, 317, 327
intercession, 312
meetings, 320
origin, 309
sentinels, 316
size, 309
therapy, 312

H

Haiti, 236
Hausa, 243
Hausa-Fulani, 244
Head Start, 134
Health, 231, 234
aged, 232
child, 232
definition, 303
Hierarchies, 44
History, 341
acceleration, 89
race, 132
Holy War, 257
Homicide, 148
Hominids, 72
Homo erectus, 72
Homo sapiens, 75
Humor, 97

I

Ibo, 244
Id, 62
Identity, 181, 184, 198
crisis, 141, 243
group, 191
Illusions, 106
Images, 327, 330
Implication, 97
Income, national, 219
Industrialization, 228
Infant Mortality, 303
Information, 341
Inhibition, 15
Injustice, 183
Inputs, 53

Insights, 184
ethologic, 158
psychodynamic, 155
Instinct, 5, 51, 158, 187
death, 155
programming, 158
Intention movements, 9
Intercessor
communication, 315
functions, 318
qualities, 314
International Association of Social Psychiatry, 300, 355
Investment, 122
Isolation, 334

J

Jehovah Witnesses, 245
Judges, 177
Jurisprudence, USSR, 214
Justice, 106, 144

K

Kenya, 322
Kibbutz, 201
Kikuyu, 244, 246
Kinship, 243

L

Labor, 120
surplus, 217
Language, 75, 78
body, 61
Latin America, 220
Leaders, 199
Learning, 51, 53
Lebensraum, 129
Life
expectancy, 303
sanctity, 175
Lysergic Acid Diethylamide, 12, 60, 342

M

Machismo, 168, 236
Madness, 87
Mali Federation, 252
Malnutrition, 134

Psychiatrists, distribution, 304
Psychiatry
　community, 211
　cultural, 208
　dissent, 181
　dynamic, 181
　ethology, 49
　evolution, 50, 278
　family, 271
　obstacles, 233
　sciences, 308
　social, 5, 49, 157, 186, 192, 293, 355
　training, 208
　USSR, 211
Psychoanalysis, 182
Psychodynamics, 157
Psychotherapy, 60
　group, 289
Punishment, 151
Purpose, 84

R

Race, 131, 134
Racism, 134
　tribal, 253
Rank, 44
Rape, 148
Reality Principle, 183
Reason, 95
Recovery, Inc., 284, 287
Reflexes, 54
Refugees, Jewish, 257
Regression, LSD, 60
Releasers, 6
Relationship, 106
Relaxation, 55
Religion, 341
　loss, 347
Repression, 52
　Black, 128
Responsibility, 291
Revolution, 338
Rights, 344

S

Satyagraha, 150
Security, 108

Selection, natural, 63
Self-awareness, 82
Sex, 37
　jealousy, 82
　socioeconomic, 39
Signals
　economic, 120
　psychosomatic, 9
　sociosexual, 43
Sinks, behavioral, 45
Skepticism, 140
Slavery, 131
Smiling, 54
Socialism, 296
Society
　origins, 243
　roots, 62
　traditional, 228
Somalia, 322
Songhay, 243
Sophists, 92
Speech, origin, 81
Stimulus, key, 6
Stoicism, 140
Strikes, 127
Subjection, 109
Succorance
　animal, 351, 354
　experimental, 354
Sucking, 54
Suez War, 261
Suicide, 154
Superego, 55
Superman, 88
Superposition, 11
Synanon, 284

T

Technoculture, 142
Technology, 89, 216, 338
Ten Commandments, 96
Territories, 44
Terror, 264
Theory
　dialectical, 106
　games, 128
　human relations, 105
　psychoanalytic, 182